D0596458

THE DISTINGUISHED CARNEGIE COMMISSION ON THE FUTURE OF PUBLIC BROADCASTING:

A PUBLIC TRUST

The Report
of the
Carnegie Commission
on the
Future of Public Broadcasting

BANTAM BOOKS
TORONTO · NEW YORK · LONDON

A PUBLIC TRUST: THE REPORT OF THE CARNEGIE COMMISSION ON
THE FUTURE OF PUBLIC BROADCASTING
*A Bantam Book / published by arrangement with
Carnegie Corporation of New York*

PRINTING HISTORY
A Bantam Book / April 1979

ISBN 0–553–12284–3

Published simultaneously in the United States and Canada

*Bantam Books are published by Bantam Books, Inc. Its trade-
mark, consisting of the words "Bantam Books" and the por-
trayal of a bantam, is Registered in U.S. Patent and Trademark
Office and in other countries. Marca Registrada. Bantam
Books, Inc., 666 Fifth Avenue, New York, New York 10019.*

Contents

Foreword

Every age leaves its mark. With temples, pyramids, gardens, cathedrals, tall ships, opera houses, galleries, libraries, laboratories and universities have successive generations recorded their own creative aspirations and claimed the attention of generations to come. By looking at the best of what they left we know what they sought to be.

What of our time?

Our age is known for violence. It has been marked by alienation. It has spawned bureaucracy. It has embraced cynicism. Yet human beings yearn for alternatives; they long to matter. They hunger for a community of shared values reflecting the triumph of intelligence and the life of the spirit. The members of this Commission deeply believe that in the decades ahead the most creative expressions of the human endeavor will come through the arts of communication.

We believe public radio and public television can lead the way. Intelligently organized and adequately funded public broadcasting can help the creative spirit to flourish. It can reveal how we are different and what we share in common. It can illuminate the dark corners of the world and the dark corners of the mind. It can offer forums to a multitude of voices. It can reveal wisdom and understanding—and foolishness too. It can delight us. It can entertain us. It can inform us. Above all, it can add to our understanding of our own inner workings and of one another.

In the conviction that it can be so, we make these recommendations.

1

...s received VHF allocations before 19...

In noncommercial television... years most of... were assigned to educational institutions interested in providing instructional... As television became more popular, however... community organizations also applied for and received licenses.

Preface

Twelve years have elapsed since the Carnegie Commission on Educational Television recommended a strengthened system of television stations, to be called public television. In the intervening years public radio and television have become established as major American institutions. This year larger audiences than ever before, easily three times the size of those a dozen years ago, will tune into a public radio or television station. This is also the year in which stations will be interconnected by satellite, beginning another decade of technological change. Despite such successes, public broadcasting continues to be plagued by many of the problems it faced a decade ago, as well as new difficulties that have emerged as the system has grown.

It was with this balanced view of public broadcasting that the boards of the Corporation for Public Broadcasting (CPB) and National Public Radio (NPR), and other concerned citizens, approached Carnegie Corporation of New York in mid-1976. They believed the time had come to reappraise the condition of public broadcasting in the United States.

In response, Carnegie Corporation created a small task force to analyze the problems and to determine whether or not a new commission on public broadcasting would be useful. The task force worked intensively for more than six months, meeting with over two hundred people involved in and knowledgeable about public broadcasting. On the task force's recommendation, the board of trustees of Carnegie

3

Corporation established this Commission on the Future of Public Broadcasting in June 1977.

With Carnegie Corporation as our sole supporter, the Commission has been fully independent of existing interests in public broadcasting. Furthermore, from the beginning, Carnegie Corporation insisted that we need feel no commitment to the positions, philosophies, or statements of either the original Commission on Educational Television or the Carnegie task force.

Throughout the course of our inquiry, we have benefited from the trust and cooperation of the public broadcasting industry. Indeed, without remarkable assistance from the men and women in public broadcasting, our deliberations would not have been possible. We have made extraordinary demands on their time—for information and for the benefit of their experience—yet their doors have always been open.

Outside the public broadcasting system, support and assistance have been no less remarkable. Independent producers, scholars, spokespersons for public interest and minority groups, people working within commercial broadcasting, telecommunications, foundations, and the federal government have all generously contributed their time and knowledge.

These men and women in their strength, vitality, and willingness to put aside their own work to assist ours, have been our greatest source of optimism for the future of public broadcasting.

The Carnegie Corporation has given continuing encouragement and unstinting support for our work. Special thanks are due to President Alan Pifer, and to Vice-President David Robinson, our liaison.

We have been exceptionally fortunate in the competence and dedication of our staff. The executive director, Sheila Mahony, gave the Commission professional guidance of the highest caliber. She and her staff organized our meetings, seminars, and public hearings. Through all these discussions and innumerable staff papers, Ms. Mahony and her associates have done much to inform our study and to frame the substance of this report. We are happy to acknowledge the contributions of Richard Beatty, Ted Carpenter, Nicholas DeMartino, Dennis Dort, Michael Goldstein, Peter Low, Deborah Mack, Laura Perkins, Richard Polsky, Robert Stengel, and Andrew Solowey. Our support staff, Mary Abadie, who copyedited this report, Yvonne Maneates, Linda Muscara, and Carol Portnoy, who met every deadline for the Commission's work, generally under heavy pressure and always with admirable skill.

The work of the Commission began in earnest during September 1977, when we gathered for the first time at the New York headquarters of the Carnegie Corporation to listen to the report of the latter's task force and to hear the reflections of Dr. James Killian, who had led the renowned "Carnegie I." During that first meeting, we identified four distinct areas of study around which issues clustered: programming, public participation, financing, and technology/dissemination. This analysis helped to structure our research and subsequent discussions, but from the beginning the connectedness of the four areas of study—the seamless web—was apparent.

Our second meeting was convened in Washington, D.C., in October 1977. The Commission at that time established a form of inquiry that was to continue for the next 9 of 15 monthly meetings that took us from coast to coast. During the early stages of our work, we made an extensive effort to visit the principal centers of public broadcasting and to receive the views of its professionals. These meetings typically lasted two full days. The first day was reserved for testimony and discussion with invited participants in a forum open to the public and the press. The meetings were structured around the important themes of the Commission's work. In these meetings we benefited from the insights and testimony of 227 people. Indeed, through the course of this testimony, the issues and problems facing public broadcasting clearly emerged.

The second day of each meeting was taken up by internal discussion and debate of the issues, staff presentations, visits to stations, meetings with station managers from the region, and dinners with local community leaders and station board members. It was an exhausting but rewarding enterprise.

There were nine such public meetings, supplemented by four additional public hearings, and two private seminars, between October 1977 and June 1978.

The formal activities of the Commission were punctuated by frequent meetings between individual Commission members and the staff, as well as a number of station visits by individual commissioners. Throughout, the staff was in constant touch with the public broadcasting industry, its observers and critics, and a variety of experts in related fields. In all, several thousand people were contacted, resulting in nearly one hundred staff papers and memoranda. (See Appendix A for a full listing of our consultants, those who testified or participated in formal meetings, and a partial listing of the many people who guided our work through informal discussion.) Additionally, we received literally thousands of items of correspondence and written testimony. We retained 22 consultants whose papers and presentations have substantially aided our work. And we were much informed by the results of a survey of public broadcasting viewers and listeners conducted by an indomitable staff. Commission members, our consultants, and staff visited Great Britain, Japan, Canada, and 25 stations within the United States.

In July 1978 we undertook the second and crucial stage of our work, the difficult task of hammering out our recommendations and drafting this report. The report represents our best effort to design a new structure for public telecommunications that can accommodate the divergent yet clear needs of American public broadcasting in the decade ahead: stronger stations to serve hundreds of different local communities, a strong and protective national leadership representing the system to the public and guiding its growth, and finally, a carefully protected institution for supporting the delicate creative work that forms the heart and mind of the system.

Respectfully, we submit our recommendations for the future of public broadcasting in the report that follows.

MEMBERS OF THE COMMISSION[1]

William J. McGill, Chairman
President, Columbia University

Stephen K. Bailey
President
National Academy of
Education

Red Burns
Executive Director
Alternate Media Center
School of the Arts
New York University

Henry J. Cauthen
Director
South Carolina Educational
Television Network

Peggy Charren
President
Action for Children's Television

Wilbur B. Davenport, Jr.
Professor
Massachusetts Institute of
Technology

Virginia B. Duncan
Board Member
Corporation for Public
Broadcasting

Eli N. Evans
President
Charles H. Revson Foundation

John W. Gardner
Common Cause

Alex P. Haley
Author

Walter W. Heller
Professor
University of Minnesota

Josie R. Johnson
Board Member
National Public Radio

Kenneth Mason
President
Quaker Oats Company

Bill Moyers
WNET/13

Kathleen Nolan
President
Screen Actors Guild

J. Leonard Reinsch
Chairman
Cox Broadcasting Corporation

Tomas Rivera
Executive Vice-President
University of Texas at El Paso

---

[1]Bill Cosby, actor; Carla Hills, a former secretary of housing and urban development; and Beverly Sills, opera star, voluntarily resigned from the Commission during the course of this study as their participation became limited by other professional commitments.

Summary
of
Findings and Recommendations

Although few of us recognized it in 1965, an era of American dominance was coming to an end just as public broadcasting was coming to birth. Perhaps as acutely as any other American institution, the system of public broadcasting was caught in the transition from an American outlook that we could do anything we chose, to today's anxiety that we may have chosen to do too much. Public broadcasting was conceived as a major new national institution, an ambitious concept that would transcend the limited fare, centered principally on public education, offered by several hundred noncommercial television and radio stations then in existence.

In less than a dozen years, among the most turbulent and pivotal in our history, public broadcasting has managed to establish itself as a national treasure. From the backwaters of an industry long dominated by commercial advertising, the public system has come into its own. Millions now watch and hear, applaud, and criticize a unique public institution which daily enters their homes with programs that inform, engage, enlighten, and delight. In that sense, the ideal has been realized: public broadcasting has made a difference.

Public broadcasting is now firmly embedded in the national consciousness, financed by the people who use it, as well as by an array of organized elements within

9

society, including businesses, state, and local governments, universities and school boards, foundations, and, of course, the federal government. It was the Congress and President who, in 1967, set up the organizational framework and turned on the flow of much-needed federal dollars supporting the operations and programs of public radio and television as we know them today.

There is a necessarily ambivalent relationship between public broadcasting—a highly visible creative and journalistic enterprise—and the government. The dynamics of a free press and a democratic government are unpredictable enough without adding the additional complication of federal financial support.

Herein lies the fundamental dilemma that has revealed itself over and over again in public broadcasting's brief history and led to the empanelment of this Commission: how can public broadcasting be organized so that sensitive judgments can be freely made and creative activity freely carried out without destructive quarreling over whether the system is subservient to a variety of powerful forces including the government?

Commercial broadcasting's entire output is defined by an imperative need to reach mass audiences in order to sell products. Despite the evident need for an alternative addressed more realistically to the problems and the triumphs of American life, public broadcasting has yet to resolve the dilemma posed by its own structure.

Upon the framework of the 1967 legislation a complex institution has been constructed, one that has not always been able to cultivate the creative in preference to the bureaucratic. Financial worries upstage creative urges, even among the best of institutions. And this one has experienced considerable financial worries. By 1970, the skeleton of a national structure was in place. The Corporation for Public Broadcasting (CPB) —a nonprofit leadership institution created by Congress and governed by private citizens appointed by the President—would receive federal and other funds, disburse them to stations and producers, and support a wide range of activities to strengthen and expand the system.

Two national, nonstatutory organizations created

by CPB—the Public Broadcasting Service (PBS) for
television and National Public Radio (NPR) for radio
—would interconnect the stations, distribute programs,
and provide other services to enhance the national and
local programming mission. And there were the stations themselves, upon which the national system was
built. Independent and diverse institutions scattered
throughout the land, the public radio and television
stations are the focal point for audiences because only
they can determine the mix of programs that best serves
the unique characteristics of their own communities.

There are high and low points in the telling of
public broadcasting's first full decade—the 1972 veto
of federal funding for the system, the reorganizations of
PBS and NPR, multiyear funding in 1975, the development of the satellite and the Public Telecommunications
Financing Act of 1978, not to mention innumerable
programming successes and much-improved service.

Nonetheless, we find public broadcasting's financial, organizational and creative structure fundamentally flawed. In retrospect, what public broadcasting tried
to invent was a truly radical idea: an instrument of mass
communication that simultaneously respects the artistry of the individuals who create programs, the needs of
the public that form the audience, and the forces of
political power that supply the resources.

Sadly, we conclude that the invention did not
work, or at least not very well. Institutional pressures
became unbalanced in a dramatically short time. They
remain today—despite the best efforts of the thousands
within the industry and the millions who support it—
out of kilter and badly in need of repair.

Our proposal is an attempt to balance the manifold pressures within and upon an institution that in
many ways mirrors the complex divisions of today's
America, providing the means with which the system
can reach its fullest potential for creative excellence
and program diversity. We necessarily concentrate upon
the design of national organizations, their relation to the
station system, and the funding mechanisms by which
all components of the system can enjoy a stable source

of funding without threat of interference with programming independence.

The practical outcome of this proposal will be the establishment of institutions and the implementation of fiscal and management policies. However, our objective transcends this level of detail. Throughout our investigation and our report we return to a central theme: this institution, singularly positioned within the public debate, the creative and journalistic communities, and a technological horizon of uncertain consequences, is an absolutely indispensable tool for our people and our democracy.

The power of the communications media must be marshaled in the interest of human development, not merely for advertising revenue. The outcome of the institution of public broadcasting can best be understood as a social dividend of technology, a benefit fulfilling needs that cannot be met by commercial means. As television and radio are joined by a host of new technological advances, the need becomes even more urgent for a nonprofit institution that can assist the nation in reducing the lag between the introduction of new telecommunications devices and their widespread social benefit.

The future for such matters is almost impossible to comprehend, much less to predict. America has entered a new era in telecommunications. Increasingly our work, our leisure, and our capacity to relate to the world are served and shaped by many electronic tools such as satellites, computers, microcircuitry, and wire and glass-fiber television distribution. Public broadcasting as an institution will be challenged and transformed: some say its future is here and that the institution is in fact already evolving rapidly into a public telecommunications complex of extraordinary importance to the future of our society.

As of now, a properly constructed and effective public broadcasting system can unleash the tremendous potential of America's creative artists so that the programming that comes into our homes can better educate and inform, entertain and delight.

While the system sometimes seems unwieldy and frustrating to those working within public broadcasting, the rewards are substantial: a sense of dedication and service, the opportunity to communicate and motivate, the rare coincidence of purpose with craft.

We have attempted, in designing improvements of the present system, to sort out the forces that encourage such creative efforts from those that frustrate it. The act of creation is not so much a mystical event as it is the intersection of inspiration and opportunity. The system must locate, at the center of its enterprise, the incentive to create—a sustained commitment to genuine artistry based upon ingenious uses of these powerful media.

1. *The Trust.* We conclude that there must be a structural reorganization of public broadcasting at the national level. For a variety of reasons, we believe that the existing national leadership organization, the Corporation for Public Broadcasting, is unable to fulfill this role. We recommend that the Corporation for Public Broadcasting be replaced by a new entity called the Public Telecommunications Trust. The Trust, a nongovernmental, nonprofit corporation, will be the principal fiduciary agent for the entire system and all of its components, disbursing federal funds to stations for operations and facilities expansion, as well as setting goals for the system and helping to evaluate performance. In addition, the Trust will supervise a wide range of leadership, long-range planning and system development activities.

One of the primary responsibilities of the Public Telecommunications Trust is to provide the system with protection from inappropriate interference in the sensitive area of program making that will occur both in and outside public broadcasting.

The Trust will also be charged with the responsibility of administering activities designed to improve the system's service to the public, especially as the effects of social and technological changes are felt in the 1980s. Included among these responsibilities are expansion and improvement of facilities and signal coverage, broadening of station involvement with minorities and women, expansion of employment opportunities, development of sophisticated training programs, establishment of both accountability criteria for federal funds and informational and research activities.

The Public Telecommunications Trust will be governed by nine presidentially appointed trustees with staggered, nonrenewable, nine-year terms. We recommend that the President make his selections from a list of names presented to him by a panel, chaired by the Librarian of Congress, drawn from governmental institutions devoted to the arts, the sciences, the humanities, and the preservation of our heritage. In addition, in order to involve the public telecommunications system in this process, the panel would include two representatives drawn from the system.

We call this new organization a Trust and its board members Trustees to underscore our conviction that the nine people who guide the course of the noncommercial telecommunications field in the next decade hold a trust for both the people working within the system and the public that benefits from its services.

2. *The Endowment.* We also recommend the creation of a second statutory organization, the Program Services Endowment, to be established as a highly insulated, semiautonomous division of the Public Telecommunications Trust. The Endowment will have the sole objective of supporting creative excellence and will underwrite a broad range of television and radio productions and program services, including public affairs, drama, comedy, educational and learning research, and new applications of telecommunications technology.

We recommend that the Program Services Endowment be governed by a 15-member board appointed by the trustees of the Public Telecommunications Trust from candidates nominated by the board itself. Three members of the board must come from the public telecommunications community. All board members will serve staggered terms of three years, renewable once. Nominees for the initial Endowment Board will be proposed to the trustees by the nominating panel. The Chief Executive Officer of the Endowment will be chosen by the Endowment's Board.

Behind the recommendation of the Program Services Endowment is a desire to create a safe place for nurturing creative activity, which will otherwise become a casualty of the many other institutional priorities of this complex enterprise. It seems clear to us that there must be at least one place in the system offering to artists and journalists the principal prerequisite for creative achievement, the freedom to take risks.

3. *Funding*. The full-service public telecommunications enterprise we envision will require substantially greater funding than the system now receives. We realize that adequate funding alone is not a guarantee of complete success, but without it, success is unattainable.

We recommend that by 1985 total funding for America's public broadcasting system grow to about $1.2 billion annually. We believe that the combined total from state government, viewers and listeners, the business community, and other nonfederal sources should rise from $347 million in 1977 to $570 million by 1985. We believe that the remainder of the estimated $1.2 billion overall public broadcasting system —about one-half of all funds—should be provided by the federal government.

We recommend that federal support to stations be disbursed by the Trust in direct proportion to the nonfederal support each station generates. At two federal dollars for every three raised locally, the $570 million in nonfederal support will generate $380 million in federal money.

The Program Services Endowment will automatically receive federal funds equal to one-half the federal funds going to stations, or $190 million.

In addition, we recommend that the Trust receive federal funds of $20 million annually for its operating costs and activities, and $50 million in each of the next five to seven years to support facilities expansion.

We recommend general revenues as the principal source of federal funds for public telecommunications. We recommend the establishment of a fee on licensed uses of the spectrum, with the income from this fee used to offset in part the increased requirement for general tax revenues.

We have designed this carefully balanced funding arrangement to accomplish several essential objectives. We believe our recommendations will provide nearly automatic support from the federal government, free to the maximum extent possible from partisan politics. We have made funding recommendations that ensure the industry adequate levels of support generated from a variety of sources, but fatally dependent on none of them.

4. *Television Programs and Services.* The highest priority for the television system is the improvement in its capability to produce programs of excellence, diversity, and substance. Accordingly, we recommend that stations spend the bulk of their new resources on programming, locally, regionally, and nationally through aggregation of some of these funds. To emphasize this, we recommend that Community Service Grants—the federal matching grants to stations—be viewed as Program Service Grants. The Endowment will also supplement station efforts, by supporting innovative and untried programming ideas in a wide range of genres devised by producers working inside and outside the present system.

5. *Public Radio.* The top priority for the public radio system is the completion of the system so that it fully serves the nation in both large and small communities. In addition, the existing and the new stations must have a solid financial and community-support structure buttressing the service function that each licensee performs in its community.

Under the overall leadership of the Public Telecommunications Trust, we recommend the development and activation of an additional 250 to 300 public radio stations. The addition of new stations will result in improved national coverage for the public radio system, greater diversity among licensees, and broader local programming choice in many markets through multiple outlets.

The Trust, in cooperation with other elements of the public radio system, will develop a strategy of system expansion that includes regulatory reform activities and a radio development program that will assist in upgrading existing stations, activating new stations, and purchasing existing commercial or underutilized noncommercial stations.

We recommend that federal funds to public radio stations derived via our proposed matching formula be used for two purposes: improvement of local service and operations, and the financing by station consortiums of programming that transcends strictly local needs. We recommend that the Program Services Endowment support additional national radio programs, particularly new and innovative projects. The Endowment will also provide transitional support for the present National Public Radio programming services until such time as stations are able to aggregate funds to support programs of their choice.

6. *Technology.* In studying new telecommunications technology and public broadcasting's role within it, our goal has been to devise ways in which all the people can have full access to the products of a public telecommunications system. While we have examined the new technology, we have concentrated on ways it might be used by public broadcasting to meet human needs.

We have concluded that it is unwise for us to attempt to chart the future course of public broadcasting as it continues to interact with new technologies. We are convinced, however, that it is essential for public broadcasting to have both the money and the flexibility necessary to enable it to chart its own course as it responds to the future.

To help the industry fulfill this responsibility, we make three recommendations: that public broadcasting and government join together to bring public television and radio service to at least 90 percent of the population over the next five to seven years; that public broadcasting move rapidly to develop a stronger, integrated research and development capability so that it can use new technologies for the public good; and that public broadcasting adopt a broader and more flexible approach to the ways its programs and services are delivered to the public.

7. *Education and Learning.* American public broadcasting had its origins in instructional radio and television. We recommend that the industry recommit itself to providing programs and services that assist in the education of all Americans. Because education in America is primarily a local matter, the major responsibility for this effort rests with the stations.

However, the quality of American education is also a national concern, and because we believe radio and television to have an important role in the process, we recommend that the Program Services Endowment initiate a major research effort to identify what radio and television can teach best, and to develop these capabilities. This is fundamental research, and the potential benefits of it for the entire society are immense.

We also believe that the Program Services Endowment should assume a central role in the creation of new instructional and educational programs. Consequently, we recommend that the Endowment finance and stimulate the development of quality programs that both test and demonstrate the potential of telecommunications for learning. We recommend that the Endowment, acting as a catalyst, allocate $15 million per year for such research and demonstration programs on radio and television. This money might be used to fund several promising educational programs or series, or it could be used as a match for licensee money in coproduction efforts.

8. *Public Accountability.* Because public broadcasting and the emerging public telecommunications industry enjoy widespread public support, stations, which are the focal point for interaction between the institution and the public, must provide serious opportunities for individuals to participate in and understand the system. Mechanisms for public participation in sta-

tion planning and development should be continued and strengthened. These include greater commitment to equal employment opportunity, broadened access by minorities, public involvement in station governance, more complete financial disclosure, and community ascertainment. These measures of public accountability should be devised so as to preserve the station's responsibility to maintain editorial freedom.

These methods, however, are not enough to provide stations with a systematic way to determine whether certain well-defined interests and needs of the public are being satisfied. We present a plan for the use of audience measurement data that will assist the public system in designing programs to meet a broad and diverse audience.

This report, as well as the process by which it was developed, is a testimony to the significance public broadcasting has come to assume in America today. Thousands of committed people within the industry are supported by a diverse, sometimes critical cross section of admirers from all walks of life. As listeners and viewers, as policymakers who will help mold the future of the system, as advocates of causes both great and small, as leaders of the many fields public broadcasting touches and illuminates, they came before us to express their views about an institution that matters. The true greatness of America lies in the strength that emerges from this kind of diversity of religious, racial, or cultural heritage. Public broadcasting must create an enterprise that attracts their continuing administration and support if it is to survive and flourish.

The revelation of diversity will not please some, notably the book burners and the dogmatists among us. It will startle and anger others, as well it should. But we have discovered in our own time that anger yields to understanding. America needs, perhaps even more than healing, a sense of understanding, something that is impossible if we each continue to wall ourselves within the corner of society that we find safe, appealing, and comfortable.

Unless we grasp the means to broaden our conversation to include the diverse interests of the entire society, in ways that both illuminate our differences and distill our mutual hopes, more will be lost than the public broadcasting system.

I

Changing Goals in a Changing World

Americans now watch television for nearly 6½ hours per day in the average household. Americans today each listen to an average of 3½ hours of radio. Many of us spend more time with the electronic media than we spend with other human beings, much less reading or learning. These are facts that we may deplore but can hardly ignore. The ubiquity of the electronic media forces us to ask fundamental questions about how and why they operate.

Societies structure their ways of communicating to reflect their dominant values. Our constitutional freedom of the press bears witness to this nation's early commitment to robust political debate and grass-roots limitations on state power. Press freedom embodies a fundamental American value: access of our citizens to the full range of information available from an uncensored marketplace of ideas. The Marxists, on the other hand, see their press as an agency serving the aims of government. The difference in outlook is fundamental.

Yet, for all our resistance to censorship, there is a sense in which Americans are denied what other societies consider vital: a flourishing public communications service uncensored by commercial imperatives.

The United States is the only Western nation relying so exclusively upon advertising effectiveness as the gatekeeper of its broadcasting activities. The conse-

21

quences of using the public spectrum primarily for commercial purposes are numerous, and increasingly disturbing. The idea of broadcasting as a force in the public interest, a display case for the best of America's creative arts, a forum of public debate—advancing the democratic conversation and enhancing the public imagination—has receded before the inexorable force of audience maximization. In their early days, television and radio experienced brief "golden eras" when relatively small and critical audiences encouraged the profession to foster inventiveness and to pioneer new forms of journalism and mass entertainment.

As television moved into virtually every home, our nation has become increasingly dependent upon it. But, because broadcasting is largely based on commercial sponsorship, it must address itself primarily to attracting the largest audiences, and therefore, also the largest advertising revenues. What these developments suggest about our national life and our dominant values is a matter of concern to many thinking Americans. It led to the establishment of the first Carnegie Commission on public television in 1966.[1]

Although some radio and television channels had already been "reserved" for noncommercial use by the government in 1945 and 1952, respectively, the idea of a national system, funded in part with government funds and aimed at the deficiencies of commercial media, was spearheaded by the work of the first Carnegie Commission in the mid-sixties. With the 1967 Public Broadcasting Act as the codification of the Commission's provocative study, the government was saying, in effect, that if commercial broadcasting must serve purposes other than the public interest, let us create a broadcast system that can serve the untapped potential of the electronic media for public understanding and enlightenment. As Father Theodore Hesburgh, president of Notre Dame University, has said, "The modern miracles of communications have been used to transmit

---

[1] *Public Television: A Program for Action, the Report and Recommendations of the Carnegie Commission on Educational Television* (New York: Harper & Row, 1967).

vulgarity, triviality, and violence. They might better be used to enable great master teachers to transmit hope and access to a better life."[2]

And so, American public broadcasting as we know it was conceived in 1967 with the involvement of the federal government in supporting an independent, noncommercial, diversified system of radio and television stations serving local communities. These elements were to be forged into a national institution serving all those who hungered for an alternative to the increasingly vulgarized commercial fare.

Today, 12 years later, public broadcasting is at the center of an even more momentous debate about communications policy, one that is fundamental to the life of this nation and the world in the late 20th century. Imperceptibly, but in less than 60 years, the means by which we perceive ourselves and the world around us have been totally transformed by the electronic media. The technological revolution, that catchall cliché promising to bring utopia to every home, has changed us all in an unspectacular, but nonetheless revolutionary fashion. We ask ourselves whether the transformation is utopian or Orwellian.

Already with us are even more remarkable technologies: wide-band cable and glass fiber dissemination of information, communications satellites, microprocessors and computers, videotape and videodiscs, digitalized audio and video. These developments are upending the economics of information processing and delivery and will further transform the way Americans live, work, think, and conduct their public affairs. The infant public broadcasting industry has been tossed into the arena with telephone companies, broadcasting networks and station groups, movie studios, newspaper and media conglomerates, the cable television industry, electronics manufacturers, and even the aerospace industry. All these giants have a commercial stake in the future of the telecommunications and information-processing industry.

---

[2]Remarks made at the installation of Joshua Lederberg, president of Rockefeller University, Oct. 16, 1978.

Will the next wave of the communications systems that are becoming increasingly central to our lives leave a place for the creative inspiration and unique learning that we have come to associate with the best of public broadcasting during the last decade? Does the emergence of a new technological context for public broadcasting radically alter the institution's mission? How can public broadcasting survive the stresses it will surely encounter during the next decade from extremely well-financed commercial alternatives?

This soul-searching on the future of public broadcasting is being conducted perhaps more strenuously than any examination of media policy the country has yet seen. We have heard it in committees of Congress, within public broadcasting and the major networks, in testimony before this Commission, in the press, and elsewhere. Not only are professionals in the commercial and noncommercial media industries concerned about the future of telecommunications in America, but a variety of citizen groups have developed considerable expertise which they have sought to use on behalf of constituencies hitherto excluded from national debates on communications policy.

Such citizen and lay concern is the result of more than a decade of disillusionment with powerful institutions in America, and "the media" in particular. Following the lead of the civil rights movement, citizen groups have focused on the power of the media to determine the national agenda and to establish the outlines of our public debate. While citizen activism originally centered on commercial television in protests against violence, sex, and overcommercialization, the media movement soon expanded to encompass public broadcasting as well.

Many public groups, once staunch supporters of public broadcasting against the blandness and vulgarity of commercial broadcasting, began to express disappointment about the record of public broadcasting on programming for minorities and women, public participation in station governance, equal employment opportunity, clandestine commercialism via corporate underwriting, and the use of so many British imports.

Perhaps criticism was inevitable, given public broadcasting's very limited resources. Expectations of a system that calls itself "public" are necessarily broad, and perhaps overambitious at a time when many conflicting voices claim to speak for the public interest.

Hence, as public broadcasting enters its early adolescence, it suffers from chronic underfunding, growing internal conflict, and a loss of a clear sense of purpose and direction. Concerns over new technology and continuing redefinition of its public responsibilities have only unbalanced what was none too stable a personality in the first place. Roughly handled as an infant industry by repeated and enervating survival struggles, public broadcasting is only now able to consider its long term future.

If we are to rediscover purpose and direction, we must somehow reach a consensus on a question with an almost infinite number of answers: *What is public broadcasting?* What distinguishes it from its commercial counterpart and justifies extensive public support? Without audience ratings and profitability as the criteria of success, how do we determine what public broadcasting should attempt to do? During a year and a half of extensive public hearings and spirited internal discussions, the Carnegie Commission has sought to answer these questions for itself. What then do we believe to be the functional characteristics and goals of American public broadcasting?

First, *public broadcasting must be noncommercial.* Unlike commercial radio and television, most print media, and many new communications services, public broadcasting creates programs primarily to serve the needs of audiences, not to sell products or to meet demands of the marketplace. This ideal demands that public television and radio attract viewers and listeners whose tastes and interests are significant, but neglected or overlooked by media requiring mass audiences. The noncommercial nature of public broadcasting has important implications for its programs, its relations with creative talent, and its mission to unserved audiences.

Equally important, *public broadcasting must be independent.* Both at the local and national levels, public broadcasting must create and maintain distance between its funders and the content of its programs—particularly when matters of journalistic and artistic judgment are at stake. Whether financial support is derived from the federal government, local or state governments, foundations, businesses, or viewers themselves, the institutions responsible for making programs must be prepared to fight for their journalistic and artistic integrity. Public broadcasters and program makers should be considered instrumentalities of the press, specially protected by the First Amendment as an integral part of the democratic process. They should speak out with the courage and integrity of a free institution. No statute can confer such freedom. It must emerge from the energy and the will of public broadcasters fully aware of their responsibility to teach and inform.

Public broadcasting must become public telecommunications. All communicators are today in a profession whose fundamental assumptions are challenged by new technological developments and by the social and political consequences that accompany any broad redefinition of mission. The deliberations of commercial broadcasters regarding their investments and market strategies only obliquely concern service to the public. Public broadcasting, by involving itself more deeply in the evolving telecommunications opportunities, could reflect the people's need for an information context that will not only enhance their lives but their citizenship as well.

We expect the years ahead to be a period of unrestrained competitive upheaval. Public broadcasting may well be the only vehicle within the communications infrastructure that will be capable of dispassionate evaluation of programming and new telecommunications services without a constant and chilling eye on the bottom line or the fortunes of a particular corporation. Classical and jazz music services, extensive national radio news commentary, original American drama, documentaries, programming in science and the arts, and public education have already proven unappealing for commercial network distribution. Even more disturbing is the trend for stations and networks to regard newsmakers and newscasters as personalities available to enhance ratings like any other program element. Today's public broadcasting and tomorrow's public telecommunications should try to strike a different note.

Additionally, public broadcasting should be able to pioneer applications of new technologies shunned by the marketplace as unprofitable or disruptive of existing investments. As an example, today's public radio and television system is implementing distribution of the program schedule via satellite, even though the commercial networks have as yet not done so. Public broadcasting has pioneered digital audio and captioning for the deaf. It is studying teletext. These are all technological achievements shunned by commercial broadcasters as impractical or threatening.

Tomorrow's public telecommunications system must develop new leadership encouraging institutional, functional, and technological rearrangements as the public's needs for information and entertainment shift, a process that will entail a flexible and expansive definition of what has heretofore been called public broadcasting.

Public broadcasting must consistently set a standard of excellence for America. Whenever noncommercial broadcasting addresses itself to its work, it must aim to excel. Free of the unrelenting demand to meet a standard of taste attractive to mass audiences, public broadcasting should permit American talent to fulfill the potential of the electronic media to educate and inform, as well as to entertain and delight.

It is clear that the communication of creative excellence is a difficult challenge, one not easily mastered by any institution. A call for excellence is not a retreat to elitism. Cultural and journalistic excellence should provide opportunities for the diverse groupings of the American people to define a pattern of programming unattainable in commercial broadcasting. These alternatives to fare suitable for mass audiences are not programs centered on the preoccupations of a privileged elite. Public broadcasting should bring to Americans the highest accomplishments of our society and civilization in all of its rich diversity.

To do so, of course, means that public broadcasting must create the institutions that will nurture creative excellence. If commercial broadcasting, by pursuing conformity defined by advertising, has stifled the full vigor of America's creative artists and journalists, we must say as well that public broadcasting has exhausted them in a Kafkaesque search for disappearing funds.

Television and radio production are art forms that flourish in an environment that rewards excellence and stimulates achievement. The act of creation is not so much a mystical event as it is the coincidence of inspiration and opportunity. Public broadcasting ought to become a major source of opportunity for inspired craftsmanship, shaping an electronic artifice into an extension and enhancement of human perception.

The medium has yet to develop the resources necessary for a sustained commitment to genuine artistry, regardless of genre. The creator, animated by love of the medium, and by the delight of discovering new pathways within the form, must be central to any successful creative enterprise. Public broadcasting must be able to find and sustain the inventive and inspired people who are capable of making the American scene into a hallmark of excellence acknowledged by the rest of the world. We are certainly capable of it. Only the resources seem to be lacking.

By providing a uniquely constructed special window on society, television and radio shape it and define it. Public broadcasting can easily bring together, face to face, people who might otherwise never meet in daily life. Such communication provides breathtaking potentialities for our sense of community. It can harmonize us in our local concerns. It can bind a nation together by constructing a common catalog of the best in our own society and world culture. A hundred years ago, such experiences were the preserve of a wealthy elite. Now they can be made available to all. The determination to do it is necessary.

Another corollary of public broadcasting's investment in the creative spirit is the necessarily diverse cultural and political spectrum that results. What a complex nation we are, and what a severely circumscribed view of it emerges from commercial broadcasting! The commercial news centers in New York and the entertainment centers in Hollywood homogenize our experience and stultify our critical faculties because their principal objective is to see that the advertising messages get through. How much truer a vision of America and the world could we have were television images to conform to the diversity and richness of life itself rather than consumer acceptability. How much greater understanding of the many racial and religious strains that comprise our nation would be possible if public broadcasting were an active agent of intercultural communication.

These visions of the role of public broadcasting in widening and deepening America's understanding of itself are in no way intended to be confined to any given form of radio or television programming. As we have already emphasized, the electronic media will continue to transform themselves during the next decade in directions that are only dimly visible today. Certainly, the goals of creative excellence, cultural pluralism, and individual expression can be applied equally to drama, children's programming, minority self-expression, and electronic education of every kind. We believe that public broadcasting must be a full service system offering a sufficiently wide range of viewing and listening experiences to attract virtually every segment of the population on a regular basis. Some programs will be extremely popular, and that is good. Other programs will have highly specialized appeal. This, too, will manage to attract significant numbers of viewers and listeners who would otherwise search in vain for interesting program materials.

But there is one objective that public broadcasting must locate at its center of its activity if it is ever to be considered a mature voice in society. Public broadcasting must have a strong editorial purpose. *Without this strong editorial purpose expressed in diverse, even controversial ways, and without an ability to construct a context for understanding the events that occur around us and the meaning of history, public broadcasting will never be taken seriously.*

Journalism has been the greatest area of peril for public broadcasters. In the early 1970s, public broadcasting's outspoken public affairs presence prompted a powerful demand for conformity from the Nixon administration. Once burned, the system, substantially financed by tax dollars, was less tempted to seek controversy or to perform a journalistic role that occasionally earns the displeasure of local pressure groups and government itself.

Yet, while it has a difficult course to chart, public broadcasting *must* develop a strong professional and independent public affairs presence if it is to be respected as an important public voice. Without becoming an agent of propaganda for any ideological position or any geographical elite and without setting itself up as an arbiter of taste or of cultural orthodoxy, public broadcasting must become a journalistic enterprise that calls events as it sees them.

There are some within public broadcasting who will actively resist this recommendation, preferring the blandness that raises no one's hackles. This is not the life of the serious artist or journalist. We certainly do not advocate that public broadcasters should be granted unlimited license to sensationalize or distort in order to titillate audiences, but rather that they be allowed to become a free institution that disciplines itself by constant comparison with truth.

Public broadcast journalism must be carried on by professionals prepared to accept and live by the requirements of responsibility that go hand in hand with freedom. We believe, for example, that a mature journalistic role for public broadcasting will require that the institution speak out on matters of public policy, attempt to uncover wrongdoing, and occasionally criticize those in high places. Such criticism must be truthful and fair, but we believe that appropriate standards should be allowed to develop within the system, rather than by statute.

We believe that public broadcasting has the re-

sponsibility to use these most powerful communications media as tools to enhance citizenship and public service. The noncommercial nature of public broadcasting permits dissemination of informational and educational activities that can elevate the level of public debate and understanding of our ever more complex local, state, and national activities.

Public broadcasting currently provides many such services over the air—legislative coverage and analysis, hearings coverage, call-in programs, professional and special-interest training via state or regional networks, special forms of instruction and information access. We believe that expansion into the nonbroadcast technologies will greatly increase the system's capability, especially on the local level, to discover new forms of public service and provide them to a wide range of professional and interest groups.

Public radio and television have pioneered creative programming for special audiences, particularly children. Such programs as *Sesame Street, The Electric Company, Mister Rogers' Neighborhood, Zoom,* and *Spider's Web* have had an extraordinary impact on American life, especially in urban centers where they have helped to mitigate the effects of poor-quality schools.

Public telecommunications must continue to break new ground in the education of all Americans—children in their classrooms and at home, adults in lifelong learning and professional training, and the general public. We recall here such highly enjoyable and educational programs as *Civilisation, The Adams Chronicles, Nova, National Geographic,* and *The Cousteau Odyssey.* Moreover, we believe public broadcasting must be prepared to devote substantial future effort and resources to the creation of first-rate programs that present to the broad audience the cultures and concerns of other specialized groups. The system must go beyond the reactive support of particular programs to "satisfy" special-interest groups and begin to apply talent, time, and money to innovative programming that celebrates and illuminates the diversity of American culture. Our understanding, for instance, is that public broadcasting was unable to develop a program about blacks with the appeal and quality of *Roots* because it lacked funds for a project of such magnitude. We must try to change that.

Such commitments will always find themselves in competition with other important objectives, and there will never be enough money or time to perform every valuable service, particularly in a climate of careful scrutiny of public funding. But public broadcasting must resolve to develop a creditable approach to American life, American creativity, and American public service. Such a commitment, dynamic and changeable as it may be, is a prerequisite for system growth and progress that will eventually earn the interest and support of millions of people in every corner of the country.

Finally, we observe that a strong and mature public broadcasting institution will become increasingly indispensable during the next decade as our fragmented and troubled nation attempts to rebuild its self-confidence, to heal its wounds, and to discover the strength that emerges in the wake of a shared ordeal.

America has become, for better or worse, a society that is mediated by many forms of electronic apparatus. Public broadcasting, and soon public telecommunications services, can do much to transform that technological intercession into a process of reconciliation. With the development of many narrow, "one-issue" constituencies in modern America, each serving its own interests and seeking its own gain, the need for such reconciliation grows. There is always the danger that propaganda can ultimately prove more satisfying than understanding, and that in the end we may cease communicating altogether. Public broadcasting, constructed along the lines recommended in this chapter and set forth in succeeding chapters, can help prevent that, and thus can prove to be of fundamental importance in the preservation of our democratic ideals.

II

The Rise of Public Broadcasting

Broadcasting in America developed under commercial auspices. In contrast to many other Western nations, the United States government awarded broadcast licenses to private firms which sold advertising time in order to finance the costs of producing and delivering programs and to provide a return on investment. Noncommercial broadcasting emerged only after this pattern had become solidified.

One of the most significant forces shaping public broadcasting's early history was the failure of the 1934 Communications Act to give special consideration to noncommercial broadcasting. Not until 1945 did the Federal Communications Commission (FCC) set aside the 20 FM radio frequencies currently reserved for noncommercial and educational users. After great pressure by educational and public groups the FCC, in 1952, reserved 242 noncommercial television channels.[1] The failure to provide adequately for noncommercial broadcasting at the outset has had lasting effects. Noncommercial radio has been largely confined to the FM band, and even there it has suffered from

---

[1]This was later increased, so there are now 655 television channels (127 VHF and 528 UHF) reserved for noncommercial educational use.

33

government restrictions imposed by the FCC. Many noncommercial television stations are forced to broadcast in the hard-to-receive UHF band[2] as a consequence of the head start gained by commercial entrepreneurs who received VHF allocations before 1952.[3]

In noncommercial television's early years, most licenses were assigned to educational institutions interested in providing instructional programs. As television became more popular, however, nonprofit community organizations also applied for and received licenses. These community licensees, deriving their funding from private contributions, auctions, and foundation grants, began to broadcast programs of both general cultural and educational interest. During the 1950s and early 1960s, many educational television stations benefited from the financial support of the Ford Foundation, which, among other things, financed the production and distribution of programs of national interest via the independent National Educational Television (NET).

In 1962 Congress provided initial federal support for the system through the Educational Television Facilities Act of 1962, which authorized $32 million over five years to aid the construction of educational television stations. By the end of 1966, 126 stations were on the air.

With the success of the federally supported facilities program, educational broadcasters began to look to the federal government for a portion of their operating support. Their efforts led to the creation, in 1965, of a

---

[2]Ultrahigh-frequency (UHF) television channels (14 through 83) are transmitted on higher frequencies than very-high-frequency (VHF) channels (2 through 13). Simply stated, UHF signals are more difficult to receive because, during a broadcast, they are more vulnerable to interference caused by physical obstructions such as smog and fluctuations in terrain. Moreover, most television sets sold in the United States before 1964 could not receive UHF channels. (In 1962 Congress passed the All-Channel Receiver Act, which required that all television sets sold in the United States after 1964 be capable of receiving UHF as well as VHF channels.) Because of these factors, UHF channel allocations have always been less desirable than VHF allocations.

[3]Educational television received no VHF reservations in 69 of the top 100 markets, including such cities as New York, Washington, D.C., and Los Angeles.

private commission on noncommercial television, to study and make recommendations for its future.

The Report of the First Carnegie Commission

Members of the Carnegie Commission on Educational Television quickly became aware of the needs and problems of educational television as it stood on the threshold of developing into a national institution. There was a need to improve and expand services to the public and greatly to increase the flow of funds to the system. At the same time, some persons in educational broadcasting feared that a large increase in federal funds would lead ultimately to government control. The Commission sought to unify the interests of those who advocated centering noncommercial television on instruction and education and those who advocated a broader public-service role. It also recognized the tension between the stations seeking to preserve their autonomy and the desire of national entities, such as NET, to develop a national interconnection and program service.

The Carnegie Commission's 1967 report[4] articulated a new and broader mission for noncommercial broadcasting. A new term, "public television," was introduced to dramatize the emphasis on programming for general enrichment and information, as well as for classroom instruction. The Commission's plan also emphasized the importance of developing a national public television system, and proposed a new leadership organization and funding process for public broadcasting.

Among the Carnegie Commission's major recommendations were:

- Creation of a private, nonprofit organization to receive and disburse private and federal funds for public television under the guidance of a 12-member board of distinguished citizens. This Corporation for Public Television was to provide programming and leadership for the system,

[4]*Public Television: A Program for Action* (New York: Harper & Row, 1967).

shield it from improper governmental and political pressure, and undertake a variety of other activities to improve public television's ability to serve the public.

- Establishment of a tax on the sale of television sets to generate increased, stable, and insulated funding for the activities of the Corporation. Proceeds from the tax would be made available through a trust fund.
- Direct funding by the Corporation of program producers, including at least two major production centers.
- Establishment by the Corporation of interconnection facilities to permit simultaneous broadcast of programs nationwide.
- Distribution of federal funds by the Department of Health, Education, and Welfare to stations in support of general operations.
- Federal funding of a facilities program through HEW in order to extend public television service nationwide.

The Commission's report was well received by the public, educational broadcasters, Congress, and the White House. Many persons endorsed the Commission's eloquent statement of the opportunity to turn the miraculous instrument, television, to its best uses. E. B. White's exhortation that "noncommercial television should address itself to the ideal of excellence, not the idea of acceptability . . ."[5] was widely applauded and supported. For the first time, a federal plan for noncommercial television was on the verge of adoption.

The Public Broadcasting Act of 1967
Although the basic intent of the Carnegie plan was embraced, some of its recommendations were altered as the White House and Congress responded to public debate, pressure from noncommercial broadcasters, and other interested parties. The legislation which resulted —the Public Broadcasting Act of 1967—differed from the recommendations of the Carnegie Commission in several important respects:

---

[5]Ibid., p. 13.

- Carnegie recommended that station operating funds be provided through the Department of Health, Education, and Welfare and that the Corporation focus on programming, research, interconnection, and other national functions. Instead, Congress decided that stations should receive operating support from the Corporation to insulate them from pressures that might be applied by HEW, a government agency.
- The Commission recommended a 12-member board for the Corporation, with six members appointed by the President and the remaining six selected by the board. Under the act, the board was enlarged to 15, all presidential appointees subject to Senate confirmation.
- In proposing a dedicated tax on the sale of television sets, the Commission sought an insulated, long-term source of federal funding for the Corporation's programming activities. The objections of television set manufacturers, opponents of any federal support for public broadcasting, and those in Congress and the Administration who viewed this form of dedicated tax as rigid and regressive, doomed the Carnegie proposal from the start. Instead, the Corporation was given annual appropriations by Congress as if it were a government agency, while the White House pledged to develop another plan for long-term, insulated funding.
- Carnegie called for the Corporation for Public Television to establish an interconnection of stations. Fearing the establishment of a "fourth network" if the Corporation not only financed programs but also had the power to advertise them and make them available for simultaneous use by stations, Congress prohibited the Corporation from operating the interconnection.
- The Carnegie Commission did not consider public radio. In the legislation, radio was made a partner of the federal support system. Thus, the new entity to disburse the federal money was named the Corporation for Public Broadcasting (CPB) to dramatize the inclusion of radio. CPB was given the task of developing national programs, arranging for interconnection, and dispensing operating funds for the radio system. The HEW

facilities grant program was expanded to include radio.

Thus, in responding to a variety of pressures and interests, Congress rearranged some of the Carnegie proposals and altered or eliminated others. The new federal support and national structures would result in achieving some of the objectives the first Carnegie Commission and others had set for the system. But in retrospect, it is fair to say that each of these policy changes set in motion conflicts which could not have been predicted at the time.

Implementing the Public Broadcasting Act of 1967

Enactment of the Public Broadcasting Act of 1967 was the most important event in the history of noncommercial broadcasting. The Act acknowledged the importance of an independent, noncommercial broadcasting system as a national institution, and established the federal government's commitment to supplement funds from state, local, and private sources. A fundamental tenet of the legislation was the need for insulation from governmental interference. The Corporation for Public Broadcasting (CPB), with a distinguished board, was the primary means for providing that insulation. Perhaps most important, the Public Broadcasting Act dramatized the promise of public broadcasting as an alternative to commercial radio and television.

By the end of 1969 CPB had received its first federal appropriation of $5 million and had made its first program production grant to National Educational Television for the production of *Black Journal*. It also commissioned a study of public radio. CPB then moved rapidly to establish its policies in three crucial areas— the interconnection of stations and the program-funding process in television, the interconnection of stations and program funding in radio, and operating support grants for stations.

To comply with the congressional prohibition of CPB's interconnecting the stations, it established a study group of executives from CPB, the Ford Foundation and station managers. The group recommended, and CPB accepted, the establishment of a new private entity, the Public Broadcasting Service (PBS), to operate the interconnection for television stations. PBS would be a membership organization, financed by CPB but controlled by the stations through a governing board that also included representatives of CPB, NET, and the public. PBS began distributing programs to stations in the fall of 1970.

CPB began to finance programs for national distribution to all television stations, although at this time the Ford Foundation was still the principal funder of public television's national schedule. In making program grants, CPB came to rely on PBS to survey the stations on their needs and priorities, and to contact producers on their proposals. This arrangement was logical. PBS was the stations' organization, and with an awareness of what programs stations actually used from the interconnected program service, it was in a position to make suggestions based on experience. In addition, to meet its interconnection responsibilities, PBS worked with producers of programs as they were planned, funded, and delivered for distribution. Thus PBS came to occupy a crucial role in funding and distributing national programming, although CPB retained final authority over what programs would be financed with federal funds.

The period from 1967 to 1972 was one of extraordinary growth and improvement in public television. The number of television stations increased from 126 to 233. New sources of funds were developed, and more stations began to tap them. University stations began to generate viewer contributions. Community stations turned to new private sources, as well as to local and state government support. Total income to public television stations grew from $58 million in 1966 to $158 million in 1972, with federal support increasing from $7 million to $31 million during that period.

The greatest accomplishments of this improved public television system were in programming, where a wide range of offerings—from the irreverent approach to public affairs taken on *The Great American Dream*

Machine to drama in *The Forsyte Saga* and such children's programs as *Sesame Street*—developed a new awareness of public television which attracted significant audiences. Between 1970 and 1972, the total prime-time public television audience increased more than 30 percent.[6]

A different division of responsibilities was established for public radio. National Public Radio (NPR) was launched in 1970 by CPB as a station organization operating the interconnection. Unlike PBS, however, NPR was also empowered to *produce* programs for its member stations. NPR was financed by CPB through annual grants for programming, interconnection, and other activities.

CPB implemented its legislated responsibility to provide operating support for television and radio stations by establishing the Community Service Grant (CSG) program. Stations were eligible to receive a modest amount if they met certain minimum operating standards. These criteria were attained by virtually all noncommercial television stations. However, many noncommercial radio stations operating only part-time, at very low power, or with a very low budget, were unable to qualify for operating support.

During its first five years the Corporation also experimented with direct grants to radio and television producers, established and supported professional and minority training programs, and began to involve itself in new technologies.

In this fashion, CPB and public radio and television established the framework for future growth and progress. The CPB board would act as an intermediary between Congress and the stations, since it had no direct operating control over programming. When political pressures arose, it was expected that the CPB board would act as an impartial, responsible buffer. CPB involved stations directly in programming and entrusted operation of the interconnection to station organiza-

---

[6]By the fall of 1972, 36.1 percent of the households in the country tuned at least once to a prime-time public television station during an eight-week period. (Data from A. C. Nielsen Co.)

tions. With station organizations involved in these important activities, it appeared likely that station reluctance to cooperate in working toward national objectives would be reduced.

By the early 1970s an institutional framework was in place. Yet several important elements of the vigorous and free national system that the first Carnegie Commission envisioned were still lacking. The most important of these was stable federal funding to provide insulation and effective planning. Related was the need for greatly increased support. The Corporation had actually commenced its work with private support while awaiting its first federal appropriation. As the size of the federal appropriation grew in the first few years, CPB nevertheless found itself with relatively meager resources to meet its heavy responsibilities. Table 2–1 shows the growth in appropriations to CPB and the facilities program administered by HEW.

Finally, the Corporation's ability to carry out its broad mandate depended greatly on the quality of the presidential appointments to its board. Unless the board members were capable of nonpolitical leadership of the public radio and television systems, the system might well falter. This objective was not appreciably advanced by a legislative requirement that a bare majority of the board be drawn from one political party.

The Watershed: President Nixon Vetoes a Funding Bill

Recognizing that the Public Broadcasting Act had not solved the question of funding, public broadcasters and government officials attempted to develop a plan for long-range funding of public broadcasting. Preliminary discussions were held with the White House Office of Telecommunications Policy, but by 1971 it became clear that some in the White House were displeased with developments in public broadcasting. Administration officials believed that public television had become a vehicle for political criticism of the administration. They asserted that public television had turned its back on localism and was attempting to create a fourth national network through increasingly centralized

Table 2–1

Federal Appropriations for Public Broadcasting

Fiscal Year	Corporation for Public Broadcasting	Federal Appropriations (thousands) Educational Broadcasting Facilities Program (HEW)
1963	—	$ 1,500
1964	—	6,500
1965	—	13,000
1966	—	8,826
1967	—	3,304
1968	—	0
1969	$ 5,000	4,375
1970	15,000	5,083
1971	23,000	11,000
1972	35,000	13,000
1973	35,000	13,000
1974	47,750	16,500
1975	62,000	12,000
1976[a]	96,000	12,000
1977	103,000	15,000[b]
1978	119,200[c]	19,000[b]
	$540,950	$154,088

[a]Includes the transition quarter.
[b]Includes $1 million appropriated for telecommunications demonstration grants.
[c]Includes a supplemental appropriation of $12.25 million.

programming and scheduling functions administered by CPB and PBS. This attitude coincided with the views of many stations that were concerned about the possibility that an eastern liberal bias would come to dominate national programming in public affairs. They desired greater control over program funding.

During the first year and a half of PBS operation of the interconnection, disputes had broken out among the stations, PBS, and NET (by then merged into WNET, New York) over the content of programs such as *The Great American Dream Machine* and *Banks and the Poor.* Stations were pressuring PBS to limit controversy on public television. PBS, in an effort to balance the desires of broadcasters and their producers, took steps that were viewed as insufficient by CPB board members who had also heard complaints about offensive programming.

Despite White House opposition, however, a two-year, $155 million authorization for CPB was passed by both houses of Congress and was sent to the White House in June 1972. President Nixon vetoed it. In his message accompanying the veto,[7] the President cited evidence that public broadcasting was deserting the concept of localism, and asserted that until the industry could return to this basic mission, long-term funding was unwise.[8]

---

[7]Richard Nixon, "Veto of Public Broadcasting Bill. June 30, 1972," *Public Papers of the President: Richard Nixon, 1972* (Washington, D. C.: Government Printing Office), p. 718.

[8]The veto was the subject of discussion on a television talk show in early 1973 on which Patrick Buchanan, a White House speechwriter, said:

> Now, last year the administration proposed an increase of $10 million in the budget for Public Educational Television, from $35 million to $45 million. It got down to Capitol Hill, and the fellows in Public Television went to work and they elevated that up to $165 million for two years.
>
> Now, when that came down to the White House, we took a look at it, and we also looked at the situation over there. I did personally. I had a hand in drafting the veto message. And if you look at the public television, you will find you've got Sander Vanocur and Robert MacNeil, the first of whom, Sander Vanocur, is a notorious Kennedy sycophant, in my judgment, and Robert MacNeil, who is anti-administration. You have the Elizabeth Drew show on, which is, she personally, is definitely not pro-administration. I would say anti-administration. *Washington Week in Review* is unbalanced against us, you have *Black Journal*, which is unbalanced against us . . . you have Bill Moyers, which is unbalanced against the Administration. And then for a fig leaf they throw in William F. Buckley's program. So they sent down there a $165 million package, voted 82 to 1 out of the Senate, thinking that Richard Nixon would therefore—he would have to sign it, he couldn't possibly have the courage to veto something like that. And Mr. Nixon, I'm delighted to say, hit that ball about 450 feet down the right field foul line, right into the stands and now you've got a different situation in Public Television. You've got a new ballgame at CPB. You've got a new awareness that people are concerned

Some assert that the President's veto resulted principally from the size of the congressional authorization, since early discussions with White House representatives involved a much lower figure.[9] However, we view this use of presidential authority as consistent with President Nixon's campaign against concentration of power in other broadcast media. We believe that the administration sought to curb public affairs programming[10] in

---

about balance. And all this Administration has ever asked for on that, or on any network television, frankly, is a fair shake.

Now, until we get that fair shake, network television can expect to be criticized. And I might add, we have had our say, network television has had its say, and over the last three years there has been a greater collapse in public confidence in the objectivity and the balance and in the fairness of the network television, than in all of our previous history of it.

When this transcript was read at a Senate hearing later in 1973, Senator Pastore retorted, "And the remarkable thing about it is that every program that Buchanan mentioned has been knocked off . . . Except the *Black Journal*, and I don't think they had the courage to do that." U.S. Senate, *Hearings on S. 1090 and S. 1228 Before the Subcommittee on Communications of the Senate Committee on Commerce*, 93d Cong., 1st sess., 1973, p. 8.

[9]The administration had requested an appropriation of $45 million in 1973, $10 million more than CPB had received the previous year.

[10]The following is the full text of a memorandum sent by Clay T. Whitehead, then head of the Office of Telecommunications Policy, to H. R. Haldeman, then White House chief of staff, on November 24, 1971:

With the controversy between the Administration and the Corporation for Public Broadcasting becoming more visible, you might be interested in what we are doing behind the scenes on the Vanocur/MacNeil situation.

After Vanocur and MacNeil were announced in late September, we planted with the trade press the idea that their obvious liberal bias would reflect adversely on public television. We encouraged other trade journals and the general press to focus attention on the Vanocur appointment. Public television stations throughout the country were unhappy that once again they were being given programs from Washington and New York without participating in the decisions. My speech criticizing the increasing centralization of public television received wide coverage and has widened the credibility gap between the local stations and CPB. It also has brought more attention to the acknowledged liberal bias of CPB and NPACT.

We then began to encourage speculation about Vanocur's and MacNeil's salaries. As a result of the increasing public controversy, several reporters and Congressman Lionel Van-

public television. Remarks by Clay T. Whitehead, the President's chief telecommunications adviser, before a convention of the National Association of Educational Broadcasters, condemned the system's alleged centralization of program decisionmaking and the consequent capacity to generate political criticism.

The veto destroyed the fragile arrangements under which CPB, PBS, and NPR had operated up to this point. As a result of the veto, CPB President John Macy, and many of his top aides, resigned. CPB Chairman Frank Pace declined to stand for reelection and was replaced by a former congressman, Thomas B. Curtis.

With the appointment of Curtis, President Nixon had appointed or reappointed 11 of the 15 members of the CPB board. The latter brought in Henry Loomis, a career public servant, as president. Loomis had previously worked closely with James R. Killian, chairman of the Carnegie Commission and a charter CPB board member.

Relations between CPB and PBS began to deteriorate. Three particular CPB board actions precipitated a major reorganization of PBS and a confrontation which substantially transformed institutional relationships within the entire public broadcasting industry. First, the CPB board voted to discontinue funding of all public affairs programming, except for *Black Journal*. Second, it rescinded a staff commitment to

---

Deerlin asked CPB to release the salaries. Macy refused, but after pressure increased, quietly made it known that Vanocur receives a salary of $85,000 a year and Robert MacNeil $65,000.

We plan to do two things in the next few weeks to continue to call attention to balance on public television, especially NPACT. We will quietly solicit critical articles regarding Vanocur's salary coming from public funds (larger than that of the Vice President, the Chief Justice, and the Cabinet) and his obvious bias. We will quietly encourage station managers throughout the country to put pressure on NPACT and CPB to balance in their programming or risk the possibility of local stations not carrying these programs. Our credibility on funding with the local stations is essential to this effort: "Memo for Mr. H. R. Haldeman" (Washington, D.C.: Executive Office of the President/Office of Telecommunications Policy, Nov. 24, 1971).

provide multiyear funding to the National Public Affairs Center for Television (NPACT). Finally, in January 1973, the CPB board unanimously voted to take from PBS certain legal, research, public awareness, and programming functions, including "the decisionmaking process, and ultimate responsibility for decisions, on program production support or acquisition [and] the pre-broadcast acceptance and post-broadcast review of programs to determine strict adherence to objectivity and balance in all programs or series of programs of a controversial nature."[11]

The leadership of the stations and PBS regarded these actions as an objectionable assertion of centralized control. Accordingly, they reorganized PBS to consolidate their own power and to provide public leadership within PBS to counter CPB. Guided by Ralph Rogers, Texas industrialist and chairman of KERA, Dallas, the new PBS incorporated its own station management board with a division of the National Association of Educational Broadcasters and the Governing Board Chairmen, comprised of laymen involved in station governance.

At the urging of key congressional officials, PBS and CPB began negotiating their differences in early 1973. At the eleventh hour, CPB Chairman Curtis resigned, claiming White House interference in CPB affairs. He was replaced by Dr. James Killian, who was widely respected in the industry because of his role in the first Carnegie Commission and subsequent legislation. In May, Killian and Rogers announced the CPB-PBS partnership agreement, designed to provide a framework for mutual trust and industry-wide consensus.

The partnership agreement provided that PBS would continue to operate the interconnection on behalf of its member stations under the direction of its station-controlled board. CPB would finance only technical operations through a contract with PBS, and would leave to PBS's station members the financing of

---

[11]"Resolution of the Board of Directors" (Owings Mills, Md.: Corporation for Public Broadcasting, Jan. 10, 1973).

such activities as programming, promotion, public information, research, and representation.

The agreement also established a significant increase in CPB's discretionary funds—Community Service Grants—to stations. These unrestricted grants to television stations were to rise to 50 percent of the CPB appropriation once it reached $80 million. The consequence of increasing the amount CPB "passed through" to stations was to reduce the amount of money and discretion that CPB itself had for programming.

The third significant feature of the partnership agreement altered the program-funding processes employed by CPB and PBS. While CPB was permitted to make all final decisions about programs financed through its TV activities department, the staff was instructed to consult on program decisions with the programming staff at PBS. PBS and CPB have never agreed on the precise meaning of the program-funding provision of the partnership agreement, causing a continuous stream of disputes over programming between the two groups. Charges have often appeared in the press and caused criticism of the industry in Congress and among public interest groups.

Immediately following the signing of the partnership agreement, however, a renewed spirit of cooperation between PBS and CPB led to the passage of a two-year, $110 million authorization for CPB. This time the legislation was signed by President Nixon, who praised the bill for furthering the cause of localism because it increased discretionary funds to television stations. In 1973 stations had received about 14 percent of CPB's funds; as a result of the partnership agreement, in 1974 they received about 32 percent of a much larger appropriation. Table 2–2 shows the division of the federal appropriation between program funding and unrestricted grants to television stations before and after the partnership agreement.

Because CPB would have less money to spend on national programs and the stations would have more discretionary funds, PBS devised a process for the stations to pool their own funds and select national programs without CPB approval. With financial support from CPB and the Ford Foundation, PBS established the Station Program Cooperative (SPC)[12] in 1974. Many of the public affairs programs once funded by CPB were now selected and funded by the stations' own decisionmaking processes.

Table 2–2

Flow of Federal Funds Through Corporation for Public Broadcasting Before and After Partnership Agreement

Fiscal Year	Total CPB Appropriation (millions)	Allocations to TV Programs (millions)	Allocations to TV Stations (Community Service Grants) (millions)
Before partnership agreement:			
1973	$ 35.0	$13.7 (39%)	$ 5.0 (14%)
After partnership agreement:			
1974	$ 47.8	$12.7 (27%)	$15.2 (32%)
1975	62.0	8.8 (14%)[a]	25.4 (41%)
1976[b]	96.0	10.4 (11%)[c]	46.5 (48%)
1977	103.0	14.6 (14%)	51.7 (50%)

Source: CPB Management Information Systems.
[a]Includes $4.1 million for Station Program Cooperative.
[b]Includes the transition quarter.
[c]Includes $4.2 million for Station Program Cooperative.

These essential features—the SPC, greater station discretionary funding, a reorganized and stronger PBS, and decreased programming funds at CPB—constituted a major reorganization of the public television system. The single most dramatic event of this period, the veto of federal funds by President Nixon, served to stimulate a host of forces already at work in the system, notably the split between the localism advocates and those interested in central decisionmaking. The period provided the clearest test of the industry's structure.

We believe there are two major lessons to be drawn from the 1972–73 events. The first lesson is that the CPB board failed to provide leadership and in-

---

[12]A more detailed discussion of the SPC appears in Chapter V.

sulation for the public broadcasting system, one of its major mandates from Congress and the first Carnegie Commission. Without attempting to judge the motives of the board, we observe that the board took action to downplay public affairs programming in order to avoid placing the entire federal appropriation in jeopardy. Rather than fight for the system's independence from political interference, CPB's decisions about NPACT, various public affairs series, and the takeover of PBS functions seem to us to have been an attempt to mollify the administration in order to maintain the funding that was now life and death to the system. The stations themselves were divided on whether they wanted CPB to resist the administration, since success in the administration's quest for localism would decentralize programming decisions and provide the stations with more money. While one might argue that CPB's decisions were arrived at independently, they did, in fact, coincide with the expressed objectives of the administration and were widely perceived as concessions.

Furthermore, by becoming increasingly involved in program-by-program decisions in controversial areas, the board sacrificed its role as a buffer between the government and program makers responsible for creating and delivering programming for the public. Because of this, many stations have come to lose respect for CPB leadership and to regard the corporation as a government agency.

The second major lesson was that there is potential strength in stations working together. They developed an important role for themselves as programmers for the system, and continued the public affairs presence on the system. They also developed strong leadership when they needed it, in opposition to what they viewed as a move to centralize authority under a politically vulnerable statutory organization.

We recognize that interpretations of the events surrounding the veto differ and that there may be more than one plausible explanation of this period. The one inescapable conclusion, though, is that public broadcasting was then and is today an extremely fragile institution that found it almost impossible to overcome the force the presidential veto represented. And the kinds of adjustments the system felt compelled to institute diminished public broadcasting's capacity to strive for journalistic and artistic excellence.

This period came to a close in an extraordinarily ironic way. Public broadcasting, the object of considerable criticism from the Nixon administration, offered gavel-to-gavel daytime coverage of the Senate's Watergate hearings in the evening. It is unlikely that commercial television would ever clear its evening schedule to provide such coverage. Public broadcasting could and did. This historic event became a personal experience for people who might not otherwise have seen or heard it. To many close observers, this coverage redeemed the system and brought it new audiences, as well as new respect.

Public radio was also adversely affected during this period of conflict. CPB's attention was primarily on television, and with no increase in federal funds as a result of the veto, the growth of public radio was slower than it might have been. And in resolving the conflict between CPB and PBS, little attention was paid to the needs of radio. It is curious that public radio—also criticized by Whitehead, in his NAEB speech, for what was in fact a far more centralized program production process—survived the period virtually unaffected by the political battles. Perhaps this was because public radio, underfinanced and with few outlets, posed little real political threat. Nevertheless, in 1973 public radio did follow the example of television stations by establishing a separate organization, the Association of Public Radio Stations (APRS), which they controlled and financed to represent their interests before CPB, Congress, government agencies, and other national entities.[13]

Thus we see public broadcasting, in the first seven years of its history, shaped less by the goodwill and good intentions of its supporters than by the attacks of

---

[13]APRS became a part of what is now NPR as a result of a merger of the organizations in 1977.

its enemies. The weakness of its board leadership, and the evolution of institutions which more often responded to crisis than to carefully laid and coherent plans, played a key role in the outcome.

Multiyear Federal Funding in 1975

One of the positive results of the 1972 veto and the ensuing conflict was a rededication by Congress, the administration, and the public broadcasting industry to development of a funding arrangement that would be stable, long-term, and insulated. As a result of their efforts, legislation was signed by President Ford in 1975 which authorized significant increases in funds over a five-year period. Equally important, Congress was willing to appropriate funds to CPB three years in advance, or through 1979. This advance funding enhanced public broadcasting's insulation and its ability to engage in long-range planning. (Table 2–1 shows the history of federal appropriations to CPB.) The amount of federal support under the new legislation was based on the ability of the system to raise nonfederal support for its programs and services. The federal funds—$1 federal support for every $2.50 nonfederal—resulted in an overall appropriation for CPB, not a station-by-station match of locally generated funds. The theory behind this "match" system was one of ensuring that public broadcasting would be responsible to the community and that its federal support, determined by community support, would be relatively protected from political attack. The legislation also included a "pass-through" formula similar to the one that had been adopted by CPB and PBS in the partnership agreement, that is, half of the federal appropriation would be distributed to stations as unrestricted grants.

The 1975 legislation marked a twentyfold increase in federal funds in less than a decade and provided an improved system for long-range and insulated funding. The federal appropriation to CPB increased from $5 million in 1969 to $119.2 million in 1978, as shown in Table 2–1. Nonfederal income grew significantly in this period too, largely due to the stronger public broadcasting system made possible by increased federal funding and the incentive of the matching requirement. Total income of public broadcasting increased almost fourfold from 1970 to 1977 ($109 to $482 million). Table 2–3 shows total federal income (mostly the spending of CPB and the EBFP, but also relatively limited spending by other federal programs), total nonfederal income, and total income from all sources for public broadcasting.

However, the new legislation also created new problems. First, the 1975 act created a climate in which all the money CPB had to spend came to be viewed by the stations as "their money," since the level of federal funds was determined as a match of the stations' locally raised funds. This situation led the television stations and PBS to oppose a CPB plan for strengthening public radio, since television licensees, that raised most of the nonfederal funds, saw radio expenditures as a diversion of their own hard-earned funds. It also led PBS and the television stations to question many CPB program-funding decisions, as well as the Corporation's allocation of funds for nonprogramming activities.

Table 2–3
Public Broadcasting Income

Fiscal Year[a]	Federal Support (thousands)	Nonfederal Support (thousands)	Total Income (thousands)
1970[b]	$ 13,648	$ 95,685	$109,333
1971[b]	24,669	128,274	152,943
1972	59,812	174,493	234,304
1973	55,585	210,953	266,538
1974	67,005	230,968	297,973
1975	92,341	277,472	369,813
1976[c]	112,646	303,154	415,800
1977	135,269	364,825	482,094

Source: Corporation for Public Broadcasting.

[a]1969 not available.

[b]Figures for 1970–71 reflect income reported by stations and are not directly comparable to figures for other years.

[c]Figures for 1976 include the transition quarter.

Public Broadcasting Today

The events of 1972–73 slowed the growth of public broadcasting and left a psychological scar on the stations—an enhanced sensitivity to perceived threats to their independence—which persists even today. Yet the ensuing reorganization and the new multiyear funding plan helped stimulate public broadcasting's recovery and renewed development.

The number of television stations increased from 216 in the beginning of 1972 to 280 in 1978, with the system now providing a signal that is viewable in over 80 percent of the nation's homes. The breadth and quality of programs increased, attracting larger audiences and criticial acclaim. The number of Americans viewing public television at least once a month has risen by 28 percent since 1973, increasing to 46 million, or 63 percent of television households by March 1978. Subscription income in the 1972–77 period increased from $10.4 million to $45.2 million, a 335 percent increase. Federal funds in the same period grew from $31 million to $114 million, a 267 percent increase. Total income reached $417 million, up from $158 million in 1972, a 163 percent jump.

Equally impressive, the number of qualified public radio stations grew from 103 in 1971 to 198 in 1978. The public radio audience nearly doubled in the four-year period from 1973 to 1977, growing from 2.2 million to over 4.2 million regular listeners. Funds to support public radio increased from $12 million in 1971 to $66 million in 1977.

From 1966 to 1977, the average length of the television broadcast day grew from roughly 8 hours to approximately 14 hours; in radio, the broadcast day grew from 13¼ hours in 1971 to more than 18 hours in 1977. The schedule of national programs made available to local television stations increased from 20 hours per week in 1970–71 to approximately 90 hours per week in 1977–78. In radio, it remained steady at approximately 40 hours per week.

Public broadcasting has created new and highly

successful programming for children, altering the American public's hitherto passive acceptance of the activities of commercial broadcasting in this area. Opera, dance, and drama have all been made available to millions of Americans through public radio and television. One performance of *La Bohème* telecast live from Lincoln Center in New York on March 15, 1977, was viewed by 5.1 percent of American households, an audience that would otherwise require 2500 sold-out performances of the Metropolitan Opera. In scores of small communities, public radio has become the only broadcast link with our musical heritage. In small towns and major cities, public radio has become the vehicle for the communication and preservation of uniquely American art forms: jazz, blues, and bluegrass. Even more than public television, public radio has created for itself a strong journalistic voice in its daily news magazine, *All Things Considered*. Public radio has revived radio drama, told stories to children, and has become the broadcast medium of record in its coverage of important congressional proceedings and other national events.

Beyond public broadcasting's programming efforts, multiyear funding and the reorganization in the mid-seventies allowed the system to move forward on other fronts. The 1975 Act encouraged the system to experiment with and develop new technologies for public purposes, and under the leadership of CPB and PBS, important initiatives were launched. Most significantly the Corporation, after initial planning by PBS and others, played a leading role in implementing public broadcasting's conversion to domestic satellite interconnection.[14] By employing satellite rather than terrestrial networking, public broadcasting will have the potential to expand greatly the quality and range of its program service and multiply the sources of program origination.

As awareness of public television and radio rose

---

[14]Public television's conversion to satellite was virtually completed in late 1978, while public radio is expected to take another year.

and as the federal appropriation to CPB—$103 million in 1977—increased, public broadcasting was confronted with new difficulties. Some in the administration and Congress became increasingly concerned about a perceived lack of financial and public accountability, limited access to the system by minorities[15] and independent producers, and continuing fractiousness among CPB, PBS, and NPR.

The FCC opened investigations of what some observers thought was excessive commercialization of noncommercial broadcasting. New financing legislation was proposed by President Carter in October 1977. The Carter proposal was modified through initiatives of Senator Ernest F. Hollings and Representative Lionel VanDeerlin, chairmen of their respective Communications Subcommittees, and legislation was enacted in 1978 which sought to address many of these concerns, while increasing federal support to $220 million in 1983. While pleased with the increased funding, many public broadcasters resented what they saw as new "strings" attached to federal funds, threatening their independence. In the legislative process leading to the 1978 Financing Act, we have observed that the three national public broadcasting organizations could not always put aside differences and work toward a common objective.

The events of 1977–78, as well as the lingering weaknesses of the system exposed in 1972, led many in public broadcasting to call for a reassessment and internal reexamination of the industry's problems. To understand those problems and weaknesses it is helpful to focus separately on the four components of public broadcasting.

---

[15]A report on equal employment opportunity in public broadcasting issued by the House Communications Subcommittee in April 1977 threatened that public broadcasting would receive no further authorizations until the Subcommittee's recommendations had been met. House Subcommittee on Communications of the Committee on Interstate Commerce, *Summary of Findings and Recommendations on the Enforcement of Equal Opportunity and Anti-Discrimination Laws in Public Broadcasting* (Comm. Print. 95-12, 1977), 95th Cong., 1st sess.

The Corporation for Public Broadcasting

The Corporation was designed initially to be the leadership entity that would allocate federal funds to the system and insulate it from political attacks. CPB has been unable to achieve its purpose for several reasons.

In the Commission's view, a major flaw in the design of CPB was the combining of system leadership and programming responsibilities in a single organization. We do not believe that any organization can exercise the leadership and dispassionate evaluative role essential to a healthy public telecommunications system if it also administers program funds on a day-to-day basis. A direct programming role for a central leadership organization in such a highly visible and sensitive enterprise as public broadcasting impairs its ability to provide insulation and constructive criticism for a system of dispersed stations.

This involvement in programming has become particularly sensitive since Congress has increased CPB's responsibility to certify that all funds—including the operating support it passes through to stations—are spent responsibly and in accord with public policy. The change in institutional personality, brought on by new regulatory responsibilities, has had a chilling effect on CPB programming activities. The chill has often driven CPB away from controversial program content, and from a willingness to take risks, to seek untried program sources, to initiate programs without the support of other funders. With distrust from stations, as well as pressure from Congress and others to alter the image of public broadcasting, CPB's programming activities have too often been subordinated to its regulatory responsibilities.

CPB's television program funding record is disappointing. With responsibility for station support money as well as programming funds, CPB is hesitant—perhaps correctly so—to jeopardize federal support for stations by giving critics the easy target of a programming disaster. In radio, CPB's record has been better, largely because it has delegated much of its programming responsibility to NPR. Overall, though, the result has been that CPB failed to function as the catalyst for creative programming envisioned by the first Carnegie Commission and the Public Broadcasting Act.

The Public Broadcasting Service

PBS is a membership organization representing and providing services to the stations. PBS also operates the interconnection and promotes and schedules programs nationally, but does not control the stations' schedules.

While PBS provides important support services to the stations, it has not been able to assume an effective national leadership role. It has fought bitterly—and often publicly—with CPB for programming supremacy, and, with virtually no funds of its own, has reached a stalemate at best. When it has tried to make policy on its own, PBS has often been opposed by many of its member stations which prefer it to be merely the clearinghouse for decisions made locally. The stations, themselves, licensed to different types of entities, have found it difficult to give their organization clear guidance in many policy matters. The result has inevitably been strife between station factions and their national representatives.

PBS's involvement in the programming process and its responsibility to represent the stations politically before Congress and the administration has sometimes created the perception of an unhealthy commingling of functions.

The leadership vacuum has been especially clear in the programming area. While PBS operates the SPC for the stations, with few exceptions it has been unable to expand its program role beyond coordinating the Cooperative's complex decision process. With only limited delegation of responsibility by the stations, PBS has acted largely as a follower of decisions made by others including corporate and foundation program funders, CPB, and federal agencies such as the National Endowments for the Arts and Humanities.

It is a matter of conjecture whether PBS, organized as a broadly based membership and representation organization, could fill a role as a funder and stimulator of major and innovative program ventures.

The reluctance of the stations to permit PBS to exercise a national leadership role can be illustrated by PBS's promotion and advertising activities—essential elements of a national broadcasting service. PBS has generated only limited funds for promotion and advertising, despite research showing audiences to be small and nonviewers generally unfamiliar with public television fare. Stations pool very little for this needed activity, fearing that national advertising will diminish their right to determine their own schedules. This has made public television reliant on the advertising efforts undertaken by the corporations and foundations which now fund many of the system's national programs. This has created the public perception of a system dominated by corporate underwriting. This vacuum of leadership has kept many fine programs from reaching a significantly broader viewership.

The Television Stations

The stations are, as is often said, the bedrock of the system.[16] They are responsible for deciding what is broadcast to their viewers and listeners, and they raise funds to support station operation. The station is legally and ethically responsible only to its audience and the public interest.

---

[16]The first Carnegie Commission's statement that "the local stations must be the bedrock upon which Public Television is erected" has often been inaccurately quoted as an assertion that the system should rest upon a "bedrock of localism." That Commission stated no such thing. Indeed, the rest of the paragraph in which the term "bedrock" appeared reads as follows:

> But there are needs that the local stations alone cannot meet. There must be effective leadership for the system as a whole. There must be means by which the stations communicate with each other, and with the public. There must be a means of performing services, as in the development of experimental programs and the recruitment of manpower, which are likely to be more efficiently carried out by an organization that can act for Public Television. There must be a system-wide process of exerting upward pressure on standards of taste and performance. (*Public Television: A Program for Action*, p. 36.)

The station can most effectively fulfill its responsibility to the public when it is not controlled by the government, its funders, special interests, or other forces. Again and again stations have defended their right to determine what programs their communities will receive. In view of the diversity of the country, this stout insistence on local control is not necessarily objectionable.

The stations have developed funding mechanisms to enable them to exercise their editorial responsibilities to their communities without external control. Increasing proportions of federal funds have gone to the stations where they may be used at their discretion. Moreover, the stations themselves established the program selection and funding system of the Station Program Cooperative (SPC) to make it possible for them to determine a major portion of their national programming.

On the other hand, although stations have resisted political attacks at the national level and have received increased federal discretionary grants, they have failed to develop a complete programming service. The SPC, thus far, has largely been limited to funding the mainstream programs with proven track records, a process that has consumed most of the available program funds. It does not have a good record of financing provocative and powerful drama or public affairs. These activities require large investments of money, and hence substantial risks. Stations are understandably reluctant to take risks with their scarce funds. Moreover, it is not clear whether the SPC would be effective in these potentially controversial areas, even if the necessary funds were available. Many observers feel it would not.

There is a related problem. The absence of a dynamic program production and selection function under station control has meant that public television's programming has become subject to external interests, especially the interests of the corporations, foundations, and government agencies that fund much of the national schedule. The stations, alone, do not admittedly have the resources to become a fully self-directed editorial medium serving the public. Curiously, the increase in federal funding has exacerbated this problem. With the federal funds determined as a match of nonfederal support, incentives for outside funding have increased.

Stations have found that the best vehicles for fundraising have been programs that do not threaten the audience's sense of well-being. Opera, light classics, science programs, travelogues, imported drama, and the like have as a result become programming staples. They please large numbers of people, bring membership money to the stations which air them, and are easily underwritten by outside funders who desire a good public image. It is a situation that is not uncommon among institutions dependent on public support. State colleges, for example, are often hard put to defend controversial professors. This is not to say that public broadcasting has been led by its funders to make programs that are not properly a part of the mission of public broadcasting. It is not the programs that are made, but the programs that are not made, that cause concern. Public broadcasting is obliged to serve all of its audience; the program underwriters are obliged to serve only their own interests. The system of dependence on underwriters has created little incentive for local public affairs programs, for programs that serve small or less affluent audiences, or for controversial programs that may offend.

The stations do not bear all the responsibility for these failures. The dependence on outside underwriters need not have been so great had the stations had sufficient funds to create the missing programs.

Funds will always be inadequate to finance *all* the possible services a public telecommunications system might provide. Despite this reality, joint efforts among stations at the national and regional level must become common. Stations must develop leadership to undertake these efforts and to provide the flexibility essential to deal constructively with the new opportunities and challenges ahead as technology changes and expands.

The Public Radio System

In 1977 the public radio trade association, APRS, merged with the CPB-financed interconnection and production agency, National Public Radio, to form a new NPR. NPR, therefore, now combines national production and distribution capability with political representation, in a way which many feel is unthinkable for television. In addition, the production activities of NPR are funded directly by CPB and are not, therefore, entirely controlled by the licensees.

Unlike the situation in public television, the public radio stations have been quite willing to have national program production and distribution centralized and under the financial oversight of CPB. Public radio stations supported the creation of NPR from the beginning, and they retain control over it through its board. Sorely underfinanced, the stations have recognized the benefits of centralizing program functions. With no station able to produce major national public affairs programs of consistently high quality, NPR has built its program service around *All Things Considered,* the highly acclaimed nightly program which stations are delighted to use, at least in part. As a single organization with a relatively large budget, NPR has been accorded considerable programming autonomy by CPB, which has worked to the great advantage of public radio. Overall, the NPR program system seems to have worked quite well.

The major reason we have not witnessed the strain within public radio that has characterized public television over the last few years is the underdeveloped nature of the system. NPR distributes only 40 hours a week to stations, compared to the 126 hours stations must broadcast. And many of the programs distributed by NPR are recorded concerts or discussions, programs which can be produced on a local basis. Thus, radio is a locally programmed medium, for the most part, and national programs make up only a small share of the broadcast day. Even though NPR services are limited now by inadequate funding, the emphasis on local programming by most radio stations limits the amount of reliance they will ever place on a national program entity. Moreover, carrying only insignificant funds for promotion and advertising, NPR programs are not broadcast by many stations. Also simultaneously inhibiting the creation of a strong national presence for NPR is the poor quality of the land-based system for distributing programs, which encourages programs not requiring high fidelity.

This situation has begun to change, and it is likely to change much more rapidly in the near future. Armed with more resources for programming and promotion as well as a satellite distribution system that provides a high-fidelity means of distribution, NPR is likely to contribute an increasing number of diverse programs. With several programs available on the satellite at one time, it is likely that stations will be able to select from a greater mix of the national programs distributed by NPR. NPR will not only be a major producer of national programs, but it will become the "gatekeeper" for the satellite.

Efforts to manage this change will be a major challenge in the years ahead. It is not clear how the inherent economy of radio will affect this problem. On the one hand, stations will desire more high-quality national programs which they can share, thus achieving significant economies on a per station basis. On the other hand, even though they are sorely underfinanced today, most public radio stations are still able to produce most of their schedules locally and are desirous of improving local service. Moreover, they may resist domination by a better-financed NPR. Thus they may seek more funds passed through to the stations, with an attendant decline in funds available for national programs.

The outcome is unclear: there may be one or several major producers of national programs and there may be one or several major distributors of those programs. Public radio is on the threshold of an important new era in which it can expand services and its contribution to our society.

The signs of this change are already apparent.

Groups of stations with similar interests or in a single region have increased their efforts to work together. At the national level there have been significant strains. Only 198 of the nearly one thousand noncommercial radio stations have met minimum operating standards required to obtain a Community Service Grant from CPB. Many stations believe they have been unfairly excluded from these support grants. CPB has attempted to accommodate to this criticism by instituting a special grant program to help stations reach this minimum level, but this has not eliminated the perception of unfairness.

There are other tensions. The strong role played by CPB in program sustenance has led to an NPR policy that is subject to much criticism. NPR membership and, therefore, the ability to share fully in NPR-produced programs, are limited to stations which can meet the criteria developed by CPB for financial support. Only 217 of the noncommercial stations in the country are NPR members. CPB's requirement that public radio stations operate in accord with fairly high professional standards in order to qualify to receive operating support has no necessary relationship to eligibility to receive NPR's programs. As a result of NPR's policy of restricting its service to CPB-qualified stations, many Americans are perhaps unnecessarily deprived of valuable program services.

Finally, while CPB funds are derived by matching funds raised by both radio and television stations, the radio system receives funds in greater proportion than it contributes. This policy has generated much public strife between radio and television over proper funding levels for radio, and has aggravated the public perception of the public broadcasting system as a fractious collection of self-interested stations, unable to work together for the public interest.

The System's Approach to Creativity and Programming

The foregoing assessment of public broadcasting's evolution is largely a political and institutional one. It tells of the internal and external pressures upon a diverse group of local entities and their national organizations, and their response to those pressures. It does not chronicle all of public broadcasting's successes—or its failures—but instead focuses broadly on its development and the interplay of its major elements.

Perhaps this history informs most of all in what it does *not* disclose. It discloses no serious, transcending effort to construct in public broadcasting the conditions for sustaining creative work. No systematic effort to establish the circumstances under which public radio and television could consistently achieve programming excellence seems possible under the present circumstances.

We have seen only sporadic efforts to permit artists access to the system; only rarely has the system been in a position to seek out the finest American talents, so that the public might benefit by their endeavor. Instead, we see independent producers required to "affiliate" with a station in order to gain access to the system.

Absent, but for a few exceptions, are successful efforts to encourage undiscovered talent to enter public broadcasting. We see instead a system where only a handful of people, usually with proven track records and tested formats, are trusted to exercise discretion in program making.

At the same time we see a system that has been unable to devise a rational and fair program-funding process that encourages program innovation and creativity. Testimony before the Commission characterized CPB's television program funding activities as irrational, arbitrary, and bureaucratic. It is a view held by both the unknown, aspiring documentarian and the established Hollywood producer. Moreover, the stations' own cooperative program development process has too often preferred the safe and has discouraged individual achievement.

It is perhaps this situation—the absence of conditions under which creative work in the electronic media can flourish—that is the most disturbing legacy of public broadcasting's first decade. Despite the hard work of many, and in spite of many isolated program successes, the tensions within public broadcasting and the lack of sufficient funds have conspired against the development of programming excellence that ought to be the hallmark of the public system.

The creation and communication of artistic and journalistic excellence is a complex and sensitive process. As commercial broadcasting demonstrates all too well, excellence cannot be mass-produced by formula. Yet some artistic enterprises—publishing houses, art galleries, symphony orchestras, and magazines and journals, for example—have balanced the conflicting pressures and objectives inherent in such a process.

Programming excellence in public broadcasting requires not just talent, but money, time, and risk taking. It requires a tradition and a structural framework hospitable to creative endeavor. We must discover the organizational, financial, and public policies that permit the public telecommunications system to protect its creativity in an era of great technological and social change. With the lessons of public broadcasting's history in mind, it is to these matters we now turn.

III

Reorganizing Public Broadcasting

We recommend the creation of a new statutory institution for public telecommunications, the Public Telecommunications Trust, a private, nongovernmental, nonprofit corporation. It will provide leadership, long-range planning, evaluation, and system development. In addition, it will provide financial protection both for broadcast licensees and for a highly insulated, self-directed division of the Trust, the Program Services Endowment. The Endowment will be dedicated to excellence, and will underwrite a broad range of television and radio program services, including public affairs, drama, comedy, education and learning research, and new applications of telecommunications technology. The Trust will replace the Corporation for Public Broadcasting, and administer the facilities program, thereby consolidating into one entity national leadership, planning, and development activities.

We recommend that the Trust and its Endowment be governed by separate boards.

The nine trustees of the Public Telecommunications Trust would be appointed by the President from a list of nominees recommended and screened for financial conflict by a distinguished nominating panel chaired by the librarian of Congress. The trustees will appoint the board of the Endowment from nominations provided by the Endowment board itself. We recommend a special process for the initial selection of both boards.

Overview

It is crucial that the public telecommunications system be organized so it can balance competing national and local responsibilities within an institution that is both publicly funded yet quintessentially private. The events outlined in Chapter II have led us to conclude that the existing configuration of national organizations makes it almost impossible for the system to meet the legitimate expectations of the American public, to resist inappropriate pressures, or to provide conditions under which creative achievement in programming will be sustained.

We recommend, therefore, a new national structure for public telecommunications, one which provides responsible private leadership for independent initiative in the production of national programs and for protection from inhibiting pressure. Our proposed reorganization will allow the system to remain essentially local, but enable it to meet national responsibilities. Figure 3–1 is an illustration of our proposed system.

The national structure will be centered on a new institution, the Public Telecommunications Trust. Within the Trust we recommend the establishment of a self-directed Program Services Endowment. In this chapter we describe the mission and governance of these new bodies.

It is central to our conception of the system that the stations remain autonomous and strong. Under our proposals they will have strengthened ability to form regional and national associations to meet their respon-

Proposed System Organization

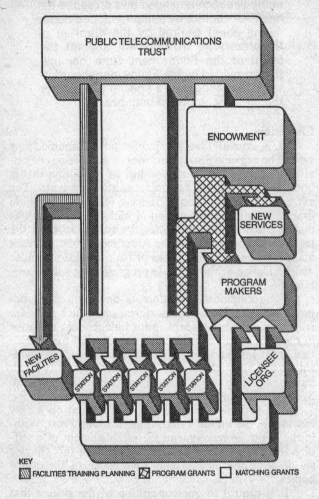

Figure 3-1. Proposed System Organization.

sibilities as they see them. We do not, therefore, recommend any specific form of governance—local or national—for the stations. Chapter V, however, contains our suggestions for effective station implementation of station-determined objectives.

A National Structure for Public Telecommunications

1. The Public Telecommunications Trust

We recommend the new statutory structure with clear delineation of powers and improved governance in order to accomplish what we believe should be the principal goals of the public telecommunications system as it evolves in the 1980s.

Foremost among these goals is the ability of the public system to create programs and services of the highest quality. In order that those responsible for programming decisions can support creativity without fear of reprisal either from political forces or from the timid within public broadcasting itself, we suggest the establishment of a Program Services Endowment funded with a guaranteed and nontransferable source of income protected by its parent institution, the Public Telecommunications Trust. The Endowment, unencumbered by the pressures of operating the system, would have the single mission of supporting national programming activities.

The Public Telecommunications Trust is designed to meet a second principal goal: to provide nongovernmental public leadership that will help develop long-range goals, evaluate the industry's performance, and supervise activities that improve the system's service to the public in a time of rapid social and technological change.

Under the leadership of a nine-member board of trustees, the Public Telecommunications Trust will administer the disbursal of federal funds to stations for operations and facilities expansion. It will also receive both federal and private funds on behalf of the autonomous Program Services Endowment that functions under its protection. The Trust has been designed as the system's chief fiscal institution in order to provide financial accountability to the public. At the same time, as a private institution, it will be a suitable conduit for federal funds. This new organization will offer protection from inappropriate interference in sensitive creative and journalistic activities whether it originates inside or outside of public broadcasting. If the trustees act as protectors and fiduciaries for the public telecommunications system, the integrity of their performance will generate the principal justification for widespread and continuing public support.

The Trust will also be expected to undertake national efforts to improve the system's service to the public, particularly as the effects of social and technological change are felt during the 1980s. These responsibilities include the expansion and improvement of coverage and the advancement of technical capabilities; the broadening of licensee involvement with ethnic, social, and racial minorities; the expansion of employment opportunities and the development of new training programs; the establishment of procedures for accounting for federal funds; coordination of system-wide institutional change, informational and research activities; and other mandates identified by the Congress and the trustees themselves. In short, the Trust will be the system's national center of public fiduciary responsibility.

Because of the key role we foresee for the trustees, we strongly recommend a refinement of the current leadership appointment process that we hope will attract the highest-caliber individuals to these posts. It is no secret that in recent years appointments to the CPB board have become highly politicized, a trend which we believe has damaged the system. Necessary reform can be accomplished by specifying a nomination procedure in the enabling statute, guaranteeing a steady flow of nominees through a process that improves upon the current appointment system. Our plan is to empanel a group of seven distinguished Americans under the leadership of the librarian of Congress, to recommend to the President a slate of potential appointees. The staff of the librarian would also perform financial investigation to guard against conflicts of interest, obviating the necessity of full public disclosure.

The Trust's Purpose: Public Leadership. The unique genius of the American system of government has been in balancing institutions to forge a national vision while respecting the vitality and geographical diversity of its many constituent parts. The strength of federalism comes from our ability to move onward despite—or perhaps because of—competing interests within the nation.

Public broadcasting, too, must find a way to balance local and national institutions to meet local and national needs. It must develop a tradition of governance that can serve the public as a whole, while giving the television and radio stations the power and freedom to determine the character of their service to their communities.

Many of these stations pioneered the concept of noncommercial educational and community broadcasting years before the federal government became committed to the system's improvement and expansion in the 1960s. The stations continue to operate as unique local or statewide institutions, financed primarily by nonfederal sources, serving publics that vary from community to community. The stations have established various means of determining local programming needs, and each has responded with programs and services that are remarkable for their diversity. The stations remain the legal entities responsible for the program schedules available to viewers and listeners throughout the land.

And yet, the stations have many common needs that must be provided on a nationwide basis. To one degree or another, all public stations are dependent upon the costly programs created for national audiences. Since 1970 the radio and television stations have been interconnected so that they could simultaneously receive programs—especially coverage of live events. Federal support for stations is provided through central organizations under the provisions of laws that express policy objectives of the entire nation; planning, and technological innovations such as satellite distribution, require nationwide implementation.

The 1967 Public Broadcasting Act sought to resolve such local-national tensions by establishing the Corporation for Public Broadcasting. The act emphasized the private nature of this corporation, and the benefits that could be derived for the stations and the public from the leadership of CPB's board, which was to be comprised of distinguished men and women devoted to the improvement and growth of the noncommercial broadcasting system.

CPB was to support the operation and improvement of the station-based system, while providing national leadership, planning, protection from federal interference, support for national programs, and the interconnection of stations. CPB has not provided the national leadership we believe the system and the public require. Nor did an effective leadership emerge from the diverse station system.

Without leadership that is respected at the grass roots and is respectful of local processes, the system as a whole is incapable of defining its mission to serve the public. Such definition is doubly difficult in public broadcasting, which is a nonprofit enterprise without the quantitative measures of advertising success.

What is a "successful" program? What is a suitable program service? What is the appropriate mission for public broadcasting? What posture should the system take toward new technological advances?

We have detected a profound uneasiness, both inside and outside the system, regarding the processes by which these and other critical questions are answered in public broadcasting. Without the bottom line criteria provided by ratings and profits, public broadcasters have difficulty in evaluating their performance and defining their goals. This presents a major challenge. Their ability to look into the short- and long-range future is regularly impaired by temporary crises, often related to funding. Thus, we have seen severe limitations on the stations' capacity to resolve conflict in a manner emphasizing the broad public interest rather than narrowly defined self-interest.

Hence the operating entities—the stations and their organizations—are inappropriate agents of publicly responsible national leadership in public telecommunications. They are too diverse, occasionally timid, and often at odds with themselves. As we observe the examples of how the system has reached consensus and moved forward on major matters of policy despite its problems, we are convinced that such progress can be substantially improved if leadership and support are properly constructed. As James MacGregor Burns notes:

> What may seem to some principled leaders to be parochialism, inertia, perversity, or apathy, may be, in fact, highly charged leader-follower relationships with their own tradition, structure, logic and morality. Only with time, determination, conviction, and skill—and with the indispensable element of conflict—can followers be drawn out of these narrower collectivities and into "higher" purpose and principle . . .[1]

The Public Telecommunications Trust must provide such leadership to balance support of all elements within the system with the larger public interest. While conflict and tensions are inevitable, coercion and stalemate are not. We call this organization a Trust and its board members trustees to underscore our conviction that the nine people who will guide the course of public telecommunications in the next decade and beyond will, in fact, act as fiduciaries both for the people working within the system and for the public that benefits from its service. The trustees will be accountable to both the industry and the public. The trustees must neither act in the immediate self-interest of licensees and their existing institutions, nor seek to impose a shifting political will upon a creative enterprise involved in most sensitive matters of aesthetic, journalistic, and educational judgment.

These trustees must protect the rights of stations and producers occasionally to criticize the government, while taking the government's money. They must assure the public that their money is spent wisely, without

---

[1]James MacGregor Burns, *Leadership* (New York: Harper & Row, 1978), p. 425.

interfering in delicate programming decisions. They must encourage the industry's managers to respond to the reality and idealism of social change by broadening access and participation of minorities and women. They must use their prestige to protect programming of the highest caliber in the arts and public affairs. The trustees must help lead the industry into an unknown future, one which may seem to make the goals of the system even more difficult to achieve.

We do not believe that such leadership belongs within agencies of the federal government. Unless the trustees can assert an independent leadership in a responsible way, the linkage between federal funding and the goals of public policy will surely shape the system into a cultural and informational ministry devised by the government. We can and must avoid such an outcome.

Unlike many other public-service activities performed with the partial support of the federal treasury, public broadcasting encounters a constitutional dilemma when it accepts federal support. Public broadcasting is a creative, potentially controversial artistic and journalistic enterprise that is highly visible to taxpayers, lawmakers, and government officials who may occasionally find themselves displeased by the activities of the system. Yet the ostensible purpose of public broadcasting is to ensure an additional agent of the free press and of artistic integrity. If the government enters the area of content regulation, either by direct interference or by the use of financial disbursement policies to exercise a subtle effect on programming decisions, the system will forfeit its independence and will be in danger of becoming a federal broadcasting system.

Some have argued that public broadcasting should receive no particular special treatment, the First Amendment notwithstanding. They ask why this institution should be spared the responsibilities of implementing federal policies. Furthermore, some would ask, if the stations cannot defend themselves, why should they have a special organization that is designed to "insulate" them from pressures and responsibilities that go with life in the real world?

The problem is that the first instincts of individual licensees in defending themselves are not necessarily those that serve a free society. It is easy to conform when a public dispute arises in which a specific local interest is not at stake. But if it is to have any integrity at all, public broadcasting must act as a unique instrument of a free society—a free press sponsored in part by the government. We cannot say forcefully enough that instruments of the press *are* different from less sensitive institutions in the society. Such instruments are protected by the Constitution itself as an integral part of the operation of democracy, whether supported by federal money or allowed to earn revenues by virtue of a federally bestowed broadcast license. Public broadcasting should, like all elements in American society, be committed to national requirements for social policy. But care must be taken lest public interest regulation become a method for government interference in program content. Hence we recommend that federal funds must continue to be disbursed by a private, nonprofit entity incorporated in a fashion similar to the Corporation for Public Broadcasting. We believe, however, that CPB should be replaced.[2]

Despite a number of major achievements, the Corporation for Public Broadcasting has not succeeded in three fundamental responsibilities with which it was charged by the Congress, the first Carnegie Commission report, and the public. These are the provisions of insulation from federal pressure, the effective leadership of the entire public broadcasting system, and the consistent support of excellence in programming.

Chapter II contains our view of the system's history. It highlights a complex evolution of forces in order to establish the background to our recommendations for system improvement. While considerable emphasis has been placed on the destructive events of 1972–73, the failures of CPB are not ancient history. The Corporation today continues to operate with low effective-

---

[2] The entire Commission agrees on the need for a new structure for public telecommunications. Two members of the Commission believe that the structure might best be brought into being through evolutionary changes of the present CPB.—W. J. M.

ness and credibility in the programming and leadership spheres. Its present board continues to display a direct operating presence in programming rather than provide insulation for system activities. While some of these problems are the legacy of the early 1970s, the institution as a whole seems enmeshed in a bureaucratic stalemate with much of the rest of the system. We believe this struggle has impaired its ability to achieve its most important goals.

We do not make this recommendation lightly. We are aware that the Corporation and its employees have contributed substantially to the growth of public radio and television during the past decade. We have concluded that the establishment of a new institution with fresh leadership unencumbered by the burdens of history is in the long-range interest of the system.

No one can guarantee that the new trustees selected under the suggested appointment procedure will perform more effectively than the excellent people who have faithfully served CPB as board members and staff over the past ten years, but the framework in which they will work and the context of their mandate for leadership will be quite different. Nothing can substitute for a tradition of leadership, independence, and fiduciary responsibility among the trustees of the new Public Telecommunications Trust.

2. The Program Services Endowment

Before detailing the full range of activities to which the Public Telecommunications Trust will be devoted, we wish to describe its involvement in national programming.

The production of programs for a national audience is the most serious issue in public broadcasting today. Earlier we described our understanding of the pressures that have made public broadcasting's production systems so ineffectual. Our funding recommendations and suggestions for concerted station action will enable local production and station-determined production of higher quality. In our judgment these improvements are not enough.

Public broadcasting must have an institution for

the support of national production for radio and television that is devoted to this single mission, neither governmental nor station-based, insulated from outside pressures, and adequately funded.

The Endowment's Purpose: Creativity in American Production

The Program Services Endowment will be established within the Public Telecommunications Trust as a well-insulated patron of the creative artist, journalist, educator, and communicator. Its only mission will be to support the development by the American creative community of programs and services of the highest quality with a diversity of styles, genres, and contents.

No organization currently exists in public broadcasting with the exclusive mission of supporting the creative activity necessary for better programming services. One producer told the Commission: "Instead of seeing how one can clean up the top, please figure out what is it that creative individuals need in order to make programs. It is the individuals rather than institutions that make programs, and it is institutions that must be created that will support those individuals."[3]

The achievement of excellence in any field is rare. It requires specialized and rather single-minded effort, a broad and constantly renewable pool of talent, and devotion to the process of creation rather than to maintenance of bureaucracies and turf. To institutionalize this vital activity is the challenge that has eluded public broadcasting over the years.

Jacques Barzun once pointed out that the artist should be viewed as the natural enemy of institutionalized society.[4] Yet despite this, all of us recognize that

---

[3] Michael Ambrosino, testimony before the Carnegie Commission on the Future of Public Broadcasting (open hearings, New York, Nov. 18, 1977).

[4] Jacques Barzun, "The Enemy in the House: Art in Modern Society" (lecture, Columbia University, New York, Jan. 29, 1973).

society cannot grow or even survive without its artists. Television and radio are the most highly visible artistic enterprises in our society, involving not only such creative and potentially controversial arts as drama, comedy, and entertainment, but also the education of our youth and the enlightenment of the populace through news and public affairs programming.

Creative activity, of course, does exist in public radio and television today and we applaud and encourage these remarkable efforts. Yet nowhere has a sustained and supported vision of programming excellence, in either traditional or experimental forms, managed to flourish. That sustaining role seems to have been left to the large private foundations. The rule within public broadcasting as advanced by its sensitive and vulnerable licensees has been safe, evenhanded, even boring programs rather than the visionary, the challenging, the ground-breaking efforts that raise the level of the entire medium. One observer has told us: "To anyone possessing even the most rudimentary knowledge of the arrangements in other communication arts that have stimulated original achievement, the structures and procedures of public broadcasting seem almost consciously designed to block such achievement. To repeat: the individual creator remains, in the eyes of this medium, The Enemy."[5]

Behind the recommendation of establishing a Program Services Endowment is a desire to create a safe place for nurturing creative activity, which otherwise will become a casualty of the many other institutional priorities of this complex enterprise. It seems clear to us that there must be at least one place in the system offering to artists and journalists the principal prerequisite for creative achievement, the freedom to take risks. We are fully aware that risk taking implies that mistakes will be made, and failures will occur. But without the capacity to take chances, to try new ideas, we will never

---

[5]Benjamin DeMott, "Towards a New Vernacular: Notes on the Future of Public Broadcasting" (essay prepared for the Carnegie Commission on the Future of Public Broadcasting, Amherst, Mass., Nov. 11, 1978), pp. 14–15.

experience success. For public television and radio to set and expand the standards of excellence for the entire telecommunications field, there must be an agent whose exclusive domain is the search for and support of excellence in the electronic media.

This goal is particularly important if we seek to increase the volume and variety of public television programs that are produced in the United States. Excessive reliance upon imported programming is primarily the result of the present system's inadequate funding base. To acquire a program already produced overseas is less costly than to produce it here. With substantial new funds concentrated in the Endowment, however, the public broadcasting system should be able to increase its commitment to American talent—writers, directors, actors, technicians, producers, film- and videomakers, as well as educators and communicators able to develop the frontier of telecommunications.

Program production professionals working in a wide range of genres and subject areas are entitled to expect the support and leadership of an institution that can concentrate its full attention, skills, and funds toward the achievement of programs of true distinction. Much of the remainder of this report details our findings and suggestions for the improvement of the system in such major fields as public affairs, the arts, children's and educational programs, and new applications of telecommunications media.

We feel confident that the Endowment can be planned so as to accommodate a broad and changing vision of program excellence, provided that the following principles are included in enabling legislation and defended strongly by the management and boards of both the Endowment and the Public Telecommunications Trust.

A Single Mission. The single reason for the Endowment should be the underwriting and development of programs and services. While we believe strongly that such services must include applications of new communications technologies beyond broadcast radio and television, the Endowment must not become entangled in the functional improvement of the system outside the programming area. The Endowment should not be asked to undertake research on training, development and enforcement of qualifications standards, audience measurement, facilities development, or system planning. It should not report to Congress. These are activities which we believe to belong under the administrative aegis of the Public Telecommunications Trust, and through the Trust, with the licensees themselves. The separation in policy authority between the Trust and the Endowment is intended to provide further insulation for the integrity of programming decisions.

Insulation. If creative risk taking and ventures into sensitive content areas of journalism and education are to involve more than rhetoric; the Program Services Endowment must be protected from the rougher forms of political struggle, including struggles over station and institutional territory. We are recommending that the Endowment have its own governing board and chief executive officer. However, we think it unwise to make the Endowment an entirely independent body, separate from the protection of the Trust. Such a separate entity, dependent upon congressional action for its resources, would become too concerned with congressional opinion. There would be, even in the absence of direct congressional or executive pressure, an inevitable effect on programming.

We recommend, therefore, that the Endowment be housed within the Trust, even though the direct policy responsibility for its programming decisions will rest with its own board. The trustees will have the responsibility to report to Congress on the financial activities of the Endowment, but will stand aloof from questions about controversial programming decisions. The chief executive officer of the Endowment will be twice protected from extraneous pressures—once by the Endowment board itself, and ultimately by the trustees.

The Endowment is protected as well from the sort of station pressures which have made the programming efforts of CPB and PBS so often merely reactive. This is not to say that the Endowment will not work co-operatively with stations. Of course it must, and we trust it will inevitably do so. We are recommending that three members of the Endowment Board be representatives of the public telecommunications system. Moreover, the system will have a strong voice within the nominating committee which will find and recommend the leaders of the Trust. These mechanisms, in addition to the good judgment of the chief executive officer of the Endowment, will ensure cooperation between the Endowment and the system it will provide with programs.

We must be frank, however, in forecasting that some programs will be disliked by some stations. Such conflict is inevitable. If, in the best judgment of the chief executive officer and his board, the program should be made, our structure gives them the freedom and the flexibility to do it and makes them responsible for the outcome.

Nontransferable funds. The many bona fide needs of the telecommunications system will inevitably nibble away at the resources of the Endowment unless a concerted effort is made to ensure the nontransferability of its budget. To that end, we recommend that the Endowment be empowered to spend funds derived from two sources: income from private funds held as an actual endowment by its parent organization, the Trust, and funds provided by Congress to the Trust according to a statutorily established formula.

Well funded and appropriately structured, the Program Services Endowment should stimulate a historic increase in domestic program production in public affairs, documentaries, education, drama, and comedy in both serial and single-program formats. Program makers will receive support providing them the ability to experiment with new formats and styles. Talent previously uninvolved in public television or radio will be brought in. The Endowment should also play a vital role in the development of public service applications of non-broadcast technologies as alternatives to the dominant modes of disseminating information and entertainment.

The Other Activities of the Trust

In addition, the trustees will supervise a number of major areas of responsibility for the public telecommunications system, many of which will change as the system itself changes during the next years.

The principal responsibilities include:

- Representation of the system to the Congress and the public, explaining the work of the entire system and insulating the system from direct government involvement in programming activities.
- Financial accountability for the federal funds that support the full range of activities of the system, including the two fiscal areas specifically established by formula: (1) station support grants, and (2) the federal funds dedicated to the Program Services Endowment.
- Establishment of policies for the administration of system activities, including the station support grants, training programs, archives, information and research, and long-range planning of facilities and expansion programs.
- Acceptance and disbursement of federal funds in the expansion of the system and development of criteria for radio stations and new telecommunications entities, in cooperation with other elements of the system.
- Establishment of policies encouraging wider use of American talent.
- Provision of equal employment opportunity.
- Supervision of long-range planning for the entire public telecommunications system, including planning introduction of new technology.
- Protection of the independent programming activities lodged within the Program Services Endowment; holding of all Endowment funds including those budgeted annually from federal sources; and prudent investment of private funds held in trust for the Endowment.

We are fully aware that technological changes could easily add new responsibilities to those we now deem necessary for this national institution. As the needs of society and the system change, Congress may well ask for special initiatives to help the system meet those needs. The Trust will have the ability to undertake these obligations as well.

We mean to define the role of the trustees in the actual *operations* of stations and the Program Services Endowment as essentially one of general supervision and policymaking. For this reason, we recommend that funding levels be set by statute, and that funds be seen as nontransferable between the Endowment and station support activities. The trustees will undoubtedly pay very serious attention to the lessons of the past. Direct involvement by the trustees in the planning or development of new program activities is an inappropriate exercise of their fiduciary role. The use of fiscal authority as a way to enter into content decisions can only lead to a confusion of roles that will weaken the trustees as well as public broadcasting.

This fiduciary role is quite well understood and accepted by boards of universities, hospitals, and fine-arts centers everywhere in the United States. A great deal is at stake for the future of public broadcasting in the effective development of a tradition of ethical restraint among the board members of the Public Telecommunications Trust.

The long-range policy decisions lying within the purview of the Public Telecommunications Trust will have crucial importance in the future growth of the system. In the past the glamour of involvement in TV programming decisions has detracted from CPB's ability to concentrate such long-range policy evaluation, and the system has suffered. In some instances the licensees were compelled to organize their own planning groups to fill the vacuum at the national level.

Several fundamental issues have emerged in the last several years meriting the immediate attention of the new Public Telecommunications Trust. They will offer the first real test of the trustees' leadership qualities.

For example, there is the issue of the nature of the licensee organizations. The Trust, as a statutory protector of the public system, can provide a forum for resolving many of the difficulties among existing radio and television licensees and their national and regional organizations. Similarly, the proliferation of organizations involved in development and delivery of non-broadcast telecommunications services raises significant questions about the management of federal funds intended for such development purposes. As the institution responsible to Congress for the disbursement of public funds, the Trust should undertake a study and develop a five-year plan providing for an orderly progression into the new telecommunications environment with initiatives determined by the system rather than Congress.

We have based our funding recommendation, detailed in the following chapter, on the central role played by the stations that currently raise the overwhelming bulk of nonfederal funds. The current broadcast system, as it evolves in the next decade, if properly guided and supported, will provide a rational and non-subjective basis for the support of known services. If, as we suspect will happen, broadcasting is outdistanced in the next two decades by the growth of new telecommunications technologies, then new methods of establishing the threshold standards for public service must be developed.

Another national goal, demonstrating the need for an organization with system-wide responsibilities, is the effective implementation of professional training and career development in public broadcasting. Without the high-salary incentives offered in commercial media, the public system must rely heavily upon intangible attractions such as the integrity of the programming process, the mission of public service, and the possibility of a more interesting and satisfying professional career. It is difficult to translate these general ideas into incentives that will attract the best of America's young talent, hold the developing talent within the system, and communicate the system's benefits to individuals outside the system. Considerably greater attention to these career objectives must be provided by the Trust in years to come.

This is particularly true in the case of recruiting and training members of minority groups and women. These groups have been the target of discrimination in the past. They constitute a percentage of high positions in public broadcasting considerably below their occurrence in the population as a whole. It must be recognized that underrepresentation of American minorities in the national governance of public broadcasting does not convey a realistic picture of the diversity of modern America and hence does not serve the public interest. We need the strengths of this new diversity everywhere in public broadcasting, but especially in the leadership positions and on governing boards of the stations or major national and regional institutions of public broadcasting.

We are hopeful that progress can be made more rapidly as federal funding grows under the proposals we are making. At present, the expansion of the job force necessary to bring in new employees is impossible for many stations because of budgetary constrictions. However, with a growing industry, a work force truly representative of modern America should emerge.

We urge the board of the new Trust to concentrate on imaginative projects designed to provide access and professional development to women and minorities in public broadcasting careers. It is not sufficient for the Trust simply to monitor or regulate the performance of stations in their efforts to secure compliance with the law. The trustees, charged with the responsibility of leading the system in such matters, must help the system provide the means to qualify candidates to pursue careers in this industry. Such projects may include sponsoring a major university degree program for public telecommunications, an expansion in the present hiring subsidy projects for special categories of employees, and assistance in refining affirmative action procedures undertaken by all licensees. These worthy projects should be widely supported by the Congress and the industry, and funded accordingly.

In the discharge of its fiscal responsibilities to the Congress and to the rest of the system, the Trust is in a special position to evaluate the financial performance of the system, administer audits, and offer the kind of accounting assistance that can make the whole system more clearly understandable to outsiders and the industry alike. We believe that such activities will enhance the credibility of the system as a fully accountable agent in the handling of public funds, and that such activities are, in this case, more appropriately performed by a private, nonprofit entity like the Trust than by the government or the system itself.

Financial accountability, however, should not be construed to extend into content of programs. We have established as a principal feature of our recommendation the sanctity of the programming funds and the Trust's protective role in the handling of those funds. The primary responsibility for granting funds to programming is insulated in a separate structure, the Program Services Endowment, the system's principal agent for fostering creative excellence.

Governing the Trust: Appointment of Trustees

We recommend that the Public Telecommunications Trust be governed by a nine-member board of trustees appointed by the President after due consideration of nominees screened by a distinguished nominating panel chaired by the librarian of Congress. Trustees will serve staggered nine-year terms, which are nonrenewable. Nominees for the initial Trust board would be proposed to the President by this panel joined for this purpose by the speaker of the House and the president pro tempore of the Senate.

One of the gravest problems during public broadcasting's first 12 years as a national institution has been the uneven and politically vulnerable process by which appointments have been made to its statutory leadership institution, the Corporation for Public Broadcasting. Because one-third of the board becomes vacant every second year, a single administration is in a position to select a majority of its members during a single term in office. On the other hand, a President can neglect the matter; indeed a total of 107 months of director vacancies in CPB's 12 years[6] were occupied by lame-duck board members.

We believe that the greatest care should be given to improving the appointment procedure, in order to assure a regular flow of nominees of the highest caliber to govern the new statutory institution we are recommending. A parallel for our recommendation exists in recent attention that has been paid to the appointment to the federal judiciary. We believe that public telecommunications merits the same seriousness in its appointment procedures.

The Nominating Panel

Central to our recommendation to retain presidential appointment is our hope that the President will undertake the vital protective role of appointing trustees only from lists prepared by a distinguished nominating panel. Except when it nominates the members of the first Trust board, the panel will consist of:

- the librarian of Congress, who will be chairman;
- the director of the National Science Foundation;
- the chairman of the National Endowment for the Arts;
- the chairman of the National Endowment for the Humanities;
- the secretary of the Smithsonian Institution;
- a representative from public television; and
- a representative from public radio.

This panel, a statutory body, will be balanced among people appointed by the President (the chairmen of the Arts and Humanities Endowments and the director of the National Science Foundation), people with public responsibilities who are appointed without government action (the secretary of the Smithsonian, appointed by the institution's board of regents, and the system's own representatives), and the chairman of the panel, who serves Congress. The members of the panel will all be people who have public responsibilities in operating institutions with missions similar to that of the Trust.

[6]Data from the Corporation for Public Broadcasting, April 1978.

Presidential Appointment of Trustees

The Public Telecommunications Trust will be governed by nine presidentially appointed trustees with staggered, nonrenewable, nine-year terms. We recommend that the President make his selections from a list of names presented to him by a panel drawn from governmental institutions devoted to the arts, the sciences, the humanities, and the preservation of our heritage. In addition, in order to involve the public telecommunications system in this process, the panel should include two representatives of that system.

While we do not recommend fettering the President's power to appoint by requiring that he be bound by the panel's nominees, we urge in the strongest terms that he respect this process voluntarily by selecting from the recommended list.

Although additional vacancies may occur, the normal course of events will result in only one vacancy on the Trust board each year. We believe that this will focus attention on the process, allowing time for serious consideration of the qualifications of nominees, and solving the problem of unfilled appointments. We feel, too, that by making the process one to which public attention will be drawn, any hint of debasement of the process will vanish.

Financial Disclosure and Senate Confirmation

At present the President submits his nominations for CPB board members to the Senate for confirmation, which requires financial investigation and full public financial disclosure. We strongly urge that this practice be amended in the case of trustee nomination for several reasons. While the disclosure of possible conflicts of interest is an absolute requirement in the case of board appointments having the stature we envision, it is also the case that public revelation of private individuals' financial holdings, or the possibility of discussions in the newspapers about the business activities of partners who are not prospective appointees, now constitutes a major deterrent to voluntary public service by people whose service we seek.

To deal with this extremely sensitive problem, we propose that a careful investigation of potential conflicts of interest be carried out on a confidential basis by the librarian of Congress, who will chair the panel. Public telecommunications appointees must be of the highest caliber. This requires that sources of income be identified so that possible conflicts of interest can be avoided. However, we do not believe that the requisite integrity of this process depends on public disclosure. The guideline for judging conflicts is simple: no one who receives substantial income from public telecommunications may serve on the board. It should be noted that lay members of station boards, under this standard, can still serve as trustees.

By making this recommendation, we realize that we are questioning what has become a commonly accepted practice. While the Trust is responsible for federal funds, it is also instructed to act in a fiduciary capacity rather than as a direct manager of such funds. It is our desire that the Trust be *less* like a federal agency than the current CPB, which is technically a private corporation as well. Because of this independent nature of the Trust, it is appropriate to differentiate between the disclosure required for government officials and the disclosure necessary for avoiding conflicts in any private corporation and achieved by standard practices in the private sector. Moreover, we know of several qualified persons who have refused board appointment because of the potential problems associated with the requirements of the present financial disclosure process.

With these objectives in mind, we believe that the staff of the Library of Congress, fully empowered to investigate the financial holdings of all potential nominees, could provide requisite assurance to Congress and the President that the names suggested for trusteeship have no financial conflicts. Such assurance does not require full public disclosure of tax returns or specific holdings. In those cases where potential nominees refuse to disclose their personal finances or some potential conflict is uncovered by the investigating staff, the name would simply be dropped.

We are certain that once our objectives are ac-

knowledged, the President and his staff would not let
vacancies languish without attention, or use trustee appointments in political trades, or even, in the worst
outcome, attempt to create a docile public broadcasting system via the appointments process. These problems have, to some extent, occurred in the past. They
must be prevented in the future. Freedom for the system can be secured by an institutionalized high-quality
appointment process, above partisan politics. We believe our proposal accomplishes this.

We recommend the librarian of Congress as the
chairman in order to place the important financial
screening process in an institution ultimately responsible to Congress. We feel that this gives a legitimacy to
the process without politicizing it.

The chairman will also be empowered to approve
the process chosen by the public broadcasting system
for selecting its two panel members. We recommend,
therefore, no special procedure for selection of the
system's own representatives, but instead ask that it be
developed by the system in cooperation with the librarian of Congress.

We are concerned that the first nine-person board
will be chosen entirely by a single President, and feel
the nominating panel should be enlarged for the selection of this first board. Accordingly, we recommend that
the panel be augmented by the two highest officers of
Congress—the speaker of the House, and the president
pro tempore of the Senate. The balance of institutions,
responsibilities, and constituencies found in this first
nominating panel, together with the President's power of
ultimate selection, form the means for attracting and
selecting the enlightened leadership we envision as the
system's trustees.

Governing the Endowment: The Appointment Process and Board Composition

We recommend that the Program
Services Endowment be governed by a 15-
member board appointed by the trustees
of the Public Telecommunications Trust
from candidates nominated by the board

itself. Three members of the board must come from the public telecommunications community. All board members will serve staggered terms of three years, renewable once. Nominees for the initial Endowment board will be proposed to the trustees by the nominating panel chaired by the librarian of Congress. The chief executive officer of the Endowment will be chosen by the Endowment's board.

For the selection of the board of the Endowment, we recommend a process analogous to that for the trustees, with two important differences. We do not recommend presidential appointment, or the presence on the nominating committee of representatives of Congress. We emphasize again that the task of supporting the production of programs should not be undertaken by those with political responsibilities.

The Endowment board will be composed of 15 people, 3 of whom should be drawn from the public telecommunications community. Board members will serve staggered terms of three years. Every year, therefore, 5 new members will be chosen, one of whom will be from public telecommunications. Members of the board may be reappointed once.

Members of the Endowment board will be selected by the trustees. For the first board, the trustees will choose from a list prepared for them by the nominating panel. Thereafter, vacancies will be filled from nominations made to the Trust by the Endowment board itself. The chief executive officer of the Endowment will be chosen by the Endowment board, and will be responsible to that board only. The chief executive's employment will be determined under a five-year contract that may be renewed once.

Conclusion

This procedure is not a simple one. Yet it represents a balancing of an extraordinarily complex set of important public responsibilities, institutional pressures, and politically diverse constituencies. The Trust and the Endowment must be institutionally tied, yet the Endowment must be free to make its own decisions. Similarly, we have learned the dangers both of placing national production funds outside the control of the stations and of giving the stations complete control over production decisions. The system will have a voice in the policies of the Endowment. There will be cooperation between the Endowment and the stations, but the latter will not dominate the Endowment. The Endowment will have flexibility to make decisions, which may be resisted by the stations.

To ensure an effective voice, not only of the stations but of the larger creative, educational, and journalistic communities, we recommend a small, but important, modification in the standards to be applied in checking for conflicts of interest. The board members of the Endowment do not have the sensitive fiduciary role of the trustees, but have another, equally sensitive role: that of supporting and understanding the processes of creativity in the media arts. Many of the best people for such a task may not meet the criteria for trustees. They should not have to. The conflict-of-interest criterion for the Endowment's board is that a member may not sit to approve grant decisions which may be of financial benefit to him. The standard will be applied as potentially sensitive decisions must be made. Should such situations arise frequently, that member must resign. This is a standard which will allow the Endowment to benefit from the experience of those inside and outside the system who understand the needs of both program makers and the public.

The structure we have described for meeting the national responsibilities of the public telecommunications system is essential to our plan for strengthening its service. Equally important are our proposals for financing the improved and expanded system we envision. We turn now to those recommendations.

IV

Funding

The first section of this chapter analyzes the level of support that we believe to be required for providing a first-class, full service public broadcasting system. The minimum necessary is approximately $1.2 billion[1] annually, from all sources.

The second section is a discussion of the principles that should govern the provision and use of this substantially enlarged flow of funds. There should be a diverse funding base, so that no single source of money can undermine the integrity of the system. Ample discretionary funds must be provided in a balanced fashion to each of its constituent parts.

A third section recommends anticipated levels from the nonfederal sources providing well over half the money in today's system. The combined total from state government, viewers and listeners, the business community, and other nonfederal sources should rise from $347 million in 1977 to $570 million by 1985. The remainder of the estimated $1.2 billion overall public broadcasting system—about one-half of all funds —should be provided by the federal government.

The final three sections include our recommendations for the allocation of federal support to the various entities within the system, governed by principles es-

---

[1] All costs and projections are in 1979 dollars.

sential for sound growth; where federal funds should be derived; and policies during the transition period. Accordingly, we recommend that the principal source of federal funding be general revenues. We believe that insulation from inappropriate federal intervention can be maintained principally through the statutory means of revenue generation rather than by dedication of particular taxes to the support of public broadcasting. After considering the difficulties of several plans for dedicated taxes, we recommend the establishment of a fee for licensed uses of the electromagnetic spectrum in order to offset a portion of the federal funds required by public broadcasting.

Because the effects of underfinancing have often been at the root of public broadcasting's other difficulties, some have suggested that this Commission should focus exclusively on remedying the system's chronic poverty. While money alone cannot guarantee excellence, creativity, and independence, we agree that this broadcasting system will never approach its full potential for service to the public without major infusions of new funds.

We believe that our funding recommendations will accomplish a number of important goals: the full construction of a national radio and television system for virtually all of our citizens; the provision of a regular and adequate flow of resources to support the ongoing work of the system; and the capability to evaluate changes in mission and operations that may result from new technological and social challenges.

Equally important is the design of incentives that we have built into our funding recommendations. We seek to make it easier, not more difficult for creative work to flourish in public broadcasting. We believe that the system should be encouraged to strike out in new directions without fear that its funding might be in jeopardy. We wish to reward innovation and risk taking.

I. Required Level of Funds

We recommend that income from all sources rise to $1.16 billion annually. We also recommend that support for one-time-only capital costs for new and improved broadcasting facilities total $350 million over the next five to seven years.

Our plan for a strengthened full service public broadcasting system that is available to virtually all Americans includes the operation of about 175 television licensees, about 480 radio stations, the Public Telecommunications Trust, the Program Services Endowment, and the various national and regional organizations serving the needs of the stations.

This system will require annual expenditures of approximately $1.16 billion, of which roughly half should come from the federal government.

Chapters V through IX set forth the considerable improvements that these funds will bring in the areas of television, radio, education and instruction, new technological initiatives, and broader public participation. Appendix D is a financial summary that discusses the costs of various improvements we recommend. We believe that a total annual investment of about $5 per person in the United States is a modest cost for such a wide range of benefits—improvements in our social fabric that we consider essential. Public broadcasting and telecommunications can touch everyone in society. The value of an effective noncommercial system is immeasurable.

For instance, in television broadcasting, our recommended level of funds will provide for substantially improved and expanded programming and promotion. At the national level, we can then have a wide range of programs—drama, comedy, history, performances, programs for children, the elderly, the daytime viewer, the many minorities within our society. For the first time, public affairs journalism would be adequately financed. Works by artists of stature and the testing of new forms of communications would advance the use of the medium. The television set can be turned into a center for lifelong learning and communications. The cost of an improved national programming effort is about $360 million annually.

Local and regional television service would also be upgraded substantially. Because each broadcasting operation will be adequately financed, it can hire talented and expert creative and management personnel. It will then be able to serve its audience with quality local programs in public affairs and the arts. In concert with other stations, local broadcasters should be able to pool funds for certain programs of greater than local interest. Broadcasters should be able to expand their means of reaching viewers through new technologies, particularly cable television, thus generating greater program choice and improving service to schools and other learning centers. With greater funds, stations will be able to improve their management and decision making. They will possess resources permitting them to seek out women and minority employees.

Taken together, the improvements to local and national television discussed in Chapter V will cost $875 million annually, a per capita cost of less than $4 nationally. For the cost to each American of a movie or a phonograph album, we can finance a rich and stimulating mix of programs and services for 365 days a year—surely a bargain, if there ever was one.

The costs of operating a public radio system that will provide equally important services to all Americans are about $240 million annually, or slightly more than $1 per person per year. Our plan requires the operation of 450 to 500 full service public radio stations, a projected addition of 250 to 300 new stations in the next five to seven years. These stations are necessary in order to reach every citizen in the country with at least one public radio station. Our proposal outlines operating costs for an estimated 480 stations in 1985, as well as a multifaceted national program service. Local operating costs are especially critical to the radio stations, because the medium remains primarily local, with the addition of various national programs to help local management define each station's format. As stations are added to the system, the demand for more diversified programming services at the national level will contribute to a more stimulating and attractive public radio system. Our recommendations for public radio are presented in Chapter VI.

The basic annual operating costs of public radio and television stations and the national programming activities of the Program Services Endowment are projected to be $1.115 billion. Additional costs for the full public telecommunications system are estimated at $45 million, including $20 million annually for the planning, leadership, and development activities of the Public Telecommunications Trust, and two special initiatives within the Program Services Endowment —the establishment of a special fund of $10 million to explore and develop new applications of telecommunications technology (described in Chapter VII), and a second fund of $15 million allocated to research and program development in learning and instruction (Chapter VIII).

The total annual operating costs of this system are $1.16 billion. Figure 4–1 summarizes these estimates.

In addition to the annual operating costs of the basic public broadcasting system, there are sizable requirements for funds to meet the capital costs of building new stations and completing the facilities of existing stations. During the next five to seven years we estimate that it will cost approximately $350 million to bring the broadcasting facilities of the system to an acceptable level and to reach virtually all Americans with at least one radio and one television signal. While substantial, we believe this estimate to be relatively conservative; it depends upon achievement of new efficiencies, more vigorous planning, and greater sharing of capital plant and distribution. Our estimates for capital investment, also detailed in Appendix D, presume that individual stations will have sufficient discretionary funds under our plan so that they can replace much of their equipment and facilities without additional federal assistance.

Both operating and capital estimates refer exclusively to the primary broadcast system, and will not pay for extensive construction or use of other technologies for nonbroadcast services. As we explain more fully in Chapter VII, the inevitable expansion by public broadcasting into the newer forms of telecommunications must be planned and designed under the direction of the Trust. We have included initial sums of money for the Trust to begin examination and planning in this field, and for the Endowment to finance experiments on applications of new technologies. We presume that once the system has defined the direction of growth that public telecommunications should follow in the unfolding future scenario, appropriate cost estimates and requests for support can be developed. It would be unwise to do so today, at a time when the broadcast system remains underfinanced, underbuilt, and underutilized.

Measured against the expenditures of today's public broadcasting system, our proposal for $1.16 billion for annual operations plus the capital costs of providing full broadcast service throughout the nation may seem high. We consider these costs to be minimum, calculated by using the low end of a range of possible costs for programs, services, and physical plant.

But measured against the costs of commercial radio and television, or the expenditures made by most other societies for their public broadcasting systems, these figures are extremely modest. Consider the American commercial broadcasting industry, for example. Each year some $8 billion is generated by the commercial television networks, their affiliated stations, independent television stations, and the radio networks and stations. The expenditures rise substantially each year. One of the three commercial television networks and its affiliates generates about $2 billion annually, which is nearly double the estimate we are proposing for all of public telecommunications—radio, television, and other activities.

Of course, a public system can be financed for considerably less than a commercial system, since it will not entail many of the expenses of a profit-making enterprise. While public broadcasting may occasionally face the same costs as commercial broadcasting for some of its programs, it will rarely pay the very high talent fees the networks often find themselves compelled

Recommended Annual Spending Level

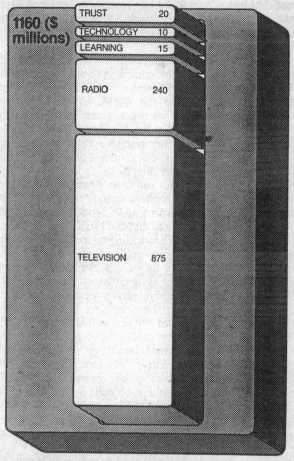

1160 ($ millions)	
TRUST	20
TECHNOLOGY	10
LEARNING	15
RADIO	240
TELEVISION	875

Figure 4-1. Recommended Annual Spending Level (excludes capital spending for facilities and expansion).

to pay in their competitive struggles. The public system does not require the same sales fees and administrative superstructure of commercial broadcasting. And, of course, it is not required to produce a dividend for stockholders. Thus, while our recommendation of $1.16 billion in annual expenditures is much smaller than comparable commercial budgets, we do not believe that the results will be inferior.

Another way to evaluate the relative costs of public broadcasting is by comparing our present expenditures with those of the major noncommercial broadcasting systems around the world. In 1975 the U.S. spent about one-third of the amount per person expended by the British for the BBC or the Japanese for the NHK. In radio, our public system is even less well off. The Japanese spent six times as much per person for NHK radio and the British spent about eight times as much for BBC radio as Americans provided for public radio. Our proposal would raise the per capita spending for American public broadcasting roughly up to the level of the BBC and the NHK.

Unless Americans are willing to meet the challenge of adequate funding, our public broadcasting system will not be able to play the role in the nation's emerging telecommunications system that we think is vital. We need a strong noncommercial system that serves the public rather than the share holders if we expect to have the full spectrum of telecommunications available in the late 1980s and beyond. It should also be recognized that the expenditure levels we recommend will not be required immediately. We have sought to project the configurations of public broadcasting in the mid-1980s. By setting their objectives for that time, Trust planners can move step by step back to today's system configuration in order to define short-term funding necessary to bring the system to full service within a decade.

We believe the basic level of expenditure to achieve this objective is an eventual annual operating budget for the entire system of $1.16 billion, plus the additional capital investment to complete the broadcast facilities.

II. Principles of Funding

The manner by which the public broadcasting industry generates its operating funds will determine to a large degree the character of its programs and the public perception of the institution as a whole. At the outset, noncommercial broadcasting was prohibited from advertising products and services as a method of raising revenues. Our proposal, which derives equal amounts of funds from the federal government and a diversified group of nonfederal contributors, rests on a set of essential principles that will have a major impact on the character of public broadcasting. The principles spring from the industry's history, and are designed to achieve a balance between the preeminent need for an independent editorial and artistic institution and the requirement that the institution be accountable to those providing its funds.

A. Insulation from Government Interference

Since the federal government legislated operating support for public broadcasting in 1967 the industry has witnessed episode after episode seeming to justify the fears of interference expressed by many stations when federal support was first proposed. While the most dramatic was the 1972 Nixon veto and related pressures on public television, we have heard testimony on numerous examples of federal agency interference in program content, pressures on the system from congressional and administrative sources, and a widespread apprehension in the system after experiencing what it perceived as threats to its survival.

Public broadcasting, as a delicate journalistic and creative enterprise, cannot be regarded as a part of the government, even though it uses federal and state funds to accomplish its goals. If government finances broadcasting, it must do so in a way that provides a sustained flow of funds with as little political pressure as the practical workings of a democratic society can guarantee. This objective is difficult to design, and even more difficult to achieve, as history has proven.

The first Carnegie Commission recommended an

independent, nongovernmental corporation to receive and disburse automatic federal support generated by a dedicated tax designed to disengage the funding mechanism from the political processes normally associated with government finance. In the system actually created by Congress, funding and institutional arrangements were altered in ways that assured legislative backing but left the system with far less insulation and independence than the first Carnegie Commission had intended.

Public broadcasting must have reliable sources of funding that do not undergo major cuts whenever political power changes in the country. Its independence must be enhanced, not limited, by the way the funds are disbursed. There should be a virtually automatic arrangement for the system to receive its federal funds, with a review of support levels on a predictable, multi-year basis.

Insulated funding is necessary from an operating point of view as well. Program development in both radio and television has not been satisfactory, largely because the system has been unable to plan and develop major projects on a multiyear basis. Lack of financial stability leads inevitably to crisis management, not planning, with attendant gaps in the program service and higher programming costs.

B. Diversity of Sources

Public broadcasting must have reasonable autonomy with respect to all sources of financial support, not just the federal government. As an examination of the present funding mix will reveal, federal tax dollars yield only 28 percent of the total system's budget, and that amount is split between the Corporation for Public Broadcasting and various federal agencies. Our recommendation is designed to encourage a balance between federal financial support and the nonfederal sources critical to public broadcasting's growth. Federal funds cannot be permitted to become the major force in the budget. Neither should public broadcasting become overly dependent upon any of the nonfederal sources—state and local governments, corporate underwriters, individuals, foundations, and others that provided most of the $482 million in total system income in 1977 (see Figure 4–2 for current funding breakdown).

The simplest mechanism for funding public broadcasting would probably be one in which stations received all their support from subscribers in exchange for programs and services. Such a plan would place substantial control in the hands of viewers and listeners without any intermediary agent capable of altering the mix of desired programs. This approach, while theoretically attractive, is in fact acceptable only if it provides a fraction of public broadcasting's revenue. Direct user financing unfortunately leads to domination by large or wealthy groups, disenfranchising poorer and smaller groups in the audience. A full service public system that responds to diversity in the population cannot rely exclusively on a funding mechanism that, in effect, caters to the largest givers.

The system that has actually evolved mixes viewer and listener financing with funds from a variety of organized interests. As shown in Figure 4–2, government, corporations, foundations, universities, and school boards supplied about 90 percent of the $482 million total income of public broadcasting in 1977. Most of this support comes with "strings"—funders provide money only when it supports a specific program or service. Only about $100 million, less than one-fourth of current income, is fully "discretionary"—that is, the funder provides support without tying it to a particular purpose or condition. The two largest sources of discretionary funds are direct gifts from audiences, and the portion of federal funds disbursed by CPB as general operating grants to stations. These Community Service Grants are discretionary, and totaled about $60 million.

The restrictions associated with other sources of funds raise a major question for public broadcasting: where is the control of such funds vested—with the funder or with public broadcasting? Just as with federal funds, restricted funds raised from organized private and nonfederal government groups carry the potential

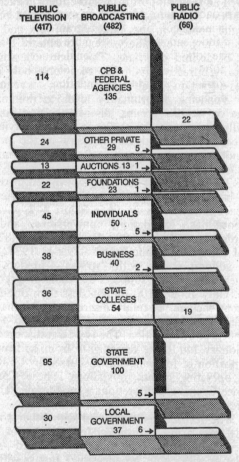

Public Broadcasting Income
1977 ($ millions)

PUBLIC TELEVISION (417)	PUBLIC BROADCASTING (482)	PUBLIC RADIO (66)
114	CPB & FEDERAL AGENCIES 135	22
24	OTHER PRIVATE 29	5 →
13	AUCTIONS 13	1 →
22	FOUNDATIONS 23	1 →
45	INDIVIDUALS 50	5 →
38	BUSINESS 40	2 →
36	STATE COLLEGES 54	19
95	STATE GOVERNMENT 100	5 →
30	LOCAL GOVERNMENT 37	6 →

Figure 4–2. Public Broadcasting Income 1977 ($ millions; may not add due to rounding).

for interference with the independence of public broadcasting.

An examination of the funding of the national television program service distributed by PBS reveals that outside funder control is a very real issue in the present system. Because stations derive about two-thirds of their broadcast schedules and an even larger percentage of their audiences from this program service, the question of independence becomes more serious.

The total cost of the national program service in 1977, shown in Figure 4–3, was $67 million. Corporations provided 22 percent, foundations 10 percent, federal agencies 29 percent, and other sources 11 percent. Stations collectively provided 22 percent and CPB the remaining 7 percent. In short, fully 71 percent of funding for the 1977 schedule was provided by entities outside the public television system.

Evidently, these other funders have a wide range of motives for contributing to public broadcasting—a general desire to support the arts, corporate goodwill, promotion of a funder's self-interest. The line between a funder's reasonable self-interest and overweening interference is a difficult one to draw.

The degree to which public television has become dependent upon outside determination of its schedule is troubling because editorial freedom does not thrive in such circumstances. At successive phases in public television's history, the domination of one funder outside the system has given substance to these concerns. When the Ford Foundation's massive financial support of public television in the 1960s made it the dominant sponsor of the system, there were numerous complaints that the institution did not have control over its own programs and journalistic activities. CPB's entrance as a major funder in the 1970s did not diminish these concerns. In recent years, as PBS and the stations began seeking an ever-widening circle of support from foundations, corporations, and federal agencies, new apprehensions were voiced about the determinative role played by corporate underwriters whose decision to fund was seen as critical in the shaping of prime-time program schedules.

Public Television National Programming
CURRENT FUNDING 1977

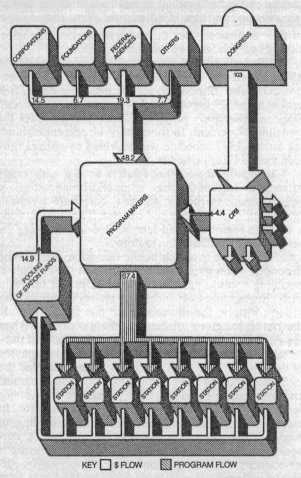

Figure 4–3. Public Television National Programming: Current Funding 1977 (PBS National Program Service).

Accordingly, corporations have become particularly visible in public broadcasting. They have enhanced this visibility with heavy promotion budgets. Many of the programs fully or partly underwritten by corporations have become the most popular on public television, including *The Adams Chronicles, Evening at Symphony, The Boston Pops,* the *Great Performances* series including *Dance in America* and *Theater in America, Masterpiece Theatre,* and *Nova,* among numerous others. Indeed, the presence of a corporate credit on public television shows has become so common that a recent survey found that most respondents believed corporate grants to be second in importance only to individual donations in financing public television.

Corporate underwriting has undoubtedly skewed the total schedule in the direction of cultural programs which are popular among the "upscale" audiences that corporations prefer. Controversial drama, documentaries, public affairs, and programs for minorities and other special audiences must then compete for remaining discretionary money. Too often, they have become casualties in a near-Darwinian competition for scarce funds.

Other funders have shown a similar interest in specifying the terms under which they will provide financial support. We heard testimony from producers about direct script control exercised by some government agencies, notably the children's series financed by the Emergency School Assistance Act. Step funding and peer-panel review of several projects financed by the National Endowment for the Humanities have resulted in disappointing creative results and limited independence as reported by the producers involved.

The fact is that public television, so dependent upon outside funders for its basic national schedule, has repeatedly forfeited its autonomy in programming. In one instance, rather than lose vitally necessary funding, programs were accepted by PBS and a large East Coast station even though PBS and the offering station did not agree with the program selected by the major corporate funder.[2]

Naturally, not all programs underwritten by corporations or government agencies carry objectionable restrictions. The public television system could not have survived and grown during the past decade without the funds provided by these outside funders, particularly for the national program schedule. It can be argued that these funders have made a significant contribution to the nascency in the arts that we have witnessed in this decade.

Moreover, the system has been able to increase the number of outside funders so that the overall funding mix for national programming and the system as a whole contain an element of balance that would have been impossible were the federal government the only funder. With diversified support from foundations, government agencies, local and state government, the Arts and Humanities Endowments, and others, the system has a much greater chance to protect itself from reliance upon any single source, private or governmental.

C. Conditions for Outside Support

On the basis of this examination of the influence of external funders, we believe that the system should continue to accept this support provided it can do so

---

[2]Testimony of Herbert Schmertz, Mobil Corporation, before the Commission, Feb. 21, 1978:

Question: You said that Mobil feels a responsibility for the content of the programs it supports. How is that different from interference?

Answer: We think we have a contribution to make in the area of program selection. We have always made recommendations concerning programs and public television is free to accept them or not as they see fit. I'll tell you one story for example. When *Upstairs, Downstairs* first became available . . . the entire public television establishment was opposed to its acquisition. We were just as adamantly in favor of it, and we said, "If you're not going to acquire it, we're going to acquire it anyway and find some way to run it on American television whether it's commercial or public." At that point public television said they would take it. I think the upshot of that is that our judgment was correct.

without sacrificing its editorial integrity and independence. The latter will require three conditions:

1. *A Balance Among Diverse Funding Sources.* The actual or perceived dominance by a single funder or class of funders can lead to the conclusion that the system is incapable of serving the public interest when the latter diverges from the objectives of those controlling the system's funds. This cannot be permitted to happen. In practical terms, diversified outside funding must be maintained in order to continue eligibility for federal matching funds. But also as a matter of policy, we believe that systematic exclusion of any class of funders, whether they be corporate or other, would force the system to become correspondingly more dependent upon the largest single funder, the federal government.

In public radio, a much greater diversity of support for national programming should be developed, since its principal funding comes from the federal government through CPB.

Similarly, local radio and television stations that receive a predominant portion of their funds from a single source—a university or state authority—should take steps to attempt to diversify their funding sources. The possibility for single-funder interference at the local level is no less worrisome than it is with national radio and television programs.

2. *Ample Discretionary Funds.* The second condition is that the system should possess sufficient discretionary money. The problem most clearly identified with outside funding is not undue influence on the content of programs, but rather that, when such attempts are made, the only recourse is refusal to produce the program. Because the system does not now have enough money to produce a controversial program entirely on its own, large contributors gain veto power. If our recommendations for levels of funding are accepted, the system will be able to refuse any inappropriate outside funder, and do so without loss of a valuable public service.

3. *Funder Guidelines.* The system must be prepared to reject proposals that violate its independence

and editorial integrity. The public must be confident that what it watches or hears on public channels is free of censorship imposed by funders or public officials.

Guidelines of the sort we recommend have already been developed by PBS. These guidelines offer a reasonable assurance that programs distributed by PBS are not just free from funder control; even the appearance of such control must be avoided. Because the underwriting decisions are published and sent to stations, a "case law" has developed. Hence stations can become more sensitive and sophisticated about local intrusions that they also should resist. Although a few cases have been highly controversial, the system on the whole has worked well.

Without explicit guidelines, abuses are likely to occur. Experience shows that funders will try to inject their views into programs and will occasionally bargain toughly by threatening to withdraw funds when their views are not accepted. In such circumstances it is always wise to have a bulwark of principle against the natural tendency of harried executives to attempt to escape the heat. Guidelines should include the following four principles:

- There should be no promotion of particular products or services.
- There should be no close connection, real or perceived, between the interests of a program funder and the subject of the program. (The public should have *no reason* to suspect that the funder has controlled the program.)
- There should be no involvement by the funder in the actual production of programs, for example, in review of scripts, choice of topics for discussion, or selection of the talent for a series.
- There should be no domination of any class of programming by a single industry or company.

III. Generating Adequate Funding

In this section we outline our recommendations for the support of public television, radio, and telecommunications from both nonfederal and federal sources.

We believe that our estimates of the necessary operating budget of about \$1.2 billion by 1985 are sound, and that a wide range of nonfederal support for public broadcasting should be used to trigger federal funding. We will treat each source separately.

A. Increased Support from Individuals

We recommend the goal of \$205 million annually in contributions from individual donors.

In 1977 the contributions of individual viewers and listeners amounted to \$50 million. While the figure has been growing in recent years, it remains a relatively small share of overall system funds—7.5 percent of radio's income and 11 percent of television's (see Figure 4–2).

The quantitative measure of this support, however, fails to indicate the value of individual donations as a measure of public satisfaction with the radio and television system. In 1977, an estimated 2.7 million individuals and families contributed to the system, an impressive record of private giving to a relatively new institution that must overcome the inclination of most viewers and listeners to regard the electronic media as "free" (even though we eventually do pay for them in the price of advertised goods and services).

We recommend that the system generate major increases in support from individuals, with the objective that this income would increase to a point where it would balance income from other sources. Viewer and listener contributions to their stations help emphasize the notion that stations belong to their communities, and illustrate how the public values its stations. The strongest stations in the system tend to be those which receive the greatest audience support. Since this support derives from many small contributors, stations can exercise discretion in their use of donor contributions.

Over the short term, on-air fund raising will probably continue to be the most effective means of seeking such support. Annoying and amateurish as these appeals may be, apparently 90 percent of those who have seen them on public television feel that they are "a fair price to pay for programming."[3] Nonetheless, public broadcasters should continually strive to make fund raising more inventive and less irritating. Individuals should be asked for support via painless solicitation methods developed by other institutions dependent on voluntary giving. These include checkoffs on payroll checks, matching gift programs, direct mail appeals based on researched mailing lists, volunteer door-to-door appeals, receptions, and testimonial dinners contrived as fund raisers, public-service announcements on commercial broadcasting stations, and other types of advertising and promotion.[4]

It will probably always be necessary for public radio and television stations to use some part of their air time for fund-raising efforts. The goal of such on-the-air activities should be to keep them nonintrusive so as not to destroy the aura of goodwill created by fine programming. It is a question of taste and proportion.

Our target for individual support is $205 million, with about $175 million coming to public television and about $30 million to public radio. Contributions will increase as audiences grow for more stations and better programs. In public television, successful stations that have established a tradition of widespread community support typically generate a $25 average contribution from 10 percent of households tuning in regularly. As

---

[3]This finding is a result of a nationwide survey of about 1100 adults conducted by Statistical Research, Inc., with support from CPB, in January and February 1978.

[4]These techniques have proven successful in many fund-raising organizations. For example, Common Cause, a broadly based and successful citizens' lobbying group, has, in addition to $2.5 million in regular dues from about 114,000 individual members in 1978, managed to raise over $250,000 from mass appeal projects such as direct mail solicitations to their national constituency and over $210,000 from special appeal projects conducted by affiliated local organizations. In 1977 local member organizations of the United Way of America raised over $745 million from voluntary checkoffs on employee payroll checks. The American Cancer Society raised about $85 million from some 37 million homes through the door-to-door efforts of volunteers.

audience levels increase to include virtually every person on a regular basis, the system should be able to raise at least $175 million from individuals and families, or about $25 from 10 percent of the nation's homes. In radio, a comparable figure where there are several public radio stations is 15 ¢ per capita, so we project $30 million when the more than 200 million persons in the country receive service.

It is not expected that each radio and television station will reach this level of support. Our projections are national estimates of total support from individuals. For example, each of several radio stations in one market will probably fail to reach this level, although together the stations might exceed it. Or a state-supported public television station serving a less affluent community might generate support from 10 percent or more of its community but at an average of less than $25. While there will be many variations, we believe $205 million in total income from individual subscribers across the nation is a reasonable goal that can be attained.

B. *Increased Support from State and Local Governments*

We recommend the goal of $235 million annually in support from state and local government sources.

State and local governments continue to be major funders of the system. Nonfederal support from tax-based sources presently comes through states and state colleges, and from local governments and other local agencies. Together these sources provided $191 million in 1977, about 40 percent of system income. Most of it was from states and state colleges, which provided 32 percent (see Figure 4–2).

These funding sources are proving difficult for public broadcasting to maintain. Except in several extraordinary state systems, licensees have faced increasing difficulty convincing school boards and governmental agencies of their continuing responsibility to finance public broadcasting. The tightening financial problems facing education and some state and local governments is partly the cause of this difficulty. Also contributing to the reluctance to fund public broadcasting is the move of the system away from a strictly instructional definition of mission to a broader one of public service, as well as the growing availability of nonbroadcast technologies that provide greater flexibility for classroom use.

State governments, in particular, must be full partners with their citizens, private entities, and the federal government in financing public broadcasting. States should increase their support of the services public broadcasting provides to education. With greater emphasis on lifelong learning by citizens, public telecommunications is an extremely cost-effective opportunity for new and valuable state services. As society becomes increasingly oriented to media, it is essential that states expand their support for school programs and services that help students of all ages to learn.

Beyond this emphasis on education, there is a critical new role to be played by states, which we believe should provide discretionary grants to stations in recognition of the valuable and diverse cultural and educational services the stations offer. These grants should be unrestricted, to enhance the independence of the system. Some states already provide considerable unrestricted support to their stations. In New York, for example, the public television stations receive about $7.5 million in discretionary support. Florida, Pennsylvania, and Ohio also provide discretionary state funding to public television stations.

We strongly urge other states to strengthen their commitment to public broadcasting via unrestricted support for stations, radio as well as television. An expenditure that would appear relatively modest by government standards can have a strong impact on the vitality and independence of the system as it serves the state's citizens. This role for states is especially critical in rural and underdeveloped areas where stations may be at a disadvantage in comparison with stations in larger metropolitan areas. Here, state support is essential to support a much-needed and highly valued public service. Moreover, increased state funding can be viewed as an investment raising the level of federal matching funds returned to local stations. Such pyramiding of state and federal resources is quite common in educational and construction programs supported under federal law.

On the basis of this recommendation for a new initiative by states and the need to expand support for the educational services of public telecommunications, we project an increase in state and local government support to $235 million.

C. *Increased Support by Business*
We recommend the goal of $70 million annually in support from business.

As described above, support from the business community is extremely important for funding public television. While public broadcasting must guard against undue dependence on corporate support in shaping the composition of national programming, we believe it to be important to increase funds from the business community if there is to be a rough balance among a variety of funding sources.

We recommend a goal of $70 million annually, up from $40 million in 1977. While corporations are likely to continue as important funders of national programs for public television, we also urge them to expand the range of their support. Public radio should generate a healthy measure of business support as its satellite interconnection system begins operation and as the number of stations increases.

The greatest increase in support from the business community should come to the individual radio or television stations. At present, many companies decline to support public broadcasting because they are unable to afford the great expense of underwriting a national television program, or because they may be local or regional firms with no interest in national exposure. With better ways of attracting local support, these companies should be able to participate in the support of public broadcasting. They should be attracted by the opportunity to provide unrestricted grants, or to assist with any number of station support projects requiring technical as well as financial assistance. To raise these funds, stations might attempt to approach a number of companies, perhaps under the aegis of the Chamber of Commerce on behalf of a certain program or activity. One-time-only efforts directed at capital support or other specialized fund-raising drives might appeal to the boosterism inherent in many local businesses. Another possibility is the use of business support as seed money to test new programs or services which, if successful, can then be sustained by appeals for viewer or listener contributions. We have already referred to business gifts matching employee contributions that have proved so successful in financing colleges and universities. Not only does this idea stimulate viewer and listener support, but it pyramids business contributions as unrestricted gifts reflecting decisions of individual viewers and listeners to support their stations.

D. Support from Other Private Sources
We recommend the goal of $60 million annually in support from several other private sources.

Other private sources including foundations, auctions, private colleges, and income from subsidiary profit-making operations provided $66 million to public broadcasting in 1977. Overall, we project that income from all these sources will remain at about this level and represent about $60 million annually. Of course, every effort must be made to increase support from these sources and to tap new sources, but we expect these efforts to yield only a constant level of income, principally because income from some of these sources —notably foundations—is declining.

Although foundations have played a much more important role than corporations in the funding of public broadcasting, this support is now ebbing. The Ford Foundation is ending its unparalleled quarter-century commitment to the establishment and development of public television. Other foundations have not come forward to fill the gap, partly because of recent declines in foundation resources. The large cost of major television series is often too much for all but the very largest foundations. Many foundations seem also to believe that Ford, with its extraordinary commitment, has tested most of the new, untried ideas of the sort that foundations typically support.

While the volume of foundation funding is likely to decline in real terms during the next decade, public broadcasting may succeed in maintaining a significant continuing involvement from foundations if it is able to develop the innovative proposals of the sort that they typically find appealing. There are important new ideas and services, especially in public radio, and with the use of new technologies in their formative stages, that are likely to continue to attract foundation support. As with corporations, new mechanisms can be devised to seek broader support from the foundation community. There might be a general program fund initiated by foundations and providing unrestricted assistance to the system or to stations. Or local costs of capital expansion programs might be financed by a group of local and community foundations acting in concert. One plan we especially endorse is the initiative of the Mellon Foundation in providing funds to PBS and several major television stations to use at their discretion in developing new programs.

Like public broadcasting, private universities face financial difficulties. With the prospect of declining enrollments in the 1980s and deepening fiscal problems attributable to inflation, these private institutions will probably reduce their support of public broadcasting, even though public telecommunications (especially public radio) may represent a new and effective means for expansion of their services and improvement of their financial base.

Auctions have already begun to stabilize at revenue levels just under $15 million nationwide. We believe this income may rise somewhat with new and more sophisticated methods but it will probably not increase dramatically.

Another source is income from subsidiary operations. We do not believe subsidiary operations can or should represent a major new source of income for public broadcasting. Nonprofit organizations are not typically successful at generating business income through subsidiary operations intended to turn a profit. Such operations often require special management efforts that seriously impair the ability of the parent organization to focus on its primary mission.

We have not identified other activities in the private sector that might be developed as significant sources of funds. We hope that we are wrong but we are aware of no significant new income opportunities.

Thus we set a goal for income from private sources other than individuals and corporations at $60 million annually.

E. Need for Federal Support

Full realization of these funding goals for income from all nonfederal sources will yield $570 million. This is a significant increase over nonfederal income of $347 million in 1977, but it is also far below the $1.16 billion we estimate to be required annually by the complete, full service system we propose. Even with increased goals in support from individuals, states, and corporations, a shortfall of about $590 million remains. (Figure 4–4 shows our targets for nonfederal income and the shortfall.)

We propose federal support to provide the required $590 million in annual operating support. We have no doubt that this level of federal expenditure can be justified. Throughout this report we express our strong conviction that a full service public broadcasting system is an essential goal of society during the next quarter century.

To proceed with the development of telecommunications without a complete and effective noncommercial broadcasting system would deprive Americans of the fullest use of their national resources, and would severely limit the quality of life and opportunities for all of us.

As a nation we have made commitments to other national priorities—education, transportation, energy, science, and arts and humanities—when a critical point in history seemed to demand it. We believe that it is now time to make such a commitment to a public noncommercial voice in the telecommunications field— now, before the vital moment is lost.

This commitment, although large in absolute magnitude, is rather small when compared with total federal spending—about one-tenth of 1 percent of the federal budget. And we cannot help but believe that a public broadcasting system costing $5 per person per year is a tiny investment in comparison with the impact a truly effective public system would have on every individual in the country.

We also recognize that even though our target sum represents a substantial increase in current levels of federal spending for public broadcasting, it will be phased in gradually. A request for $590 million per year requires an especially sound rationale in a time of inflation, and in the midst of growing concern over taxes and government spending. While our plan would postpone full funding until 1985, we anticipate, nevertheless, annual increases in support of public broadcasting based on the funding mechanisms we are recommending. This report is our rationale and we hope that it is compelling.

The commitment cannot wait. We must begin now to provide sufficient resources to realize the great promise of public broadcasting in America.

In many respects the commitment has already begun with the passage of the Public Broadcasting Act in 1967 and continuing through the Public Telecommunications Financing Act of 1978, which authorizes $180 million in federal funding for 1981. The stated purposes in justification of current increases in federal

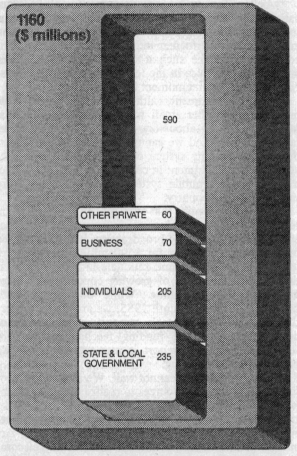

Shortfall in Recommended Annual Spending

1160
($ millions)

590

OTHER PRIVATE	60
BUSINESS	70
INDIVIDUALS	205
STATE & LOCAL GOVERNMENT	235

Figure 4-4. Shortfall in Recommended Annual Spending (excludes capital spending for facilities and expansion).

support are sound.[5] What we propose is a further commitment to the promise of telecommunications, for the purposes and objectives set forth in this report.

The improved public system that we foresee will be possible only if a wide range of interests in our society believe that public telecommunications merits sustenance. By establishing a goal of $570 million from millions of individual contributors, states, corporations, and other private sources, we are, in effect, asking the federal government to match its best efforts to theirs. Without such a broad signal from the nation, our case for federal support would not be very compelling.

With a large number and variety of funders, public broadcasting can become independent of domination by any single source. This support, and the independence that we hope can result, will be far likelier to come to the system if the crucial federal support—about half of the system's total income—can be disbursed in a way that maximizes incentives for other

[5]Section 396(a) of the Communications Act reads as follows:

Sec. 396. (a) The Congress hereby finds and declares that—

(1) it is in the public interest to encourage the growth and development of public radio and television broadcasting, including the use of such media for instructional, educational, and cultural purposes;

(2) it is in the public interest to encourage the growth and development of nonbroadcast telecommunications technologies for the delivery of public telecommunications services;

(3) expansion and development of public telecommunications and of diversity of its programming depend on freedom, imagination, and initiative on both local and national levels;

(4) the encouragement and support of public telecommunications, while matters of importance for private and local development, are also of appropriate and important concern to the Federal Government;

(5) it furthers the general welfare to encourage public telecommunications services which will be responsive to the interests of people both in particular localities and throughout the United States, and which will constitute an expression of diversity and excellence;

(6) it is necessary and appropriate for the Federal Government to complement, assist, and support a national policy that will most effectively make public telecommunications services available to all citizens of the United States; and

(7) a private corporation should be created to facilitate the development of public telecommunications and to afford maximum protection from extraneous interference and control.

contributors, and at the same time insulates the system from political interference.

To determine how best to do this, we must first consider the process through which public broadcasting now receives federal funds.

Current Federal Support. Federal support for public broadcasting currently takes three forms, principally an appropriation to the Corporation for Public Broadcasting for the support of stations, national programs, and distribution, as well as the leadership and support functions CPB performs. About three-quarters of total federal support for public broadcasting in 1977 went to CPB.

The remainder is divided between federal support for equipping and improving station facilities (the Educational Broadcasting Facilities Program), and grants and contracts by federal agencies for specific programs or services. The Department of Health, Education, and Welfare, the National Endowment for the Arts, the National Science Foundation, and the National Endowment for the Humanities finance television programs intended for distribution by PBS. As shown in Figure 4–3, this agency underwriting represented $19.3 million in 1977; facilities funding totaled $14.0 million in 1977. The history of federal appropriations to CPB provides the model of federal support that we seek for public broadcasting in the future.

Federal support for public broadcasting through CPB has increased dramatically since the establishment of the Corporation in 1968. Table 4–1 shows the history of federal support for CPB. The appropriation more than doubled from 1973 to 1976, and it will double again by 1979.

During the early '70s, federal support to CPB was determined by the regular federal appropriations process with, at best, two years advance funding in each appropriations cycle. Chapter II describes the difficulties caused by the Nixon veto of the CPB authorization bill in 1972. Subsequent events led to a change in the form of federal support. Enacted by Congress in 1975, this new arrangement provided for multiyear financing to guarantee better insulation and facilitate

Table 4–1

Congressional Appropriations and Present Authorizations
to the Corporation for Public Broadcasting

Fiscal Year	Appropriations (millions)	Authorizations (millions)
1969	$ 5	—
1970	15	—
1971	23	—
1972	35	—
1973	35	—
1974	47.5	—
1975	62	—
1976ᵃ	96	—
1977	103	$103ᵇ
1978	119.2	121ᵇ
1979	120.2ᶜ	140ᵇ
1980	152ᶜ	160
1981		180ᵈ
1982		200ᵈ
1983		220ᵈ

ᵃIncludes the transition quarter.

ᵇAuthorized amount in the Public Broadcasting Financing Act of 1975.

ᶜAppropriated amount, but subject to amendments, such as supplemental appropriations.

ᵈAuthorized amount in the Public Broadcasting Financing Act of 1978.

planning while preserving regular congressional monitoring of federal spending.

Funds were to be authorized for a five-year period, with the actual appropriations determined three years in advance. The 1975 legislation authorized the availability of federal funds up to specific levels for the five-year period 1976–80, and actually appropriated specific amounts for 1976, 1977, and 1978. As 1976 drew to a close, Congress would appropriate funds for 1979, and so on. The plan intended that there always be three-year advance funding. The course of events has not always provided for three-year advance funding, but federal support has always been provided at least two years in advance since the passage of the legislation in 1975.

Other elements of the new funding arrangement

are even more significant. Chief among these is that federal support for CPB is based on a partial match of nonfederal revenue generated by the system, up to the maximum established by the actual appropriation. This provision establishes incentives for local control and support to an independent public broadcasting system, as well as a nearly automatic means for determining the appropriate level of federal support. In 1975, the plan required that every $1 in the federal appropriation be matched by $2.50 in nonfederal income. The matching ratio has been changed most recently in 1978 legislation, which requires that each $1 in 1981 federal appropriation be matched with $2 in nonfederal income. This numerical ratio between federal and nonfederal sources provides an easy mechanism for Congress to alter the total federal appropriation that is available as a result of the stations' local fund raising. Changing the matching ratio has thus far resulted in larger federal appropriations. There is no good reason why the downward trend of the matching ratio could not be reversed, although history suggests that the possibility is remote.

The beneficiaries of this federal matching program are located throughout the country. Radio and television stations that raise nonfederal funds receive a federal return for their efforts. CPB returns about 60 percent of its total appropriation to the stations as discretionary funds, called Community Service Grants (CSGs). The size of the total federal appropriation to CPB, as well as the actual grant made to each station, is fixed by the ability of stations to generate local support. The system rewards local initiative with federal matching dollars. Because eligibility for receipt of federal funds and the amount of the CSG are determined by objective quantitative means, the system is well positioned to avoid review of program content as a condition for increased funding. This is absolutely essential when federal funds are used to support editorial and artistic activity.

Thus, licensees do not really "earn" their CSGs with any specific program or service. They have established, in the eyes of Congress and CPB, a basic eligibility for public funds by operating stations that perform a public service in their communities, and by generating nonfederal income that determines the size of the federal appropriation through the matching process.[6]

While the theory of a matching formula for funding public broadcasting is sound, the greatest advantages of the plan have not been realized in actual practice. Congress has consistently specified ceilings on the amount available under the matching formula. Public broadcasting has consistently exceeded the amount of nonfederal income necessary to reach the specified appropriation ceiling. By seeking a "supplemental" appropriation in order to honor the matching principle

---

[6]A television station receives a Community Service Grant calculated in two steps. Each station meeting minimum eligibility requirements receives a basic amount equal to 0.1 percent of the federal appropriation to CPB (for example, $103,000 in 1977, when the appropriation to CPB was $103 million) plus an amount of the remaining funds reserved for television CSGs determined by that station's share of total nonfederal income of all stations. It is this total income which determines the federal matching appropriation and which largely determines the amount of the pass-through grant to each station. In 1977 the average CSG for a public television station was $329,000. The largest station received a grant of about $3.8 million and several stations with small budgets received amounts near the minimum of $103,000.

A similar formula is used for radio. The radio CSG is divided into three parts:

1. *The base grant.* A fixed grant of $26,550 (in 1977) to each qualified station.

2. *The incentive grant.* The total amount remaining after the base grants is allocated to stations in proportion to their nonfederal income. Half this allocation is awarded; the other half is reserved for possible award as a bonus grant.

3. *Bonus grant.* This rewards stations which participate in any of the following areas:

• public participation;
• public awareness;
• development.

Stations that participate in all three areas receive 100 percent of their potential bonus grant; in two areas, 50 percent; in one area, 25 percent.

In 1977 the average radio CSG was $38,000. The largest station received a grant of $157,174, while several stations with small budgets received grants near the minimum of $26,550.

and increase overall federal support, CPB has subjected itself and the system to more appearances before the Congress. Hence, the purpose of establishing multiyear funding—the insulation from annual political review of the system—has been undermined. In practical terms the match has not been automatic, and has turned out to be a complicated and time-consuming process to administer.

Even greater inconsistencies in the matching theory can be seen at the station level. While stations raise *all* the funds that determine the overall CPB appropriation, they only receive part of that money in return as CSGs. This has led to bitter struggles between the stations and CPB. Moreover, the funds distributed by CPB to stations are allocated according to a complicated, multistep formula which minimizes the direct relation between the funds an individual station has raised and the size of its federal grant. As a result, stations cannot accurately specify the precise amount of federal support triggered by audience contributions or other sources of nonfederal funds. Grants fluctuate from year to year, according to the total amount available, the number of stations sharing it, and other provisions of the formula. Stations cannot honestly say that a viewer giving a dollar will trigger a federal grant in the proportion specified in the legislation.

The present federal funding plan has built into it an inevitable clash between the competing demands of stations, whose fund-raising efforts determine the size of the entire federal appropriation, and the necessary activities undertaken by CPB on a national level, which include its own administrative costs, national programs, television and radio interconnection, research, training, and technological initiatives. This clash is built into the formula devised by the system to divide up an appropriation that has never provided enough funds to go around. With its own national priorities in mind, CPB has limited station demands for an increased share of the appropriation. And CPB's formula and allocation policies, while altering the sanctity of the federal matching principles, have served to protect stations in smaller communities, which could never raise sufficient funds locally.

We believe that the essential theory of the match, coupled with higher federal funding and other techniques for assuring the survival of essential national services, can provide a stable overall public broadcasting system that is more rational, less divisive, and more productive for the viewers and listeners who will receive its benefits.

IV. Allocating Federal Support

A. Administration by the Public Telecommunications Trust

We recommend that the Trust receive and disburse three distinct and separate pools of federal funds, on a three-year advance appropriation:

1. Automatic matching grants to stations.

2. Automatic special formula grant to the Program Services Endowment.

3. Funds for the national activities of the Trust.

As the leadership entity for the system, the Trust would, by legislation, receive three distinct and separate funds that would not be pooled, or reallocated from one to another. Separating the leadership and other activities of the Trust from station support and programming at the Endowment will eliminate direct rivalry between the Trust and the stations or the Endowment, or both, for a larger share of the funds. We believe this separate money flow for each activity is essential to sustain the independence of the whole system and balance its constituent parts.

We have no doubt that the Trust will be called upon to use its considerable prestige and leadership to protect one or all of these three funds from politically motivated scrutiny. In these cases the Trust is expected to protect the system by doing its best to fend off inappropriate controls at appropriation time. Insulation of

128   FUTURE OF PUBLIC BROADCASTING

both stations and Endowment will be further aided by the virtually automatic flow of funds provided under this plan.

All the Trust's funds should be based upon a three-year advance appropriation in keeping with the arrangement adopted in 1975. This funding arrangement will permit the necessary advance planning for the Trust, the Endowment, and the stations. It will further strengthen the insulation of the overall system by cycling federal support three years in advance of actual use.

B. Stations

We recommend that stations receive discretionary grants of federal funds from the Trust at a match of $1 for every $1.50 nonfederal.

With $570 million in nonfederal income, the stations will receive $380 million in federal matching grants, the match being provided directly to each station. For every $1.50 raised from nonfederal sources, a station would receive $1 in federal matching funds distributed by the Trust. By providing a match directly to each station, the incentive of matching federal support will be greatly strengthened. Such a powerful incentive for increasing local support is essential to our goal of dramatically increasing nonfederal funds. Also, the direct match should eliminate the sort of destructive debate that has occurred in the past over the use of CPB's appropriation which the stations saw as "their money."

Our recommendation for increased federal support to stations builds on the soundness and success of the existing program that provides the Community Service Grants in relation to station fund raising. Local and state support triggers unrestricted federal funding, and enables stations better to meet their community responsibilities by broadcasting programs of local preference.

An essential element of this plan is the method by which distance is placed between the federal government and the public broadcasting system it helps to finance. In our model, stations are fully responsible to their local communities. The station alone selects and broadcasts the programs that best meet the needs of its community. This editorial responsibility involves production of programs of purely local interest and sometimes of wider appeal. It also involves pooling resources with other stations for programs they collectively determine to be necessary. The station is not only the gatekeeper, responsible to the community for what is broadcast, but also the funder of many of the programs it selects for the community.

The federal matching grants to stations, together with local support, will yield the discretionary funds required for these purposes. The total station funds will be $950 million, the predominant share of the $1.16 billion required for annual operating expenses. Of the $380 million required in matching funds for stations, we estimate that about $250 million will support national programming and promotion in radio and television. The balance will strengthen local and regional programming and improve overall station operations. By channeling federal funds directly to the stations on a matching basis we seek to protect program decisions of the system from federal scrutiny, and to provide a predictable flow of funds that reflect in an objective way the degree of community support for that station's activities.

Several rules and procedures will govern the disbursement of the federal discretionary funds to stations.

1. *Administration.* The Trust will administer the matching grant program. It will collect reports from stations on nonfederal income, follow accepted procedures to verify the reported income, report the total to Congress and the Treasury, and receive the required matching amount. The Trust then disburses the precise amount to each station as determined by the $1 federal for each $1.50 nonfederal formula.

2. *Appropriation.* The federal funds required to meet the match will be estimated in advance in order to enact a five-year authorization for this program. Pro-

jections must provide sufficient latitude to assure adequate funds in the event of accelerated growth of the system.

The entire Trust appropriation will be made on a three-year advance funding cycle. Reasonably accurate estimates of nonfederal income should be available at this point. Again, appropriations should slightly exceed estimates, with the proviso that federal funds will be disbursed to stations only as eligible local funds are raised. Unused funds are returned to the Treasury at the end of the year.

3. *Planning.* Because federal grants to stations represent the single largest source of funding for public broadcasting, it is essential that the stations provide complete reports to the Trust on station activities to verify both services and spending. The Trust will require such reports in order to carry out its fiduciary responsibility for the system and to be assured that public policy requirements are fully met. The Trust will also use its station reports for representing the system to Congress and others.

It is equally vital that stations work with the Trust and their own national organizations in developing plans for future programs and services. A multiyear system plan revised annually should be provided enabling Congress and others to monitor the progress of the system in meeting its goals. Such a plan should cover the use of all moneys including the discretionary grants which match nonfederal funding for the stations. The plan should, of course, be suitably flexible, permitting stations to alter their objectives as required by changing circumstances, and holding off congressional attempts to review or reverse funding decisions.

The absence of a plan for system spending and development has been one of the major shortcomings of the industry. Without a plan, the industry has given the impression of less than adequate performance and inefficient use of funds. Some have also concluded that public broadcasting is unresponsive to criticism in such areas as financial accountability and equal opportunity. Public telecommunications can expect to receive

public support only if it develops responsible plans for
improving its services to the public and if its progress
—though not its individual programs—is measured in
terms of these goals.

We reemphasize that we do not intend this recommendation to inject the Congress into specific activities of the system or stations, or to permit the imposition of purely political standards in planning. Plans
must be developed by public broadcasting alone. On
the other hand, the need for insulation from inappropriate interference should not be used as a shield to
avoid the responsibilities that go with the administration of public funds, or to prevent the system from
being accountable to the public.

4. *Eligibility.* Stations must meet defined minimum standards of operation in order to qualify for federal matching grants. Federal funds to stimulate and
support the development of stations are only appropriate where the station has the capacity and commitment to provide a full service and where the community has demonstrated strong support for the operation
of the station. Suitable standards would be applied to
areas such as the length of the broadcast day, station
governance, financial reporting and audit requirements,
personnel management, and local programming capacity.

Such guidelines for eligibility for federal funds
have governed the CSG program administered by
CPB and have been a largely positive influence on the
growth of public broadcasting. Especially noteworthy
have been the efforts by some stations to improve operations in order to achieve eligibility for grants tied to
the standards. With many small, low-power, noncommercial radio stations, the qualification standards are
critical (see Chapter VI).

C. *Program Services Endowment*

We recommend that the Program
Services Endowment automatically receive federal funds from the Trust equal
to one-half the federal grants to stations.

With $380 million in matching grants to stations, the Endowment will automatically receive $190 million.

The Program Services Endowment is so central to our plan for strengthening public telecommunications that we hesitate to endorse any other aspect of this report without its establishment. The Endowment, encapsulated within the Trust, and financed by both federal and private moneys held for its use by the trustees, is a crucial programming source counterbalancing the programming activities of the station system. While stations will use their considerable resources to provide mainstream programs and services nationwide, the Endowment will concentrate on the unconventional, creative, untested ideas in programming and telecommunication services on which the stations, acting alone or in combination, would be unlikely to risk their funds.

The support of such creative activity by the Endowment can be seen as the most critical continuing need for the system and, with this mission, the Endowment becomes essential for the justification of federal funding for the entire station system. Alongside the leadership activities of the Trust, the stations and the Endowment will form the basis for a strong and effective public telecommunications system.

We believe strongly that funding the Endowment via a matching grant piggybacked atop the matching federal grants for operating the stations, and funded at a level equal to one-half the latter, offers a secure and continuing means of support for the principal creative work of public broadcasting. The equivalent of one-half the federal funds to stations has been chosen carefully to provide a balance between the Endowment and the stations. If the Endowment were permitted to become too large as a programming service for the system, it would accumulate ongoing programming responsibilities that would ultimately defeat its role as a catalyst for new ideas and innovative programming.

Subject to reasonable rules of accountability, the Endowment should have great flexibility in the allocation of its resources. We recognize the need, however, for formal budgeting and careful accounting within the Endowment to justify its expenditures at the $190 million level. Without intending in any way to limit the flexibility of the Endowment in determining the wisest use of its funds, we envision a typical budget roughly as follows, with expenditures (including staff) for (1) national television programs and promotion, at $125 million; (2) other television programming and promotion projects at the regional level and at individual stations, at $22 million; (3) local and national radio programs and projects, at $18 million. (See Chapters III and V.) Additionally, the Endowment would expend (4) $15 million annually for research and development of programs and services in learning; and (5) $10 million to develop applications of new technologies. (These activities are described in Chapters VII and VIII and Appendix D.)

Private Income for the Endowment.
We recommend that the Trust seek other independent funds for the Program Services Endowment.

The Endowment will also receive income from a private endowment established as independent support of the activities of the Endowment, especially the development of programs. We could urge the Business Roundtable and other leadership groups within the business community to develop a plan to stimulate at least $50 million in corporate contributions. A group of foundations might consider making a large grant in concert as a challenge for matching funds raised from other private sources. The Trust would then undertake a fund drive among the general public. A federal match should be established in the Treasury as a special fund, and drawn upon by the Trust as elegible nonfederal matching funds are generated. This sort of pyramiding would offer a way to build the Endowment's initial resources relatively quickly. These start-up funds, while yielding only modest income, will help provide further insulation for the Endowment, and a cushion against total reliance on a single source of support.

D. Public Telecommunications Trust

We recommend that the activities of the Trust be financed with a direct federal appropriation, and that its responsibilities include a special plan of federal support for the capital costs of developing and extending the public radio and television systems.

The Trust is the leadership entity for public broadcasting. It will perform activities that are essential to the future of the whole system, including fiduciary responsibility for the federal funds provided to the stations and to the Endowment. Other activities of the Trust include system planning, system research and evaluation, training and personnel development, verifying nonfederal income, and various leadership activities involving the Congress, the administration, and the general public. To perform these and other leadership functions vital to the development of the public system, the Trust will require at least $20 million annually. (The functions of the Trust are described fully in Chapter III; their costs are explained in Appendix D.)

Facilities. The first program of federal support for public broadcasting was the Educational Broadcasting Facilities Program (EBFP). This program is discussed at a number of points in the report, and is fully described in Appendix E.

We recommend that this facilities program be continued in a slightly altered form by the Public Telecommunications Trust with the objective of completing the task of bringing public radio and television to virtually all citizens. We propose that the Trust have flexibility in administering this program to develop both systems in the most expeditious way. At times, for example, special grants for personnel or purchasing radio stations may be required, as described in Chapter

VI. The basic objectives of the activity as they relate to capital costs and facilities are described in Chapter VII.

We estimate the cost of establishing a complete radio and television broadcast system at $350 million over the next five to seven years. (See Appendix D.) There are many uncertainties. Capital expenditures can easily be several times as large, especially if there are major new investments in nonbroadcast facilities or other technologies. We have consciously limited our emphasis to the task of completing the broadcast system so that the diverse programs and services provided by public broadcasting can become available throughout the land. With this system in place, we would be in a sound position for a national evaluation of the wisdom of extensive investment in nonbroadcast services offering systematic enrichment of the information environment available to the public through an evolving public telecommunications system.

During the five to seven years required for completion of the broadcast system, however, it will undoubtedly become necessary to support limited investments in nonbroadcast technology. To provide modest funds for these new developments as well as funds adequate for completing the system, we recommend an expenditure of $50 million annually for five to seven years, with the requirement that at least 25 percent of the cost of any project be developed from nonfederal sources. With this measure of nonfederal involvement, we should be able to guarantee local initiative on behalf of new or improved stations. Moreover, the requirement for some nonfederal funds reduces the drain on the federal treasury for completing the broadcast system, thus providing moneys for exploring alternative means of delivering new services.

Thus the Trust will receive ongoing support of $20 million for its activities, plus $50 million annually for five to seven years to complete the establishment of public radio and television services nationwide.

We believe that a direct congressional appropriation offers the best means of financing such needs. Direct federal determination of the level of support for the

Trust, with the latter's important leadership role for representing the system to the Congress, should yield effective communication between elected representatives and the trustees acting on behalf of the total system. Disagreements between the trustees and Congress ought not to reduce funding for the stations or the Program Services Endowment, because the formula grant recommendations and the Trust's protection effectively insulate stations and the Endowment from political pressures that might develop. Congress can alter the duties and responsibilities of the Trust easily through changes in its mandated management activities and parallel changes in its appropriation. But Congress should not attempt to undermine the Trust's leadership role in the system, or to alter the automatic nature of the formula grants to stations and the Endowment.

E. A Sound Plan for Federal Support

The principal outcome of these several means for providing federal support to the stations, the Endowment, and the Trust would be an increase in federal funds for public broadcasting amounting to $590 million annually. Accordingly, as shown in Figure 4–5, the federal support will eliminate the estimated shortfall in our computation of the upper limit of nonfederal funds against the $1.16 billion estimated requirement for financing the annual operating costs of the full service system we recommend.

With federal funds for stations rising to 40 percent of their income, the stations will have greatly increased discretionary funds with which to improve their services. Federal funds will be the largest single source of support for the stations, raising fears that federal control may quickly follow. But with federal funds at 40 percent of the total budget of a station, and provided on a relatively automatic matching basis, we are confident that the independence of the stations in essential matters related to their program services will be preserved.

The Trust's leadership is an additional bulwark protecting the stations' independence. Even though financed almost exclusively via federal money, the Trust

Recommended Income Levels

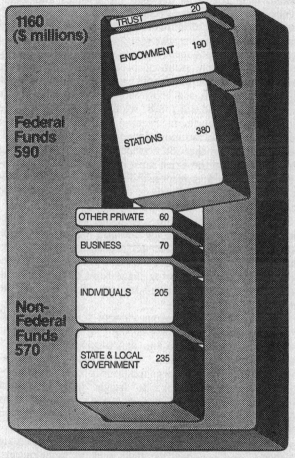

Figure 4-5. Recommended Income Levels (excludes income to finance capital spending for facilities and expansion).

and the Endowment are designed to be highly resistant to government intervention. For the extraordinarily important and sensitive programming work of the Endowment, our plan offers two protections. First, the character of the Trust's board will provide significant insulation, as will the special encapsulation of the Endowment as a separate institution under the umbrella of the Trust. Second, the automatic nature of the formula grant to the Endowment should remove such funding from the ordinary political pressures and special-interest set-asides of the federal appropriations process. While Congress has a legitimate oversight role in the expenditure of federal funds, we feel confident that the clear First Amendment function of the Endowment will create broad support for protecting its independence at least in the initial stages of its existence. The Endowment and the Trust must build traditions of independent action and responsibility if they are ultimately to become fine institutions comparable in stature to the best American universities or the BBC.

The Trust is the proper focus for direct communication of all sorts with the nation's public representatives. As the system's leadership entity dedicated to the public interest, the Trust would provide the appropriate forum for considering suggestions and complaints originating from the administration, Congress, or the general public.

What emerges from our view of this strengthened public telecommunications system is a balance of forces, not dissimilar to the constitutional democracy that has served us so well. A broad base of contributors, individuals, and organizations provide local institutions with the means to trigger federal support enhancing the editorial and creative activity that is vested in the licensee. This in turn triggers additional federal money for a nationally mandated creative force that can, with supplementary private funds, create programs and services that flow back to local outlets. With an overall financial and political umbrella that helps plan for the completion, improvement, and diversification of the entire system—a national responsibility financed by the national government—this telecommunications system can mesh its diverse functional activities with a logic and unity that will support its constituent parts successfully. The system, if constructed carefully along the lines we have recommended, is not likely to undermine itself.

V. The Source of Federal Funds

We recommend general revenues as the principal source of federal funds for public telecommunications. We also recommend the establishment of a fee for the use of the spectrum by commercial broadcasters with the income from this fee used to offset the requirement for general tax revenues.

We have considered a number of special sources of federal funding in our attempts to achieve two objectives: maximum insulation for public broadcasting, and a way to help reduce the strains on the federal budget that an increased appropriation will create. While we believe the estimate of $590 million in federal funds to be necessary for the realization of full service public broadcasting, we are also aware that public broadcasting must compete with other activities in a time of concern over rising costs and the role of government spending in fueling inflation.

We have examined a number of special sources of funds, including several special taxes, a set-aside of taxes already paid by commercial broadcasters, and a fee for the use of the electromagnetic spectrum. Of the three options, we believe that only the spectrum fee presents a viable method for returning some of the recommended increase in expenditures to the federal Treasury; this fee, a new source of funds for the federal government, would be charged to private interests for their use of a public resource. It appears to us to be a fair and reasonable levy, one in accord with sound fiscal policy, which may also improve efficiency in spectrum management. Other forms of earmarked funds for public telecommunications have been carefully considered by us and reluctantly rejected.

1. *Special Taxes.* Special taxes with revenues dedicated to public broadcasting are often suggested as an ideal means for providing secure funding while protecting the system from government interference. The first Carnegie Commission advanced such an idea when it recommended a tax on the purchase of television sets with the income reserved for public broadcasting.

After extensive study and discussion, we have become convinced that such a special dedicated tax is not an effective solution to the funding problems of public broadcasting. While special taxes would appear to provide a stable flow of support free of political pressures, they are also rigid statutory formulas not easily adaptable to the changing needs of public broadcasting. Clearly, Congress retains the right to alter or end such an arrangement, as attested by its recent decision to expand the use of Highway Trust Fund moneys for mass transit; but such alterations can be expected to bury the system in litigation from those whose support might be altered by proposed changes. Dedicated taxes are by no means a guarantee of insulation from political and other pressures.

A special tax also does not provide a stable and planned flow of funds. Proceeds from the tax would fluctuate with variations in general economic conditions and the fortunes of the activity taxed. Even more important, taxes on television sets or commercial advertising revenues would almost certainly be passed through to consumers. Accordingly they would become not only a source of inflation but a burden on the lowest income levels of the population.

Finally, a special tax could yield an amount significantly below the level of federal support required under our plan. A single tax might provide a maximum of $100 million to $200 million without becoming inequitable on those taxed. Thus a single special federal tax could at best provide a limited source of funding, perhaps identified for the Endowment—but, in the light of the arguments set forth above, such a tax would be less secure and less attractive to consumers than the alternative matching grant method we have proposed.

Accordingly, special taxes with the proceeds dedicated to public broadcasting have serious drawbacks. Each of the individual alternatives has serious practical disadvantages as well.

The tax on television sets recommended by the first Carnegie Commission would place the burden for public broadcasting on one industry even though the benefits of the system are widely diffused through society.

A tax on broadcast advertising would not place the burden so directly on one industry, since many different firms promote goods and services with broadcast commercials. It would also have the advantage of relating income for public broadcasting to the activities of commercial television and radio, where single-minded emphasis on merchandising has led to much of the need for a noncommercial alternative. But the development of a special tax on the revenues of commercial broadcasting in order to finance public broadcasting would, most Commissioners believe, lead to a state of affairs in which the extended role of commercial broadcasting in financing its own alternative would be used as a "trade-off" to reduce the existing public-service obligations of commercial broadcasters. We consider such trade-offs to be unacceptable.

The singling out of commercial broadcasters for a special tax on profits would be, in our view, extremely difficult to administer, because of the structure of the commercial system and the number of stations with little or no profit. Depending on how the tax were designed, networks and stations would be encouraged to alter their accounting in order to hide resources. For example, if only stations were taxed, the networks, as owners of several of the most profitable stations, would have a strong incentive to reallocate costs, reducing reported revenue from their profit centers. Also, as large corporations with many divisions, networks could easily shift corporate overhead to reduce reported broadcasting profits.

These difficulties are compounded by the fact that many stations, especially UHF television stations and large numbers of radio stations, realize only marginal profits, or even losses. Excluding such stations from the tax would shift the burden to a relatively small number. For example, only 353 of 638 television stations showed profits of $400,000 or more in 1976, while 101 showed losses. After-tax profits of these stations and profitable radio stations may equal something under $1 billion, clearly too little to generate a significant amount of the required level of federal support for public broadcasting.

Quite apart from administrative problems, there would be inequities when stations change hands. Original owners may well have reaped windfall profits in the sale of the station while current owners might simply earn a conventional return on investment.

A number of other special taxes that might be dedicated to public broadcasting have also been considered. We have been forced to reject each of them because of problems they raise. For example, a tax on the transfer of radio or television stations, while theoretically appealing as a means of realizing some public gain from the large increase in the value of these properties, could fluctuate dramatically from year to year as the climate for sales is altered by changes in FCC policies and other factors. More important, it would be extremely limited in amount, since total sales are not generally more than a few hundred million dollars annually.

Thus we believe that special taxes are theoretically unacceptable and impractical. Dedicating the income from such a tax to public broadcasting would not add significantly to the insulation of the system. We hope that the dispelling of our own naive faith in special taxes dedicated to public broadcasting as an automatic source of insulation and as a reliable source of income will cause others to view them more analytically and realistically. This long-held hope serves only to prolong the instability of the system.

2. *Set Aside Taxes of Commercial Broadcasting.* Another alternative we have considered is using the considerable taxes already paid by commercial broadcasters as a device to finance the public system. These taxes are estimated at $700 million or $800 million at the federal level, more than enough to finance the federal share of the costs of public broadcasting. Under this

plan, rather than increase the tax burden of commercial broadcasters through a dedicated tax or a spectrum fee, Congress would earmark some or all of these tax receipts for public broadcasting. While this funding plan would not work annual hardship on the commercial broadcasting industry, it does not seem to alter the federal funding picture because it does not generate a new source of revenue. The funds going into public broadcasting will go out of the Treasury. This seems to move funds from one federal pocket to another, without reducing any burdens.

3. *Spectrum Fee.* A fee for the use of the spectrum is an alternative which overcomes many of these objectives.

We believe that the theory of a spectrum fee is sound and reasonable. Broadcast frequencies are a scarce public resource allocated by the FCC to a wide range of businesses and individuals, including broadcasters who are required to serve the public interest in exchange for their use of the channel. Service is evaluated periodically when station licenses are renewed. It is equitable and proper for the government to charge private users of any scarce public resource, just as it charges for mining, grazing, timber, and oil exploration rights on public property. A fee for the use of the spectrum would serve to stimulate some users to seek greater efficiency because the fee relates to the portion of the spectrum occupied. Today there is no incentive to limit usage by any spectrum user. While commercial broadcasters typically use a discrete slice of the spectrum that does not vary, other spectrum users, CB radio operators for example, would have greater incentives for efficiency. Ultimately broadcasters might also be able to compress their signals if there was suitable financial incentive. Manufacturers might then be induced to design more efficient receivers.

A spectrum fee does, however, raise practical problems. It is difficult to construct a fair means of calculating the charge. Several factors, including revenues of the user and some consideration of the "scarcity value" of the frequency assigned, would probably be included in the calculation of the fee. Putting a price tag on scarcity is a difficult task even if only in a theoretical exercise; when practical consequences weigh in as well, the problem becomes even more vexing.

It is also arguable that income from the fee should be used to finance activities other than public broadcasting. The administrative costs of all regulation in the communications field, as well as efforts to strengthen minority ownership and rural telecommunications services, have already been suggested as possible uses for this money. However worthy these activities might be, they do not require any greater insulation than other government programs. The First Amendment mission of public broadcasting sets it in a different category, one that requires the greatest care in constructing its relationship to government funding.

It is this unique nature of public broadcasting that motivates us to recommend the enactment of a spectrum fee. We believe such a fee is proper and that an equitable schedule of rates can be devised by Congress. Moreover, we believe our plan for public broadcasting will be closer to realization if we can identify a new source of money to the federal Treasury along with the drain of resources required under our plan. Whether or not Congress would explicitly specify the revenues from the spectrum fee as a source of federal moneys for public broadcasting, it seems entirely reasonable to regard this new income explicitly as an offset to the added cost of a complete public broadcasting system. It would then be logically linked in both time and congressional action to the deliberations over the future of federal support for public broadcasting. Formal dedication of the proceeds of the spectrum fee to public broadcasting would be a modest plus for both insulation and reliability of funding, but we would not view it as crucial for achieving either one of these objectives.

Even if Congress does not think it appropriate to link the income from a fee on all users of the spectrum to public broadcasting, it may wish to designate the proceeds from fees charged to commercial broadcasters for financing the public system. In this way commercial broadcasting would directly contribute to the maintenance of the public system that is necessary to broaden the kinds of communications services available in the country beyond those which help sell products. The theory of a spectrum fee applied to all users appears to be sound, and this linkage between commercial broadcasting and public broadcasting seems equally sound.

The income from the spectrum fee on commercial broadcasting could not in any event provide more than a portion of the federal moneys required for public broadcasting. It is difficult to speculate without a more precise resolution of the principles of spectrum fee structure, but if we are forced to estimate we would conjecture that the fee on commercial broadcasting will probably generate no more than $150 million to $200 million, and perhaps considerably less. It would certainly be unable to provide the total $590 million required in annual operating support.

To solve these difficulties, we propose that the income from the spectrum fee be seen as an offset against the required levels of general revenues set forth in our plan. If, for example, the fee generates $200 million, the commitment of general revenues will be reduced to $390 million. Using the income from the spectrum fee as an offset in this manner does not alter the basic automatic nature of our plan for federal support, but it does provide an important new source of money to the federal Treasury, making our proposal easier for the government to finance. We also believe that the spectrum fee will, as a special source of secure funds for public broadcasting, further strengthen the insulation of the system.

Thus we recommend a spectrum fee as sound and equitable public policy. The income from this fee paid by commercial broadcasting might be designated for public broadcasting as a noncommercial system providing a necessary complement to the commercial stations and networks. To avoid fluctuation directly as income from the fee changes, we have not tied public broadcasting's budget only to the direct fee collection. Instead, we believe it should be used as a general offset to reduce the demand on the Treasury posed by our plan for federal support for the Trust, the Endowment, and the stations.

VI. Transition

The next several years must be years of dramatic growth in public broadcasting. Public awareness and support must increase significantly, and both public radio and television will require improved and expanded operations at both national and station levels.

With total income reaching $482 million in 1977, the system must have a sound and judicious plan for further development. We believe that the system, spurred by the incentive of the federal matching grants going directly to stations, can achieve our projected full service level of $1.16 billion annually in 1985.

Federal support will have a crucial role to play in this period of development. The matching grants for stations (at the $1 federal for every $1.50 nonfederal ratio) should be made available immediately. Similarly, support for the Endowment should be instituted at a level equal to one-half of federal funds to stations. If these arrangements were applied to funding in 1977, grants to stations would have equaled $232 million and support for the Endowment would have been $116 million, for a total of $348 million. Additionally, the Trust should be financed at nearly the full level of $20 million annually plus $50 million per year for several years in order to develop the needed capital expansion program leading to full coverage. Thus, as soon as possible, the federal government should increase its support to over $400 million. Federal funds will continue to rise in tandem with the growth of the system through 1985, when $590 million will be provided in annual operating support. Congress has already appropriated $200 million for CPB in 1982. We recommend that this level of support be increased to the precise amount required under our system of formula grants, and that there be an added allocation for the Trust. Only through the establishment of this leadership at the national level will our complete plan for strengthening public broadcasting become a reality. Figure 4–6 shows the current nonfederal and federal support and the levels to be achieved by 1985.

Growth in Public Broadcasting Annual Income

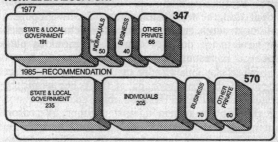

NONFEDERAL SUPPORT

1977

| STATE & LOCAL GOVERNMENT 191 | INDIVIDUALS 50 | BUSINESS 40 | OTHER PRIVATE 66 | **347** |

1985—RECOMMENDATION

| STATE & LOCAL GOVERNMENT 235 | INDIVIDUALS 205 | BUSINESS 70 | OTHER PRIVATE 60 | **570** |

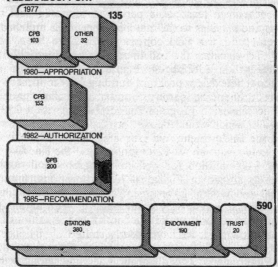

FEDERAL SUPPORT

1977

| CPB 103 | OTHER 32 | **135** |

1980—APPROPRIATION

| CPB 152 |

1982—AUTHORIZATION

| GPB 200 |

1985—RECOMMENDATION

| STATIONS 380 | ENDOWMENT 190 | TRUST 20 | **590** |

Figure 4–6. Growth in Public Broadcasting Annual Income (federal support excludes capital spending for facilities and expansion).

The Trust should lead the system in planning this period of transition and growth. The changeover from the current institutions and support mechanisms will entail some dislocations, which should be kept to a minimum. More important, the system must use its increased funds judiciously to foster its growth. It is critical that these decisions be made in a cooperative and constructive fashion, unlike the debilitating debates that have in the past surrounded decisions by CPB on allocating its resources.

Efforts by either radio or television to seek special support at the disadvantage of the other would be especially destructive. Responsible growth cannot pit one part of the system against another. A reasonable plan might provide more national programs for television along with an opportunity for public radio to expand to the critical mass necessary to realize its potential. It is especially important, as described in Chapter VI, that the development and expansion plan for radio provide a reasonable period to phase in new stations and services so the matching incentives attached to federal funds can work constructively.

To visualize the full impact of our funding plan, we refer the reader back to Figure 4–3, which illustrates national television program funding. In contrast with current financing patterns, under our plan, national public television program support would rise to $360 million, which would be met principally by the stations and the Endowment. We estimate the stations will collectively spend about $200 million and the Endowment over $125 million for national programs and promotion, as shown in Figure 4–7. Corporations, foundations, and federal government agencies will contribute the balance, a relatively small amount. With ample discretionary support under the control of the stations and the Endowment, we have clearly shifted the balance of support so there can be no excessive influence by these external funders. This illustration demonstrates how our plan will strengthen the independence and integrity of the system so that it can continue to improve and extend its services to the public.

Public Television National Programming
PROPOSED FUNDING

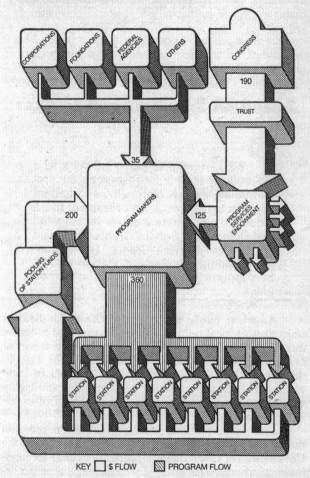

Figure 4-7. Public Television National Programming: Proposed Funding.

V

Television Programs and Services

> We recommend that stations spend
> the bulk of their new resources on pro-
> gramming, locally, regionally, and nation-
> ally, through aggregation of some of these
> funds. To emphasize this, we recommend
> that Community Service Grants be viewed
> as Program Service Grants. The Endow-
> ment should supplement station efforts,
> by supporting the innovative and untried
> ideas.

American public broadcasting is based on the dual
objectives of local self-determination and high program
quality. Accordingly, the system is faced with the most
challenging task in the communications field: how to
develop a dynamic balance between the needs of local
communities on the one hand, and the costly and highly
specialized task of producing a constant flow of excellent programs for the nation on the other.

This chapter offers some reflections on program
making in public broadcasting today, and sets forth the
Commission's views on the production and decision-
making processes necessary for achieving the improvements which we believe to be attainable in the near
future.

We concentrate here primarily on television. Radio will be discussed separately in Chapter VI, for a number of reasons. Because radio is more diverse, more local, cheaper to program, and more strictly "formatted," the strategies for improving radio program services are substantially different from those for television. Moreover, the two public systems are at different stages of development, with varying institutional structures and substantially different programming problems.

Radio's first priority, as a result, is to complete its physical facilities. As this recommendation is implemented, the need for programming will increase accordingly. We recommend that responsibility for wider-than-local programming in radio, as well as for television, be borne principally by the stations, which will aggregate funds and assign decision-making authority. The Program Services Endowment will act as a catalyst for new programming initiatives in radio, as well. Thus our discussion of the Endowment applies to both media.

The Economics of Television

The high cost of producing television programs is at the heart of the industry's structure, in both commercial and noncommercial systems. While television stations are licensed to provide local service, it would cost too much for each individual station to produce a full schedule of programs that could attract an audience. Thus, all television stations seek to share costs for at least some programs.

Commercial stations, with the goal of attracting the largest possible audiences for programs, usually try to affiliate with one of the three national networks because they supply programs with broad appeal. The networks pay for programs by selling advertising at rates based on the number of viewers watching and then pay affiliates to broadcast programs carrying these ads. Affiliates also sell spot ads within national programs. By refusing a network show, the affiliate forfeits revenues and must finance another program in its place. This virtually guarantees simultaneous network carriage for most programs.

Public television stations, on the other hand, were

created and built by grass-roots organizations, with different missions determined by circumstances in each community. Hence the "owners" of public stations are a diverse group, including universities, city and state governments, school districts, private nonprofit corporations, and a number of hybrid arrangements.[1]

Yet, like commercial stations, public stations have found it necessary to turn to a variety of national sources for their program offerings during a substantial part of the broadcast day. In the 1960s the Ford Foundation financed National Educational Television (NET) as a program supplier, a function later intended for the Corporation for Public Broadcasting with the advent of large-scale federal funding in the early 1970s.

As we have noted, the tension over local versus national control of program production and scheduling has been a consistent theme in public broadcasting. Few public television stations could manage to finance an entire weekly schedule with their own resources. Yet the local licensees insist upon the right to determine what they will run and when. They strongly resist scheduling that is outside their control.

With considerable struggle public broadcasting has evolved a unique principle for preserving local control. Instead of a national network with incentives for simultaneous scheduling by all affiliates, the public television system has the National Program Service, operated by PBS. This service balances local control of station schedules with the need for a national interconnection by offering national programs for optional use by local licensees. The programs themselves come from a variety of sources, many of them licensees striving for national recognition via major production efforts. Moreover, the stations have control over the financing and production of many of their programs. Public television stations have consistently resisted the creation of a publicly financed "fourth network." The arguments against such a network, analogous either

---

[1] In 1978 there were 280 public television stations licensed to 155 entities; 39 percent were community licensees, 34 percent university licensees, 15 percent licensed to the states, and 12 percent to local authority. Source: PBS Research.

to the BBC or to the commercial networks, are quite persuasive. Geographic and sociological diversity of the licensees provides a major bulwark against either a government-sponsored propaganda machine or a national ministry of culture. The danger of the latter grows in proportion to the development of centralized production, scheduling, and advertising. As a recent Senate Communications Subcommittee report put it:

> In such a "network" a central authority determines not only what programs will be produced for national distribution and what programs will be distributed nationally, but also when the programs will be broadcast in various communities around the country; then it promotes those programs in a coordinated fashion, so that a large, national audience may generate the substantial ratings that attract increasingly larger revenues from commercial sponsors.[2]

As we will detail later, the new multichannel satellite distribution system has already begun to affect scheduling options of public television stations. Because of greater program choice, cheaper distribution costs, and broadened access to the satellite system, stations are even less likely to form a classic national network. First, however, it is necessary to look at the way public television produces and delivers its programs today if we are to chart future improvements.

Today's Production System

All television stations assemble their own broadcast schedules through three mechanisms:

- production of programs by the station itself;
- acquiring or producing programs by pooling resources with other stations;
- acquiring programs developed and financed by one or another national entity, sponsor, or production center.

---

[2]U.S. Senate, Commerce Committee, Report 95–858, Public Telecommunications Financing Act of 1978, May 15, 1978, pp. 20–21.

Commercial television stations are either network affiliates, carrying network programs according to network schedules, or independents, scheduling mostly movies and series which are syndicated commercially for such use. In independent or network commercial television, the economic consequences of attracting the largest possible audiences at each hour of the day determine the charges for advertising time and hence the programming choices that are made. Actual program production is performed by a fairly small number of Hollywood companies dominated by the major film studios.[3]

Programming for public television is quite different. First, there is no national network or central programming entity with sufficient power to dominate local licensees as the commercial networks do. Costly programs distributed nationally are typically supported by dozens of separate entities in a bewildering process of cofinancing and joint decision making.[4]

Second, public television has developed a number of sophisticated methods by which individual stations join together to finance and decide about programs. Public television stations do purchase syndicated products, just as commercial stations do. But in the early 1960s, beginning with a regional consortium called the Eastern Educational Network (EEN), the public stations began to pool their funds in order to acquire and produce programs. The regional idea soon spread throughout the country, and was successful in establishing a number of station consortiums to generate instructional and educational programming.

But reasons other than economics forced the public television stations into collective program-financing arrangements. Until 1973 national programs were financed largely by modest federal funds under the con-

---

[3]Of the prime-time schedule for the fall 1978 broadcast season, 68 percent of all prime-time commercial television was produced by 11 production companies. Of this 68 percent, a major portion were produced by one company: MCA-Universal (*Broadcasting*, Sept. 4, 1978, p. 22).

[4]For the 1978–79 PBS national schedule, there were 39 separate corporations, government agencies, foundations, and station consortiums funding programs and services.

trol of CPB, supplemented by private sources. Following the 1973 Partnership Agreement, stations received a greater share of federal funds, and CPB's programming budget and discretion were reduced. If stations wanted to fill their schedules, they were forced to come up with a way of pooling funds to finance programs. PBS created the Station Program Cooperative (SPC), a mechanism which not only created a national programming budget for the stations, but decentralized the decision-making process. The SPC evolved as a program-by-program marketplace that insulates program decisions by giving power to several hundred station representatives, rather than a handful of centralized funders.[5]

A third feature distinguishing the public system is the production role of the local licensees. Commercial television stations may occasionally produce their own programming, but such production is usually limited to local news, talk shows, and documentaries. Even when program content is of more than local in-

---

[5]Through SPC, stations select the programs they will help finance. Each station's share of the cost of a program is calculated according to the size of its CPB grant, which is a reasonable measure of ability to pay since the grant is based on nonfederal income.

The SPC has several steps:

1. Program proposals are, in theory, generated by producers in response to an overall plan and statement of needs developed by PBS. All proposals are described in a catalog, then evaluated by a vote of all stations. PBS uses the station preferences and other considerations to select programs for the program catalog.

2. With the catalog known, PBS reviews program budgets, producers attempt to gain support for their programs, pilot programs are viewed, and the annual PBS program meeting is held to discuss new programs, buying strategies, programs available from other sources, etc.

3. PBS transforms its computerized teletype network linking all stations into a computerized market: for a series of "rounds" each station votes yes or no for each program, based on a price determined by the number of stations selecting the program in the previous round.

4. Programs are dropped from contention when no stations are willing to share their costs. Thus, after 10 or 12 rounds, the process concludes with purchase of the remaining programs by participating stations.

5. Programs are produced, sent to PBS, and then distributed. Stations may not use programs they do not purchase.

The selection process is governed by a strong "bandwagon

terest, such programs are rarely broadcast nationally.[6]

Because the public television system resisted creation of a central network to develop national programming ideas, stations emerged as producers themselves. Sixty percent of the programs broadcast by stations in 1976 were produced or packaged by the stations or related organizations.[7] In some cases, these programs originated as local efforts and "went national" when other stations expressed interest. Other programs were "offered to the system" by one station which then received underwriting support. Under this arrangement, producing stations have become highly competitive entrepreneurs, raising funds from a wide number of sources to finance production for the entire system.

---

effect." That is, as one station drops the program it becomes proportionately more expensive for others, who are more likely to drop it, and so on. Also, stations as a group tend to support the programs they know and like, leaving new offerings at a disadvantage. In order to stretch their resources as far as possible and achieve the cost advantages of nearly simultaneous, networklike usage, stations therefore tend to join the majority in selecting a program.

The stations have allocated between $12.5 million and $18 million through the SPC in each of its five years, including $24.1 million from the Ford Foundation and CPB in its first three years. Even though these funds represent about one-quarter of program funds, the SPC generally accounts for 40 percent of station broadcast hours.

[6]Exceptions include programs that go into syndication, and those produced by stations owned by group owners with outlets in several cities.

[7]This 60 percent figure breaks down as follows: 11.9 percent were produced locally by the stations themselves; 18.0 percent were produced for national distribution by four major, station-based production centers (WNET, New York; WGBH, Boston; KCET, Los Angeles; and WETA/NPACT, Washington, D.C.); 31.8 percent were produced by all other public television stations and related organizations. (These "related" organizations include SECA, a regional network of stations, and Family Communications, Inc., formerly associated with WQED, Pittsburgh, but now independent.)

Of the remaining 38 percent from nonstation sources: 14.8 percent came from Children's Television Workshop, producers of *Sesame Street* and *Electric Company;* 8.5 percent came from all other independent (i.e., nonstation or station-related) producers; 5.4 percent came from foreign productions or coproductions. The balance came from consortiums (3.4 percent), commercial U. S. (2.7 percent), and other sources (3.5 percent).

The Underlying Tension: Poverty

Underlying all these distinctive arrangements has been the relative poverty of the public television system. In 1977 each commercial network spent approximately $500 million on programming. In that year the cost of the PBS-distributed national schedule was $67.5 million.[8]

This scarcity has led to squabbles over funds and the authority to use funds for programs. The financial aspects of the partnership agreement, giving more money directly to the stations and depleting CPB's budget for its own programming activities, was written into legislation in 1975. CPB tended to follow a cautious policy in spending the resources it continued to control: an increasing share was devoted to less costly research, development, and piloting. CPB refused to provide series support beyond a second season, and it rarely financed a major series single-handedly, preferring instead to lever scarce funds by joining with one or more other funders.[9]

The station-controlled SPC system is equally cautious. While a multiplicity of decision makers clearly does provide political insulation, such decision making also tends toward the purchase of programs that are relatively inexpensive and that minimize risk and uncertainty. Hence, the SPC usually supports the "bread-and-butter" programs already proven successful and noncontroversial. These include such staples of public broadcasting as *Washington Week in Review, Wall Street Week, Sesame Street, Crockett's Victory Garden,* and *Evening at Symphony*.

---

[8]The value of the programs, however, was considerably greater. Public television produces far less original material than the networks, relying instead on lower-cost acquisitions, whose production cost is absorbed by the original sponsor or the producer.

[9]In fiscal year 1976 CPB supported the production of nine major series for national distribution past the pilot stage. Of these, seven were supported by other funders. In that same year, the television activities department of CPB spent $10.14 million, of which $4.5 million went directly for support of the Station Program Cooperative. CPB has phased out its support of the SPC, and has a projected budget for fiscal year 1978 of $18.5 million, of which $11.5 million is already committed.

The stations jealously guard their own resources, raised from local sources and matched with federal funds. They must apportion their budgets among local programs, station-operating costs, and national and regional program aggregations. Quite reasonably, they attempt to mold all programming decisions to follow their own priorities.

The station-financed national organization, PBS, possesses a small programming budget and limited discretion.[10] The only powers PBS can exercise are either delegated by the stations or derived from PBS's role as operator and scheduler of the interconnection. With foundation grants and funds provided by stations and CPB, PBS can sometimes "make a program happen," though it has been barred by stations and Congress from producing programs itself. PBS has been given discretion to facilitate a narrow purpose such as coverage of special events or support of station fundraising marathons.[11]

The final participant in public television programming is, of course, the underwriter. In a financially starved system, money speaks more authoritatively than principle. Few who testified before the Commission defended these financing mechanisms. Yet much of the best programming on the system has been made possible only through the support of corporations, foundations, and government agencies, singly and in combination. And while detailed guidelines have been established to assure that funders are not directly in-

---

[10]PBS's operating budget in 1978 was $22.4 million. About $14.5 million financed the operation of the interconnection; $3.6 million supported a program administration department and program information; another $1.2 million supported station services, including assistance for station fund-raising efforts. The balance, $3.1 million, financed general management and administration along with the costs of the board.

[11]A division of PBS, the Station Independence Program, aids stations in raising funds, especially from viewers in on-air appeals, but also from a variety of sources. Funds for programs to cover current events and other special opportunities that are timely and require immediate action are pooled at PBS through the Station Program Cooperative. This special events fund is used by PBS under the guidance of the vote of either a special committee or, if time permits, all the stations.

volved in decisions on program content, the fact that underwriters can choose the programs they wish to fund or not to fund considerably reduces the system's discretion.

Because the present public television system has such a relatively small amount of discretionary funds for the development and production of new programming, it is often easier, cheaper, and less risky to acquire programs produced by other broadcasters, particularly those in Great Britain. While the volume of British programs shown in the United States represents the cream of that country's commercial and noncommercial output, the effect on American viewers is the impression that public television prefers actors and commentators with British accents.

The problem is certainly one of public perception —such programs give rise to accusations of "elitism" and anglophilia. For the professionals involved in the domestic production industry the problem is more serious. The vast resources of the American creative community are presently underused. Except at the very pinnacle of the field, unemployment is rampant. When they do get work, writers, producers, and directors, as well as the other talent they hire, are forced by commercial television into predictable and often debased formula series. In public broadcasting, creative energies are sapped in a confusing and time-consuming search for financing.

Lessons from the Past

What conclusions can be drawn about programming in public television on the basis of the system we have described?

Foremost, perhaps, is the universal difficulty producers have had in developing programs for a system with so many different and sometimes conflicting decision makers.

It is even more difficult, as a result, for public television to produce and protect controversial or innovative programming, particularly in the public affairs and documentary areas. We have heard from producers inside and outside public television, on both sides of the Atlantic, about one absolutely vital prerequisite for creative programming: the freedom to take risks. Without risk taking, programming tends to become bland, unadventuresome, and timid.

Both the BBC and American commercial networks function effectively only because they have the money, the authority, and a fifty-year tradition permitting them to make quick, controversial program decisions. Their officials are answerable after the fact but possess the resources with which to translate their decisions into sight and sound.

We have seen in the American public television system a source of diversity and vitality at the local level which ought to be supported and strengthened— particularly since the individual stations are likely to be prime agents for experimentation in the delivery of new telecommunications services during the next decade. The diversity of these public licensees provides not only political protection and a secure base of financial support, but also a positive guarantee against the establishment of a national arbiter of taste or political perspective.

We believe that America's public system must strike a balance between the unique local service needs of each community or region, and programs of national interest designed to bring our society together. Such national programs are expensive, and must continue to be financed by a number of sources. We suggest, however, that the system must develop ways to concentrate its resources for efficient and effective national program production, both by aggregating station money and by establishing an entity whose sole purpose is the creation of innovative radio and television programming services of the highest quality.

Public television stations can be creative centers in every community—to welcome the artists and the actors, the producers, directors, and writers; to reach into the universities, museums, symphonies, ballets; to train talent and produce programs in every region, state, and community in America. A diverse nation demands diverse opportunities for its people. A new telecommunications environment represents an extraordinary challenge for every station and every region. Put funds into ideas and talent, and let flourish all across this great country the kinds of programming that will inspire the local community, educate the region, and inform the nation.

Program Costs for the Future

How much programming should be financed? What will it cost, and who will control the expenditure of funds? These critical questions are central to the design of our funding plan as set forth in Chapter IV. Funds are limited, both from public and private sources. However, unless public television can dramatically improve its ability to produce original American programs in a wide range of formats and subjects, it will not merit continued support. Thus top priority must be given to program funding during the next decade.

A typical public television station broadcasts about 85 hours weekly. More than 60 of these hours are provided to it by PBS,[12] although almost half of this—because of a shortage of new productions—is composed of reruns. The remaining 40 hours of non-PBS programming are either locally produced, or syndicated, or provided by other suppliers, i.e., regional networks and educational consortiums.

According to our estimates the average station will increase its broadcast hours to over 120 weekly. Thus the present public television system can absorb some 70 hours of new national programming weekly, so that reruns would no longer make up so much of the national programming carried by stations. This would cost about $360 million annually, including about $50 million for promotion. Another $230 million would measurably improve local and regional programming for the entire system.

As we see it, this money could be expended in two ways, governed by two sets of broad principles.

First, as set forth in Chapter III, our plan would

---

[12]Based on *Public Television by Category, 1976*, a survey by Katzman and Wirt. Of an annual total of 4542 broadcast hours per station, 69.3 percent were provided by PBS.

place approximately $190 million of federal funds for national programming in a highly insulated and specialized national Program Services Endowment, housed under the protective umbrella of the Public Telecommunications Trust. The Endowment would possess sufficient resources and sufficient independence from day-to-day station operations and the imperatives of a schedule to concentrate on the critical program needs of the nation as a whole. The fulfillment of such needs would be accomplished primarily by support directed to the most outstanding producers, journalists, educators, and artists. The Endowment must have the flexibility to support experiments and high-risk projects utilizing nonbroadcast as well as broadcast systems. The organization should be able to provide the public broadcasting system with the freedom to take risks which must exist in any serious creative enterprise.

A second method for developing national programming will be the station-based consortium model. Under the funding plan described in Chapter IV, public television stations by 1985 should generate some $380 million in federal funds, matching on a 2:3 basis an estimated $570 million in nonfederal funds. We believe that a first-rate public television system should require that approximately $325 million of those funds be aggregated for more-than-local programming. Almost $100 million more will strengthen local programming. (For a more detailed analysis of programming costs and expenditures, see Appendix D.)

Programming and Services at the New Endowment

While the consequences of any practical approach to effective federal funding show that stations will continue to have control of much of the money available for national programs, we believe there should be reserved an important role outside their direct authority. This is the Program Services Endowment, which we see to be an integral part of the overall programming development process. Neither the Endowment nor any other national mechanism can succeed for any extended period without station involvement in its governance and decision making, and station enthusiasm for its mission. Nevertheless, we believe that a healthy tension between the Endowment and the stations is useful. A system that is station-controlled in its totality would be a very limited one, just as a system which gave all money and power to a single central programmer would be a mistake. A station-based system needs to be challenged, to have the complacent views of its audience shaken occasionally by programs that it finds disturbing. Station-dominated production processes should be countered with new talent, new concepts, and innovations derived from segments of the creative community of which the stations may well be unaware. In a changing technological environment, the key to public broadcasting's future is creativity. New systems of delivery mean that broadcasting itself will become one of the many new pathways into homes, universities, schools, and hospitals. We view the Endowment as the centerpiece of interaction with the creative community in America for national programming.

The Endowment would seek to develop the best of such programming for use on public broadcasting, something which we believe it will accomplish by supplying support for the creative work of America's artists, journalists, producers, and educators. The Endowment should nurture ideas in public broadcasting that other entities reject as too risky, a process that requires room for occasional but not continuing failure. Hence, while stations may—and should—take creative risks each day, we understand that they must live with the requirement to fill thousands of hours of air time per year, as well as to respond to widely divergent interests in their own communities. The Endowment, responding primarily to the national goals of public broadcasting for creating programs and services that provide both delight and stimulation to a nation too often fragmented by the pressures of narrow constituencies, is more likely to attempt innovations in form and content.

The Endowment will serve to counter the perception of British domination of system programs by concentrating a substantial amount of funds in an institution whose single objective is the increase in creative production activity for the American public broadcasting system. It is less likely that the Endowment will spend its funds for foreign products than for American creative work for several reasons. First, other sources exist for the best of foreign programming—underwriters and stations themselves. More fundamentally, the Endowment is being established primarily as a stimulus to American creative talent, notably absent from the present system.

In fulfilling their mandate, the managers of the Endowment should have the authority to allocate funds to fulfill this broadly defined mission of public broadcasting. Funding activities will probably include support of pilots, research, production centers inside and outside the system for radio and television, individual program grants, national competitions, and subsidies for existing programs. At their own discretion, they should be able fully to fund programs, to fund jointly with other organizations, and to cooperate with station organizations in programming development projects.

The Endowment will fund programs designed primarily to enhance the national offerings of public television and radio broadcasting. Hence the station system should always have the right of first refusal. However, we can foresee, in a time of changing social and artistic concepts, that some Endowment-financed programs may be unattractive to the station-based system and hence may reach audiences via nonbroadcast technologies in circumstances where the stations exercise their right to refuse to carry the programming.

The nature of the creative enterprise is complex, and an institution established to foster program production and experimentation will necessarily explore a wide range of management processes in awarding grants and contracts.

We believe that three principles are critical for the success of the Endowment's work, no matter what procedures and mechanics are established for the funding and decision-making processes. First, the chief executive officer, once he or she is selected, should have a defined term of office and should be empowered to exercise final power of decision on all grants and contracts. Current system practices tend to militate against any identifiable party taking responsibility for decisions, with the result that decision making travels in endless bureaucratic ellipses. Production takes far too long, and decisions tend to be overly cautious. Programming derived from such decision making is more often than not tame and quiescent. Creativity is highly personal and individual, and so, too, are the processes by which judgments about creative work are made. We believe strongly that the best remedy for bad decisionmaking in creative areas is to dispense with the decision maker rather than to ensnare him in bureaucracy.

Granting ultimate authority to the Endowment's chief executive officer, however, does not mean that we suggest a programming czar for public broadcasting. A second principle that should characterize the Endowment's grant making is diversity. The chief executive officer will, practically speaking, rely upon a staff, as well as the advice and strength of the Endowment's governing board, comprised of individuals whose own expertise in various fields of creative and intellectual activity can add immeasurably to the Endowment's decision-making process. In addition, we expect that the Endowment will regularly rely upon the advice of panels of experts in the appropriate fields of production as it goes about its work of seeking the broadest group of applicants for grant programs. The clash of such diversely generated advice with the creative energies and prejudices of a skilled and decisive chief executive should provide an environment in which the statistics would favor successful programming. One of the chief advantages of the Endowment, established outside the actual station system, is the advancement of new talent, innovative or risky ideas, and pioneering program concepts. The Endowment will need all the assistance it can get in order to assure maximum participation in its program production procedures.

The final requirement in the Endowment's process is fairness. Virtually every producer testifying before us described a funding and development process that seemed arbitrary, confusing, and at least in many cases, manifestly unfair. The Endowment, in avoiding the

kind of programming by committee that has plagued
much of public television, cannot be perceived as ca-
pricious or secretive. Its processes must be open and
observable. Decisions should be explained. While every
act of creativity is, by its very nature, a subjective one,
we have no doubt that the chief executive of the Endowment will be called upon to justify his judgments.
The process should be seen as rational by producers
whose work is supported as well as by those who are
unsuccessful in securing funding for their ideas.

We have heard from individual writers, directors,
and independent producers, who almost unanimously
complained of an overly complicated structure, lack of
authority to make decisions, and bureaucratic rivalry
that stifled creativity and paralyzed the system.

In casting the recommendations in behalf of the
independence and authority of the chief executive officer of the Endowment, we were much influenced by
their testimony and by the advice of Sir Huw Wheldon,
who stated:

> If it is an original work you are after, you had
> better leave it to the individuals. . . . You help
> them, provide resources, stimulate them, possibly
> even inspire them, but fundamentally what you
> have to do is trust them. It is a simple enough
> proposition but, in practice, television officials
> simply cannot bring themselves to accept it. They
> may start with individuals but they get nervous.
> They set up committees . . .
>
> No real programme was ever made by a
> committee. You insure yourself against failure by
> having a committee, but you also insure yourself
> against triumph.[13]

We believe strongly that the Endowment and the
Trust must devote themselves to building a public
broadcasting enterprise that emphasizes programming,
not structure. We urge the Trust and Endowment to
work toward developing a public affairs tradition,
and an aspiration for excellence in drama and the arts.

---

[13]*The British Experience in Television* (London: British Broadcasting Corp., 1976), p. 12.

This can be achieved only if the funding and policy organizations, including the stations, set up procedures that respect the artists, writers, producers, and directors who make programs, and include as decision makers the outstanding members of the creative community itself.

We believe that many of those people are now in public broadcasting and that it will attract many more. For that reason we have carefully included station participation in the nominating process for the Trust and for service on the Endowment. Our reasons go directly to the lessons of the last ten years—that there is talent across the country that can be tapped for national leadership and that there is strength in the unity that will flow from such participation.

Our vision of the Endowment centers on program innovation—creating new ways to use the electronic media. These are long-range goals, determined by the Endowment in cooperation with the Trust, public broadcasters, program makers, and leadership figures in society. The design of the Endowment will develop logically around the accomplishment of various programming goals.

A number of such goals have been suggested to us. They provide illustrations of approaches that might be taken.

Drama. The Endowment may determine that during the next five years public broadcasting and the American production community should develop a pool of writers for dramatic programming comparable to that in the highly praised British system. A division of the Endowment might then plan a coordinated, multiyear grant program to support this goal, financing a radio writing workshop, a competition for television writers, university writing workshops at the graduate level, support at a number of levels for television drama production centers, cofinancing of independent films by new writer-directors, and so on.

Journalism. In entering the complex field of television and radio journalism, the Endowment might establish an "op-ed" page for television and radio, fund production units to identify and train commentators with special news skill or experience, help finance units

to produce minidocumentaries for the daily news efforts
of the system, or add to the diversity of documentary
voices by setting aside a portion of funds for new producers. Perhaps the best example of the long-term
commitment needed in innovative public affairs programming is the evolution of the so-called "magazine"
show for television. The first such program for national
television was the *Public Broadcasting Laboratory* in
1967. Shortly after the PBL experiment ended, *The
Great American Dream Machine* was created, mixing
light subjects and satire with investigatory work, using
talents of staff and independent producers. Both early
prototypes from public broadcasting were used in the
development of CBS's very successful *60 Minutes,* only
one of several network magazine attempts. It took four
seasons of refinement before that show met with audience approval, heralding a wave of imitators.

Minorities. If the delicate interaction of production team, on-air talent, audience appeal and content is
difficult in the general public affairs field, it is even more
so with special-interest programs aimed at minority audiences. Little research or promotion has gone into various television and radio programs for special audiences.
Such programs have largely failed to attract either their
intended audiences or a broader group of viewers.
There is no reason why the level of subtle analysis that
preceded *Sesame Street* could not be applied to planning
for black cultural programming or related types of special programs. This should not in any way be seen as
merely a political obligation to special interests, but
as a difficult and challenging goal aimed ultimately at
using America's diversity in order to promote inter-
group understanding. We believe that the system has
not even begun to address this national problem.

Independent Producers. In recent years the system
has heard complaints by independent producers about
lack of access and attention. We have heard them. The
goal of bringing new talent into the broadcast system
requires the creation of formats balanced between the
differing needs of producers and stations. The Endowment might finance a Center for Independent Television,
whose job would be to develop broadcast formats that

can take advantage of the range of talent among independent producers. This Center would develop contacts with the full range of independents, and provide a WATS telephone number for easy communication. The Center's mission would include the establishment of fair selection procedures, financing, support in understanding the system, rights negotiations, and a variety of related services for and communications with independent producers in both radio and television.

Children's Programming. The Endowment might support program production that can fill the gaps in children's programming that currently exist in the national radio and television schedule. While the system, particularly television, made much of its reputation on the basis of superb children's programming, there is very little production activity for children in the system now. The Endowment's programming staff would, along with its planning in other content areas, assess the need for serving the nation's youth with programs in drama, public affairs, science, the arts, and other fields. Children, as much as their parents, need programs that can entertain without condescending, and enlighten without preaching. In this vein, programs such as *The Ascent of Man, Civilisation, Nova, The Adams Chronicles,* and the *National Geographic Specials* provide children and adults with entertaining and exciting ways to learn outside the classroom context. Such programs could constitute a major area of investigation for the Endowment.

Naturally, these are only a few ideas. One principal mission of the Endowment is to innovate—to stimulate creators to create ways by which television and radio can be better used for communication and entertainment. Programming, however, is a very broad concept, and will require the Endowment to establish a number of additional divisions.

Television and Radio for Learning. In addition to production support and development of general programs for children and adults, the Endowment might pursue a major research support program in the use of radio and television for learning. As we detail in Chapter VIII, the Endowment will be positioned to make an extraordinary contribution to the current debate among programming experts and educators regarding the effect of the electronic media on actual learning and behavior patterns. Such research is needed if instructional programming, both for classroom and nonclassroom use, is to continue its improvement in effectiveness and quality beyond the use of talking heads. One of the reasons why *Sesame Street* and *The Electric Company* proved to be so expensive was the considerable amount of research used in the design, production, and alteration of the programs. As a result, the producers have documented changes in children's learning patterns from exposure to the programs. This approach involved a major creative advance in the use of television for children's education. Research of a similarly high caliber into learning can be a major contribution by the Endowment.

In addition to their research activities in developmental and classroom learning for children, the Endowment has an opportunity to take a similar role in the development of lifelong learning programs for adults. There is now much exciting activity in the system in the development of mechanisms for college instruction by radio and television. The kind of innovative research needed for children's learning is needed for adult learning too. Perhaps the best example of such an approach can be found in a series of programs, developed after an enormous amount of research and testing at the BBC, whose purpose was to teach illiterate adults to read. Designed with the twin objectives of teaching the illiterate and of removing the feelings of shame connected with the fact of illiteracy, the program has helped thousands of people overcome a serious handicap.

Technological Applications to Programming. As we shall discuss in Chapter VII, the Endowment will have a programming mission extending beyond the development of broadcast radio and television shows. It might sponsor a variety of experiments on developing technologies potentially applicable to public telecommunications. A division of the Endowment will support program-oriented innovation in broadcast and nonbroadcast distribution technologies to broaden the ability of licensees and others to become full service telecommunications entities within their communities. In addition, the Endowment might support the efforts of the system to pioneer in new technical applications: public broadcasting has already led the way in satellite interconnection, captioning for the hearing-impaired, and subcarrier radio. Such experimentation could be extended to other fields, for example, the refinement of educational uses of two-way cable or the broader uses of the satellite distribution network by additional public-service users.

While the Endowment would exercise discretion in all such matters, we might suggest the establishment of two types of telecommunications-funding procedures, both distinguished from the pure "hardware" orientation of the expanded facilities program discussed in Chapter VII. The first would be demonstration projects (perhaps at a level of $1 million) designed to launch new, experimental applications of telecommunications services which might subsequently be supported by the Trust's ongoing funding procedure. Under this plan, continuation of established and demonstrated projects could be supported. In this fashion, new and tested telecommunications concepts could be financed by the national creative arm of public broadcasting.

Radio. Finally, the Endowment will have a division devoted to the creative capacities of radio programming. (We shall discuss radio production support in more detail in Chapter VI.) While certain program activities of the Endowment may well include both radio and television components, radio will demand special attention because of its unique capabilities. This applies as well to the organized production capacity of public radio, which not only shares with television the underuse of independent producers, but has relatively few station production centers with major responsibility to feed the national system.

Endowment support of national programming for the public radio system will be critical during the first years of its existence, under the provisions of our funding proposal. Currently the National Public Radio programming budget is supported almost exclusively by the Corporation for Public Broadcasting. Our plan would ultimately transfer the principal responsibility to the licensees themselves, who, with considerably greater support grants from the Public Telecommunications Trust, will be able to establish more centers for radio production and to continue NPR at its present or greater funding levels, at their discretion. However, during the transition period it is unlikely that the radio licensees will be able to support all NPR's programming activities, as well as supporting new program sources, without some outside support—which presumably could come from the Endowment's radio division.

The goal of the Endowment is to compensate in part for the less flexible view that a collection of diverse stations might be expected to adopt toward national programming. However, we believe that it would be unwise to retain a majority of program funds at the Endowment, thereby eliminating any meaningful station role in national programming. This would not only jeopardize the Endowment's independence, but would undoubtedly lead stations to regard the latter's resources as rightly belonging to the stations themselves, instead of as a balance to the stations' own programming efforts.

We wish to emphasize the integrity of the Endowment's programming money. It does not "belong" to the stations and the money is not spent for the benefit of the stations, but for the benefit of the entire national audience. The clear separation of the Endowment from the day-to-day workings of the stations as well as from its parent organization, the National Telecommunications Trust, is vital to our plan. Such independence will not guarantee an end to the fractious disputes over resources and program authority that we have witnessed in public broadcasting in the 1970's, but there is a substantially greater opportunity for harmony and real achievement in these arrangements than in any others we have been able to imagine.

Station-Controlled Programming

Funds which the stations raise from federal and nonfederal sources must cover the operations of stations as well as a number of national activities performed by station-run organizations such as the Public Broadcasting Service and the regional networks. As we have indicated, one of the most important uses for station funds is the collective financing of national and regional programming, fulfilling criteria set down by the stations themselves.

We believe that the distribution of a substantial portion of federal funds to the stations via a matching formula provides an extremely effective way to insulate the system from centralized political control. Formula matching also offers a nonsubjective method by which federal money can support programming activities in direct proportion to local appreciation of that service.

But the stations must develop a rational plan for the aggregation and allocation of their television programming funds, as well as dramatically improved techniques for generating exciting programs. Such a plan will require significant and difficult adjustments on the part of the licensees, which have experienced problems in resolving differences among themselves.

To achieve this larger programming goal, the stations should receive substantially larger sums of federal money than are now available. With increased funding goes correspondingly greater responsibilities. These responsibilities fall into two somewhat overlapping categories, accountability and programming.

Accountability. The issue of accountability, which is discussed in greater detail in Chapter IX, has become a major concern for all institutions receiving public funding, and public broadcasting is no exception. Taxpayers and their elected officials have the right and obligation to know how public funds are spent; yet with a delicate First Amendment operation such as public broadcasting, the audit mechanisms by which the government gains such assurances can very easily intrude into the editorial or artistic content of the programs.

It is unrealistic for public broadcasting to expect special exemptions from expanding accountability requirements that now go hand in hand with public funds. The system must accept the requirement of continuous and perhaps irritating scrutiny of its budget decisions.

But the government must also underwrite the public broadcasting system's freedom to make the critical judgments that are central to the integrity of its enterprise. Occasional errors of judgment are a necessary corollary to this freedom.

Efforts will be made to force the system to abandon certain programs, and this must be resisted. Our proposal recognizes the possibility of such efforts by establishing the Public Telecommunications Trust as the protector of programming funds—both those of the stations and the Endowment.

No statute, no form of dedicated funding, no abstract principles can guarantee the freedom and independence of public broadcasting. It must be earned daily through the integrity of the system's programming decisions, and by the willingness of the system's leaders to put their jobs on the line if necessary in order to defend that integrity. This is the only way in which to build a secure tradition which will deter attacks from those who would demand conformity in exchange for federal dollars.

However, we are not suggesting that the system should be prepared to wage war with accountants and auditors in order to prove that it is really free. Struggle becomes counterproductive when it leads to symbolic rather than real arguments, while funding is held hostage. The fights must be reserved for those issues which focus on the central reason for the public broadcasting enterprise in the first place: editorial freedom and artistic expression.

We believe that this broadcasting system must act in concert to have a stronger voice than it has had in the past. Some within the industry are far too willing to stay out of controversy and avoid difficult programming decisions in an effort to guarantee the flow of federal funds at all costs. What is sacrificed in easy accommodations to loss of editorial or artistic freedom is only integrity; but perhaps nothing else is really valuable. Most people in public broadcasting instinctively recognize the mockery such sacrifice would make of the system's cherished mission.

Programming. We strongly believe that the establishment of a Public Telecommunications Trust will considerably enhance the ability of public broadcasting to engage in courageous public affairs and other adventuresome programming from which it has shied away too often in the past. The Trustees should be selected to defend the Endowment and the stations in making difficult programming decisions unfazed by fear of retribution. And while the stations must themselves develop a tradition of freedom, they should be strengthened by the knowledge that the Trustees are prepared to fend off inappropriate intrusions.

Of course, the defense of a tradition of independence and integrity can be carried out successfully only when the system generates programming that merits defense—programs of substance. We believe that the stations and the Corporation for Public Broadcasting have given far too little attention to the creation of new programming. In an effort to encourage stations to aggregate a significant fraction of the funds they receive from the federal government on programs of a local, regional, and national interest, we believe that the Trust and the Endowment should emphasize programming as the television system's top priority.

In public television especially, the major justification for increased public support is improved program service. Stations do not exist simply to continue to exist and prosper. Increased funds should end the struggle for bare survival. Thus, with the vastly enhanced responsibility of building a full-service program schedule that goes with an increase in federal funding, we believe that federal funds distributed in the past as "Community Service Grants" should be viewed as "Program Service Grants." Stations will retain total discretion over their use, but will be expected to spend as much of their funds as possible on program-related matters.

The techniques used by the television licensees to pool their resources and make decisions about what programs they decide to produce will continue to be diverse, and most appropriately should remain under exclusive discretion of the stations themselves and the organizations they designate as their agents.

Aggregation might well include procedures similar to the Station Program Cooperative, the Station Independence Program, the special events fund, regional and educational consortiums, new and established production centers for specific tasks, special minority efforts such as the Latino and the Native American consortiums, national operation of an acquisition fund, and the delegation of authority for piloting and program development to PBS and other entities.

Each of these ideas is suited to a particular objective and should be designed to play a role in a coordinated long-range plan for station-based decision making. Such a plan requires a renewed dedication on the part of stations to overcome the inherent problems of operating a creative enterprise democratically among a diverse group of licensees. In that regard, having listened to many station governors and operators, as well as their critics and supporters, we offer a few observations about how television licensees can improve the programming process as they begin to have greater responsibility and funding:

A Broadened View. In the past the stations have often acted out of self-interest, with insufficient concern for the broader needs of the system and its audience. Both at the local governance level and in the governance of their regional and national organizations, stations would be well advised to expand their horizons to embrace broader segments of the community and the nation. This expansion should not be merely cosmetic, but a genuine strengthening of the stations' commitment to the public. A number of measures to broaden governance are discussed in Chapter IX. Some stations are presently governed by absentee boards, particularly universities or other institutions headed by officials who may never set foot inside the television or radio station. They would do well to restructure their relationship to such boards so that local community representatives can be involved more directly in helping the station.

Taking Responsibility. An important corollary to a broader perspective is the assumption of power and greater responsibility for the future of the system. Because of lack of funds and occasional internal jealousies, stations have often acted to block rather than to initiate. Stations are, as we have underlined, the real strength of public broadcasting, and as such must regain the support of their natural allies in the nation by generating exciting programming, by communicating more openly, and by leading rather than reacting.

Improving Systems for National Production and Distribution. The goal of all system processes is programming. Our funding recommendation makes a clear separation between funds belonging to the stations, by virtue of their matching formula, and funds under the discretion of the new Endowment. This dichotomy is intended to mute some stations' tendency to expect other organizations to create programming "for" them. Enough money must be given to the stations to create and deliver programs which, in their judgment, meet the needs of significant portions of the American population. Effective program development cannot exist if every station insists on a voice in every decision. Some delegation of powers must be given to station-governed bodies that have the full confidence and financial support of stations.

Hence, the stations may well decide that a single station or other production agency should be designated to organize an activity such as drama production, performance programming, or news. They may well feel that PBS or any other organization should be given responsibility to receive program proposals and to fund pilots and acquisitions. These are, we repeat, appropriate decisions for the stations to make, provided no station is coerced, network-style, into carrying a program against its will.

As we have noted earlier, the new satellite distribution system will change a number of factors in the relation between stations and the various entities they control. First, when the satellite system is fully operational in 1980, each public television station will have access to any two of four available programming feeds simultaneously. Any station wishing to do so may, of course, set up additional receiving antennas to receive more simultaneous signals. Additional satellite channels are also available for rental if a sufficient number of stations have need for further program choice. This choice allows the system to provide live congressional hearing coverage to some stations and in-school instruction to others. It permits stations to tape one program while carrying another live.

Because the satellite has the capacity to distribute programs relatively inexpensively, it will be possible for programs to be offered nationwide, even if fewer than a majority of stations want a program. Thus, consortiums of stations will join together to form ad hoc networks for specialized programming needs.

The satellite also means that the imposition of an actual network-type operation is almost impossible. PBS will continue to operate the satellite system, but access to part of the capacity will be governed by a semiautonomous group of station representatives who parcel out time to other programmers, including independent producers and the regional networks. The National Program Service, and perhaps a number of subsidiary programming services, will be assembled by PBS for the stations who wish to use them. But no one should attempt to compel a local licensee to carry a program at a precise time if it perceives a community responsibility differently. By advocating the continuation of national program services instead of a network, we assure that programs that might be controversial can still be produced and offered to those stations wishing to carry them.

The Role of Local Program Services

Throughout our investigation we have seen evidence of the extraordinary range of local programming services offered by public television licensees. They range from excellent nightly and weekly public affairs series, many inspired by the *Newsroom* program, to consumer and viewer action programs, local arts showcases, live event and legislative coverage, investigative documentaries, and performances of all genres. Many of these programs subsequently become nationally or regionally distributed, and are financed jointly by station consortiums.

Just as the national public television system has

rendered extraordinary public service to its viewers by carrying important Congressional hearings and major national events, many stations regularly provide live and taped coverage and commentary about local and regional occurrences. In times of crisis—school closings, assassinations, disasters, newspaper strikes— public television stations have moved in to fill the void by providing information services in a way that commercial stations rarely can, given commitments to advertisers.

We have discovered a growing number of public stations no longer confined to the provision of services by broadcast. They seem to be evolving into telecommunications centers that make use of cable, Instructional Television Fixed Service, radio and television broadcasting, and multiple satellite links. Several prototypes are examined in Chapter VII.

Unfortunately, many stations continue to operate on very low budgets, limiting their own programming efforts, which sets up a vicious cycle. Because simpler local shows may not attract the audience or stimulate viewer donations as would glossier national programs, stations cannot budget sufficient funds to improve local programming efforts.

Of course, many stations have managed quite well, even though underfunded, to create innovative and popular local program formats. Increasingly, stations are turning to independent video producers and filmmakers who can devote time and single-minded energy to a project in a way that overburdened staff producers rarely can, particularly at smaller stations.

Both station and independent producers are benefiting from the refinement of video production and editing tools that have revolutionized the television industry in the past five years.[14] Costs are coming down

---

[14]New video formats have, however, created some controversy at the FCC, because the signal they generate sometimes falls below standards established before their widespread use. While technical quality of American television should clearly not fall below reasonable standards, we do not think the FCC should automatically preclude certain technical advances, and the programming improvements they can bring, without certainty that its existing standards are not too rigid.

as quality improves, so that producers now have in their reach the ability to deliver network-quality programs at more reasonable budgets.

By establishing local and regional production and postproduction centers, stations can attract independent talent and production grants, and provide station personnel the opportunity for greater creative interaction, as well as wider distribution for programs. We believe that such communities of program makers are a natural outgrowth of the public television system that will be enhanced by future technical developments.

Future Station Budgets. These and other local programming initiatives will be possible in the future only if a substantial increase in discretionary funds can go to each station in the system. Our proposal is designed to raise the average station budget to about $4 million per year by 1985, an increase of $2.3 million from 1977, when the typical station budget was $1.7 million. Forty percent of the average budget would be from federal funds, and 60 percent from nonfederal sources.

Station financing for national programs and promotion will represent about $1.1 million of the typical budget. Not all of this is an increase, however, since a typical station now spends perhaps $200,000 on programs via the Station Program Cooperative and other sources and since this figure represents some assumption by the stations of spending previously done on their behalf by funders such as corporations and foundations.

Stations will also bear the costs of their national interconnection, about $100,000 per station, as well as the station membership organizations representing stations and performing services for them, which we also estimate at about $100,000.

After these national programming and operating expenditures and improvements in operating efficiency, we estimate the growth in funds for new and expanded local activities to be typically between $1.3 million and $1.5 million. This is an increase of about a third over the current budget level for local activities, an increase which we believe to be essential to improve interaction of stations with their communities and to develop programs locally, regionally, or with small groups of stations, or even to acquire programs elsewhere as necessary to meet important local needs. Expanded fund-raising activities, new efforts to use television for learning, improved efforts to understand and respond to the communities' needs for programming, and other new functions will be required by stations. While these efforts will in some cases be major ones, we believe that they will require no more than half of the increase, leaving about $600,000 to $800,000 for developing less-than-national programming and promotion.

Here the stations should have total discretion. A station can determine most effectively whether these funds should be used only for local programming or for local promotion of national programs and other station activities. This additional money, along with the current budget of $1.7 million, leaves the typical station with about $3 million annually to perform the complete range of local functions of a public broadcaster.

Local needs and skills are so diverse that it would be folly for us to outline the use of this money as we have attempted to do for national programming, except to emphasize and reemphasize, as we have, the need for efficient operations. Additionally, as more stations become involved in the nonbroadcast telecommunications field, they will bring in new sources of financial support, with specialized state, federal, and local grants applicable to the federal match—powerful leverage for the development of nonbroadcast experiments and an incentive both for public stations and cooperating local institutions.

Professional Tools: Promotion and Audience Measurement

Additional money flowing into the stations and the overall system will permit public broadcasters to take advantage of a number of other professional tools to achieve maximum service to the American public. Foremost among these tools are program promotion and audience measurement. These two activities have been shunned by many public broadcasters over the years because they occupy such a preeminent role in the operations of commercial stations. Slavish use of ratings at the expense of program quality and diversity, and lavish advertising by the networks and local commercial outlets, have distorted the important role which both ought to play in the broadcast enterprise.

Ratings are an obvious way to discover who is watching or listening. As we detail in Chapter IX, public broadcasters must refine their use of measurement tools to determine a much more precise profile of audiences if they are to improve their selection of programs that meet public needs.

Promotion and advertising are prerequisites for audience awareness and the limited public awareness of the programs available on public stations is one of the main reasons for the relatively tiny size of their audiences. Commercial stations have not only more money to spend for advertising, but access to their own highly viewed broadcast time, worth millions per year, in which to tout their schedules.

Public broadcasting first saw the extensive use of program promotion for national programs financed by corporate underwriters. In what has become a benchmark for the industry, Gulf Oil Company spent $900,000 to promote the *National Geographic Special* called *The Incredible Machine,* compared to $350,000 in production costs. The program attracted the largest number of viewers in public television's history.

While public broadcasters have been grateful for such underwritten promotion, it is inadequate and erratic. Corporate backers frequently pay for advertising which produces good "image" results for themselves, and only secondarily urge viewers or listeners to tune in to the local station. More often than not, national sponsors focus their efforts on national magazines and major market newspapers, overlooking hundreds of smaller markets.

Public broadcasting has begun to develop an overall national promotion and awareness campaign in recent years. We applaud these efforts, and encourage the public and Congress to recognize that without the ability to reach its potential audience, public broadcasting will never achieve its mission of service to the broadest number of citizens.

This will be particularly true as we witness the actual unfolding of the new, more copious information environment of the 1980s. Radio has already felt the impact of a multiplicity of channels. Listeners are urged in promotion and advertising to select a particular station for its "format" or "sound," not for its individual programs. As television choices expand, public broadcasters must be sure that their audiences understand where to find the alternative services which will have been developed with so much creative energy.

Incentives to Create

Throughout this chapter, and this entire report, we have returned to a central message: public broadcasting is a national treasure, unlike any other. While it seems unwieldy and frustrating to those inside, the rewards are substantial: a sense of dedication and service, the opportunity to communicate and motivate, the rare coincidence of purpose and craft. In short, the thousands of people who bring programs into America's homes are, in one way or another, collaborators in creativity.

In order that this collaboration may occur, a complex institution has been constructed, one which does not always cultivate the creative over the bureaucratic. Financial worries upstage creative urges, even among the best of institutions.

We have attempted to sort out the forces that encourage creative effort from those that frustrate it. In public television, the most pressing need is a rededication by the people involved in all aspects of the system —producers, talent, technicians, fund raisers, managers, board members, volunteers, promoters, supporters, contributors—to make programs happen. Unlike public radio, to which we now turn, public television has a nearly completed infrastructure for communications. What the television system has tried and failed to invent is a truly radical idea: an instrument of the mass media that simultaneously respects the individuals responsible for creativity, their audiences, and the forces of control.

We know that our recommendations aim high: cooperation, efficiency, creativity, balance—all idealistic impulses that nobody will oppose. We also know that the impulse to create is ready to flourish within each of us, given inspiration and a reasonable chance to succeed.

VI

Public Radio

Like the educational television system evaluated by our predecessor Commission in 1967, public radio today is hard pressed to reach its full potential. There are too few stations to reach a large portion of America. Most existing stations are underfinanced. They pay wages too meager to attract and retain top talent and management. Facilities are not always adequate. Without sufficient funds to go around, the industry has fought over policies for allocation of federal funds.

Despite its difficulties, the eight-year-old public radio system has achieved remarkable results, and has even greater potential to revitalize the entire radio medium. We have been convinced that public radio's past successes, as well as the future benefits of a more fully developed radio medium, make this system an important national resource that deserves expansion and strengthening.

This chapter will explore the radio system and the potential that we believe it holds for informing, educating, entertaining, and interacting with a nation of listeners. Many of the fundamental principles discussed throughout our report apply equally to radio and television, such as a commitment to full service programming, wider availability of signals, diversity in programming and station ownership, accountability and responsibility to the public, devotion to creative excellence and editorial integrity, insulated funding, and adaptability toward developing technologies.

These goals, however, cannot be achieved in the same way by radio and television. The two public systems are intrinsically quite different media, exhibiting distinct institutional arrangements and varying levels of development.

A History of Public Radio

The early history of public radio is, in fact, the early history of much of radio itself. One of the very first broadcast stations in the United States—call letters 9XM—was built in a University of Wisconsin physics laboratory. Renamed WHA-AM, it remains a major station in the public radio system.

With the expansion of commercial advertising on radio in the 1920s, educational radio experienced a precipitous decline. The airwaves became crowded with new commercial stations, and haphazard licensing often relegated educational stations to undesirable frequencies. Some educational stations were bought by commercial interests; others simply went off the air for lack of funds.

The Communications Act of 1934 firmly established the basis for licensing and regulation of broadcasting in this country and effectively closed the door to further educational development of radio on the AM band. The Act, which incorporated basic elements of the earlier Radio Act of 1927, established orderly procedures for licensing of station assignments. However, Congress refused to reserve any of these channels for noncommercial, educational use. Without specially reserved channels (during the economic depression), educational institutions could not marshal the resources to compete with commercial radio entrepreneurs, who quickly secured most available frequencies. As a result, over the next two decades, noncommercial radio maintained only the most precarious existence, and was nearly inaudible to the American consciousness. Even today, only a handful of public stations can be found on the AM band.

In 1939 the government opened the development of the frequency modulation radio band—FM radio. The action had little practical importance at that time, since few home sets capable of receiving FM programs were being manufactured. When, in 1945, the FCC moved the entire FM band to another portion of the spectrum, FM began again at ground zero. The FCC also reserved 20 of the 100 FM channels for noncommercial, educational purposes. To this day, the 88.1 megahertz (MHz) to 91.9 MHz frequencies on the FM dial remain noncommercial throughout the country.[1] This reservation marked a turning point for public radio, even though it would take nearly 20 years for either commercial or noncommercial FM radio to develop into a major industry. The scarcity of receivers and the poor quality of most stations tended to reinforce this slow rate of growth.

In 1948 the FCC authorized class D, 10-watt stations in the noncommercial FM band as a way of encouraging educational institutions to enter FM broadcasting and, perhaps, to expand their commitment once they took the first step. The 10-watt power classification was significantly lower than the previous FCC standard of 100 watts. Even though these small stations could only serve a radius of two to three miles in normal terrain, many colleges and universities invested minimal capital and entered FM broadcasting.

Commercial and noncommercial FM radio developed slowly. Because demand for channels was relatively light, the FCC altered a policy that allocated specific FM frequencies for specific communities. Instead, starting in 1958, the FCC permitted a qualified applicant to build an FM station on any frequency that would not interfere with existing stations, hoping thereby to stimulate further growth.

In the noncommercial FM band, the frequencies were developed almost exclusively by educational institutions. Moreover, in 1960 the FCC formally con-

---

[1]The FCC added an additional channel at 87.9 for noncommercial use in June 1978. Technical restrictions limited its use in most parts of the country.

firmed its policy of allowing other nonprofit groups to
apply for reserved frequencies.[2] This move paved the
way for a new kind of community licensee, typified by
the Pacifica listener-sponsored stations group, which
focused on the provision of radio services to its community.

But, by the early 1960s, the commercial portion
of the FM band had begun to fill up and operators
were asking for more efficient allocation policies. In
1962 the FCC complied, providing a table of allocations for commercial FM stations throughout the
country.[3] They declined to do the same for the 20
reserved noncommercial FM channels, a circumstance
which the FCC has yet to remedy. Part of the reason
for this inaction during the 1960s was that the FCC
saw no way to determine where educational stations
should be placed so that all Americans would receive
FM service. Prior to the adoption of the goal of full
service public broadcasting in 1967, most educational
radio stations offered services that catered to rather
narrow interests. Licenses, it was assumed, would be
held by universities or special-interest community
groups, whose location was not clearly related to the
size of their potential audience or full national coverage.

The FCC's random policy toward the allocation
and award of noncommercial FM stations became increasingly unmanageable in the mid-'60s as demand for
frequencies increased. Conditions became extremely
chaotic following the passage of the Public Broadcasting Act of 1967, which called for the establishment of
a national system of public radio stations to serve the
entire country.

Into this thicket stepped the newly formed Corporation for Public Broadcasting, which in 1969 fi-

---

[2]*Amendment of Sec. 3.503(a)(2) (S. Nisenbaum)*, 19 RR 1175
(1960).

[3]A table of allocations assigns to different communities stations
of predetermined number, power, and frequency. If properly developed, a table ensures that all major communities will have the
opportunity to be served by one or more stations, and that optimal
utilization of the spectrum is achieved.

nanced, with the Ford Foundation, a study of the public radio system.[4] The report described a weak and unimpressive noncommercial radio system. Most stations operated on less than $10,000 per year with signals of only 10 watts of power. Most stations, in fact, were off the air most of the time. Almost all were serving some institutional function, such as student training or in-class instruction, rather than providing general programming for the public.

As a result of the study, with 400 noncommercial stations on the air, CPB established policies in 1970 to ensure that its limited funds would be disbursed with maximum effect. Rather than disperse funds equally among 400 weak stations, the board established grant criteria designed to create a core of well-financed, professional stations upon which a national system could be built.

Grants from CPB were to be used as an incentive for local financial development. Stations would be required to meet minimum criteria on their own before they could win CPB funds. Criteria would become progressively stricter. This policy for public radio assistance was designed to encourage stations seeking CPB aid to:

- be dedicated to general educational or cultural service, rather than strictly institutional service or religious programming;
- broadcast a full, regular schedule;
- maintain a core professional staff, a minimum budget, and adequate facilities for local production;
- operate at sufficient power to reach a broad community audience.

The second major step CPB took in 1970 was the establishment of National Public Radio (NPR) in

---

[4]This study, entitled *The Public Radio Study,* was published in April 1969. An earlier report published by National Educational Radio was called *The Hidden Medium: Educational Radio.* The report described the success and potential of noncommercial radio and helped persuade Congress to include radio in the 1967 legislation.

order to distribute programs to public radio stations, much as the Public Broadcasting Service would for television. In addition NPR was to be a production entity, since the weak public radio system had not developed sufficient capacity to generate its own original program material.

The Current System

The present public radio system has grown dramatically since its organization in 1970. National Public Radio, with a budget of $8 million,[5] produces and distributes approximately 40 hours of programming, primarily news and public affairs, per week.

NPR was reorganized in 1977 to combine its program production and distribution responsibilities with membership service and representation functions.[6] NPR standards for full membership are identical with the CPB criteria for receiving federal funds. Thus NPR membership (217 stations in 1978, 24 AM and 193 FM) includes all but a handful of CPB-qualified stations plus 19 "associated stations," which are principally outlets only capable of repeating the signals of full-power NPR stations.[7]

In addition to these stations, which are called public radio stations, another 800-odd[8] noncommercial FM stations are licensed by the FCC. Many of these stations have been built since 1970. Some 500 of these are 10-watt stations. The remaining 300 stations vary

---

[5]NPR's total 1978 budget totaled $8.1 million, $5.6 million of which was spent on programming (including $1.8 million for "engineering," principally for the interconnection); $0.3 million was spent on representation functions, and $2.2 million for administration.

[6]NPR merged with the Association of Public Radio Stations, which was formed in 1973.

[7]Precise counts for the number of NPR members, CPB-qualified stations, and total noncommercial radio stations on the air vary slightly because of differing tabulation practices of the responsible organizations.

[8]The FCC counted, as of Sept. 30, 1978, a total of 973 educational FM stations on the air (938 licensed, 35 operating under construction permits). About 200 of these are public stations, leaving approximately 775. In addition, the FCC lists 80 educational FM stations authorized, but not yet on the air.

widely in power, from 100 to 100,000 watts. Service and operations vary widely, too, from part-time, amateur efforts to round-the-clock professional work. The majority of the 800 nonqualified stations, however, have low budgets and operate primarily for student training, activities akin to student newspapers and in-class instruction.

An important distinction exists between "public" radio and "noncommercial" radio. Throughout this report, we call those stations that have qualified for CPB operating support the public radio stations. These, along with NPR and other producers, constitute today's public radio system. Noncommercial radio is a more inclusive term, which applies both to CPB-qualified public radio stations and all other noncommercial stations licensed by the FCC. Included among noncommercial radio stations and largely outside the CPB-NPR-defined public system is a small group of community licensees, 50 of which are members of another membership organization, the National Federation of Community Broadcasters, founded in 1975. Most of these stations, modeled after the listener-sponsored Pacifica station group, feature local programming, public affairs, and diverse cultural fare.

Total income of the public radio system (CPB-qualified stations plus NPR) reached $65.5 million in fiscal year 1977. Almost 33 percent of that income came from the federal government ($21.5 million), while the remainder came from a variety of nonfederal sources, the single largest being state colleges at 28.3 percent ($18.6 million). In 1977 the average station raised nearly $188,000 from nonfederal sources and received a Community Service Grant (CSG)[9] from CPB amounting to over $37,000, for a total budget of about $225,000.

The largest station in the system has a budget of approximately $1.2 million, with $150,000 coming from its CSG. The smallest station budget is about $100,000, of which approximately $25,000 is derived from its CSG.

---

[9]See p. 124 for discussion of Community Service Grants.

A number of the system's gravest problems stem from its poverty. While all of public broadcasting is underfunded, public radio is disproportionately needy. As a result, salaries are relatively low, programming is limited, and the ability to serve listeners, who might in turn provide additional support, is hindered. Public radio generates only 13 percent of the total public broadcasting nonfederal income today. In 1977 the average professional station manager in public radio earned $18,000,[10] about $10,000 less than his counterpart in public television. An average public radio producer earned $10,500 in 1977.[11]

The system's underfunding has also affected the physical plant and, as a result, the availability of public radio programming throughout the country. As a legacy of the FCC's inadequate allocation policy for the noncommercial FM band, there are not enough stations, especially in major metropolitan areas. Although precise estimates are not available, CPB and NPR have estimated total public radio coverage at about 50 percent of the United States. Thirty-four of the top 100 metropolitan areas[12] are not served by a local public station. Few are served by more than one.

A final consequence of the system's poverty is the lack of variety among public radio stations. About 40 percent of the public stations program mostly classical music, while most of the others include classical music programming with their other cultural offerings. The majority of CPB-qualified stations, 127 in all, or 64 percent, are licensed to institutions of higher education. The remainder are operated by community groups (41, or 21 percent) and state or local authorities (30, or 15 percent). In contrast to television stations, only 27 percent of which are licensed to educational institutions, radio grew up as an adjunct of the educational system. This reflects the institutional dominance of educational radio's early development, which

---

[10]For comparison to commercial salaries, see Appendix C.
[11]Data from CPB Management Information Systems.
[12]Standard Metropolitan Statistical Areas.

has been perpetuated in CPB's efforts to upgrade existing stations.

The effect of this history is a public radio system that does not reflect the pluralism that is such a highly valued characteristic of American society. Our communications policies, in particular, have emphasized diversity of ownership and programming as a means of assuring broader participation in the life of the nation. Diversity is not completely served by classical music or university licensees alone, no matter how laudable either may be. Without sufficient funds to expand the number of stations, greater diversity has heretofore been an unachievable objective.

Public Radio's Potential

When we began this inquiry, some of us asked: Why radio? Is there a good reason why a potentially obsolete technology should receive federal support? What can radio do that is unique, even critical, meriting our enthusiasm and advocacy? Why should there be an expanded *public* radio system when there are so many commercial stations around? Has the record of the system since it was established eight years ago warranted further investment and promotion?

We have been convinced by our examination that not only is public radio alive and well, but radio is a vital medium that has only begun to flourish during its second life, which began following the introduction of television in the 1950s. Public radio, during its short period of federal support, has achieved remarkable growth, impressive program quality, and has provided us with a glimpse of what is missing from the plethora of commercial radio signals. Commercial radio's failure to provide programming services for a diverse American public, coupled with the potential of public radio to perform that task, has convinced us that the society needs a much improved audio component to its public telecommunications system.

With six radio receivers per household in operation in America today, radio is ubiquitous. In homes, cars, and the workplace, on bicycles, beaches, and boats, the average American uses radio for some three hours per day. Despite the transformation that television has wrought upon the role of radio in American life, the medium remains a vital information and entertainment link for most of us.

Moreover, radio continues to be preeminently a medium of ideas. As many of us remember from days gone by, radio allows the listener's imagination to take hold without the dominating visual component of television. This is still true today. We are reminded of the experience of WHA-AM and WHA-TV, which shifted the production of an instructional painting series for children from television to radio. It was found that when instructed by television, children attempted to imitate what they saw on the screen; but when taught by radio, they were stimulated to use their own imaginations.[13] Radio drama, serious (and funny) talk, and documentaries—these are equally important uses of the medium of imagination that are now too often neglected.

Today, radio production is quite inexpensive, representing only a small fraction of television production costs. Many radio stations can afford to produce a large majority of their programming themselves, with local news and features, music and cultural programming tailored to local tastes. Often they provide exposure for local musicians and performers, or support local cultural and civic institutions. Broadcasts of local concerts, panel discussions or call-in shows, coverage of local sporting events, and community "bulletin boards" are within the technical and economic means of radio stations even in the smallest markets.

In addition to local service, the economy of radio production makes possible programming to special audiences. Minority cultural tastes and needs, be they classical music, avant-garde jazz, or bilingual service, can be—and are to various degrees—served by public radio in this country.

Finally, radio is responsive and flexible. Any telephone can serve as a remote unit. Editorial decisions

---

[13]Richard O. Forsythe, "Instructional Radio: A Position Paper" (ERIC Clearinghouse on Educational Media and Technology, Dec. 1970), p. 5. Mimeographed.

can be made based on the quality of the ideas to be communicated, rather than on the quality of the visuals, as is often the case in television. A radio producer or reporter needs only an audio cassette recorder and a bit of ingenuity.

Because of its ubiquity, flexibility, low cost, and popularity, the radio medium continues to occupy a major role in the commercial communications industry of America. The business which delivers radio signals to over 95 percent of the American public in any given week earns substantial and growing revenues. In 1977, industry revenues reached $2.3 billion.

Sixty-five percent of new sets sold can receive FM. With the growth on the commercial FM band that was made possible by the 1962 FCC allocation decision, FM has established itself on a par with the once dominant AM stations. Forty-nine percent of all radio listening now takes place on the FM band, compared to 25 percent in 1972.[14] The number of commercial FM stations rose from 2200 to 2800 between 1970 and 1978; AM stations grew from 4300 to 4500 in the same period.

Unfortunately, much of the potential of the radio medium—for local service, for service to cultural tastes outside of the mainstream, for instantaneous response to the outside world—is ignored by commercial radio in this country. Moreover, these failures seem endemic to the system, rather than incidental, and constitute the strongest argument the Commission sees for increased support of public radio.

Commercial radio, like television, survives and profits from the advertising revenues it generates. These revenues depend on the size and demographics of a station's audience: the larger the audience, and the more attractive the demographics, the more an advertiser will pay a station to run a commercial.

With the tremendous increase in the number of radio stations over the last decade, many have become specialized in order to attract audiences distinct from

[14]Source: RADAR, Fall 1978 and 1972. Copyright, Statistical Research, Inc. Used with permission.

those of other stations in their markets. However, this phenomenon has not been so sweeping as one might expect. The vast majority of commercial radio stations fall into one of five major format categories:[15] "middle-of-the-road," country and western, Top 40, "beautiful music," and religious. In general, in markets where the five top commercial formats are already represented, profits of additional stations are maximized by slightly varying one of the formats already represented rather than providing an alternative service.

Even within the less common formats, the necessity for maximizing audience size will compromise quality. A commercial classical music station may limit its play-list to "light classical" music, which is apt to attract a larger audience than music that would satisfy more specialized listeners. The need to run commercials may cause the interruption or elimination of long pieces or live broadcasts. All-news stations may eschew events coverage or lengthy analysis in favor of 15-minute news summaries, endlessly repeated for the convenience of commuters.

Commercial radio has also found it profitable to downgrade local service. Although local radio production is cheap, syndicated productions are even cheaper and can sometimes attract larger audiences. Such canned programming is easily combined with automated station operation, further reducing costs. Unfortunately, this trend has been accelerated by the growth in outlets which might have provided increased commercial diversity. With more stations to divide the audience, a commercial operator must be able to turn a profit with smaller and smaller audiences. The only way is to cut operating costs.

In its eight years of existence public radio has bucked these trends and still achieved remarkable growth in the number of professionally operated stations, audiences, public recognition, and award-winning programming.

One hundred ninety-eight stations now qualify for CPB funds; 73 received funds in the beginning of

---

[15]See p. 332 for more detailed information.

1970. Income has jumped from $9.4 million to $65.5 million between 1970 and 1977. A survey showed that by the spring of 1977, 4 million people were listening to public radio during a week,[16] an increase of over 75 percent since 1973.[17] A 1978 Roper survey showed that 28 percent of the population recognized NPR, compared to only 11 percent in a similar 1976 survey. The Roper poll also indicated that public radio's audience includes less educated and less affluent listeners of all age groups.[18]

Program services provided by National Public Radio and other production entities around the country have rejuvenated information, entertainment, and educational services in audio broadcasts. *All Things Considered,* the centerpiece of NPR's schedule, presents a daily hour and a half of news, analysis, and feature reporting. Original radio drama has been revived by *Earplay.* NPR and many of its member stations have provided gavel-to-gavel coverage of Congressional hearings.

At the local level nearly two-thirds of all the jazz and classical stations in the country are public stations, despite a 35 to 1 advantage of commercial stations overall. Many public stations serve specialized audiences unserved by anyone else. A Navajo station in Ramah, New Mexico, translates the *Albuquerque Journal* and vital weather information into the Navajo language. In parts of Alaska public radio offers a primary service to listeners often without *any* other form of communications—bringing the only source of news from the outside world, announcing births and deaths or the visit of a doctor to a remote clinic. In Buffalo, New York, public radio offers the only all-news service in the community; in Santa Rosa, California, it speaks Spanish; in Boston, it provides fine-arts pro-

---

[16]Data were gathered in a specially commissioned Arbitron survey in April-May 1977. The copyrighted survey is cited with permission.

[17]Source: CPB Radio Research.

[18]About half the listeners earn less than $15,000, and a similar number have a high-school education or less. About half are 45 years or older. Source: 1978 Roper survey.

gramming. In Minnesota the public radio system regularly broadcasts the concerts of the Minneapolis symphony, the Minnesota Opera, and the St. Paul Chamber Orchestra. Simultaneously, on a separate signal inaudible without a special receiver, "talking" book, newspaper, and other specialized services are transmitted to the print-handicapped.[19] Other public stations use these additional subchannels to broadcast medical, adult, and elementary-school instructional programs, or emergency warnings; about 50 provide special services to the print-handicapped.

Realizing Radio's Potential: The Recommendations

Given the accomplishments of public radio and its considerable potential for public service, we believe that the present system should be more fully funded and substantially expanded. The following discussion details our goals for the public radio system, the means by which we believe those goals can be achieved, and the impact of this activity on existing and new institutions during the next decade.

Our recommendations fall into three categories:

• The use by the radio station system of the increased federal matching grants at the local and national level, in combination with new funds available from the Program Services Endowment.

• Expansion of the existing system to 450 to 500 stations[20] so as to assure virtually complete national coverage by at least one public radio station, and multiple station coverage in larger markets.

• A development strategy managed by the Public Telecommunications Trust that will add the 200 to 250 additional public radio stations to the present system by means of regulatory reform, financial assistance

---

[19]The term "print-handicapped" defines potential members of an audience which includes the visually and physically handicapped, the geographically isolated, and the illiterate—those who cannot use printed material as a regular source of information and entertainment.

[20]Chapter IV and Appendix D assume 480 stations to estimate the cost of a completed system.

for present and developing stations, and the purchase of existing stations.

The emphasis of these recommendations is two-fold, revolving around the critical importance of the station in the public radio system. We believe that the radio system must be completed, so that it fully serves the nation in both large and small communities. In addition, both existing and new stations must have a solid financial and community support structure strengthening the editorial function that each licensee performs in its community.

As with television, radio stations are legal and ethical entities licensed to represent the public interest in their communities. Yet radio has special characteristics that tend to make it more local in character: its flexibility, the greater economies of program production, and the substantially larger number of outlets in most communities, affect the ways audiences use the medium.

Because of these factors, and the major impact of doubling the number of qualified public radio stations, there are perhaps even more opportunities for change within the radio system. A major influx of funds to stations, and the impact of our funding design, will transform radio rapidly. Any institution experiencing sharp growth in a short time is in danger of encountering an influx of entrepreneurs and bureaucrats who can undermine the efforts of professionals . who formerly kept the enterprise alive with more meager resources but perhaps higher spirits. We hope the devotion and dedication of today's public radio professionals will not permit this phenomenon to transform their industry. We believe their vitality is an essential component of the diversity we propose as the underpinning of a new national initiative.

> We recommend that federal funds that go to public radio stations on a direct matching formula be used for two purposes: improvement of local service and operations, and the financing by station consortiums of more-than-local program-

ming. We recommend that the Program Services Endowment support additional national radio programs, particularly new and innovative projects. The Endowment will also provide transitional support for the present National Public Radio programming services until such time as stations are able to aggregate funds to support programs of their choice.

The potential of the public radio system for increased service must be built on the base of professional, CPB-qualified stations now in place. We have come to realize that financial conditions are unacceptable at most of these stations.

In order to improve this service and provide adequate salaries, facilities, and promotion funds, we believe the cornerstone of an expanded public radio system must be an increased federal match of $1 for every $1.50 raised by stations. The funds would be disbursed on a direct formula basis by the Public Telecommunications Trust. In addition, these stations will have access to an expanded facilities program operated by the Trust.

Our funding plan embodies two new principles for the radio system: First, the system would now have sufficient funds and a new responsibility to aggregate funds for more-than-local programs. These funds would be used for the production of high-quality, innovative radio programming.

At present, NPR is the principal production center performing this function. We recommend that NPR's program service receive support from the Program Services Endowment at its current level of approximately $6 million to ease the transition from total CPB support to full station support.

While recognizing that radio stations have fewer financial incentives than television stations to pool money for common programming efforts, we believe the principle is still sound and should be applied to both media. We do not mean to imply, however, that radio licensees must use the techniques of decision making devised to solve television's programming aggregation problems. The Station Program Cooperative is complicated, and to many in radio, highly bureaucratized. It is quite conceivable that NPR member stations would continue to give money to their national leaders to provide existing, or new, programming services. At present, however, NPR receives most of its program support funds by direct grant from CPB. We believe that the Program Services Endowment should continue to provide the existing level of $6 million to NPR during a transition period until the licensees are capable of assuming financial responsibility for their national programming. It is not our desire to specify how and what stations should decide, but rather to emphasize that the authority and the funds should be under their collective control.

By our estimates, the stations should be able immediately to aggregate approximately $10 million of their own funds for the support of additional programming, a dramatic increase in the range of services which the system can offer the public. Stations will thus develop new capabilities to produce programs outside the NPR production center structure if they wish, and will be better prepared to decide which services should receive their support, as the Endowment grants to NPR are phased out.

Second, federal funds would constitute a direct formula match and would not be diluted by allocation formulas or policy initiatives of the Trust. Even allowing for the added responsibility of more-than-local services, this new policy will result in a real increase in support to every station in the system. Currently, the average station earns from its CSG about 20¢ return on every nonfederal dollar raised. Adding in the value of radio services at CPB and the interconnection grant from CPB direct to NPR raises this return to approximately 28¢. Our funding recommendation would raise each station's return to 67¢ for every dollar raised from nonfederal sources.

Proportionately, the greatest funding increase will be realized by the largest stations in the system, since the present formula provides them a lower return on

202   FUTURE OF PUBLIC BROADCASTING

nonfederal income than to small stations. Some of this
increase will be offset by a progressive fee structure
that licensee organizations should adopt. The remaining increase is perfectly appropriate, however. Many
of the largest stations are located in some of the largest
metropolitan areas, or at the preeminent institutions of
higher education in this country, with access to a broader variety of cultural, political, and social events than
most smaller stations. Already these stations carry a
significant burden for production for the rest of the
system, and we believe that under this plan they should
play an even greater role.

The smallest stations in the system will be protected under this plan, and will experience a substantial
real increase in direct support. Currently, the smallest
stations in the system receive about a 33 percent return for every nonfederal dollar raised. With an equitable fee structure at the licensee organizations, most of
the federal match should be retained by these stations,
providing a sorely needed boost to the essential local
services that they provide.

Under our recommendation the average station
budget among the present 200-odd stations would increase immediately, from $225,000 to $310,000,
based upon 1977 nonfederal income figures. In fact,
the amount will probably be larger—about $400,000,
given the growth patterns of nonfederal income.

Two classes of licensees may find this change in
funding structure troublesome: the institutional licensees, and those serving audiences that are less likely to provide adequate financial support, notably minority and specialized groups, or smaller communities.

The institutional licensees may fear direct funding
because their parent organizations—usually universities
—could regard increased federal funding as a signal to
reduce their own support. Our plan would give greater
opportunity to the stations outside the educational institutions, but it may provide an even stronger stimulus
for investment by institutions and state and local governments, who after all will be generating a substantially improved return on their money. A reduction in
automatic institutional support, if it occurs, might stim-

ulate some stations to seek autonomy, that is, to develop local governance separate from the parent group. This, too, would be an opportunity for substantial growth and change. While we recognize the dangers for some licensees, we believe that the overall strategy for funding, which will increase rather substantially, is a sound policy that will stimulate growth among all groups of licensees.

We believe that, in all likelihood, this will be true even for the smallest stations—those providing services that are not widely popular, or those in areas with few potential listener-supporters. The increase in the match, once a station is qualified, is considerably larger, providing a threshold level of stability for every station.

It is also true that coverage in less populated areas —or of particular, unserved audiences in urban areas —is an objective of public policy. We believe that state and local government support, as well as new federal programs for minority media ownership and rural telecommunications services, can be stimulated by Trust policies for radio development, which will be discussed in detail later in this chapter.

With flexibility, foresight, and an eye toward the factors which seem to contribute to successful radio station growth, we anticipate that the Trust will foster strong stations. However, if problems occur, particularly when the Trust is attempting to achieve system-wide goals such as minority ownership or small-market coverage, the Trust would have full discretion to establish additional grant programs designed to provide solutions.

As increased funding becomes available to each station in the public radio system, we anticipate a sizeable jump in the funds that they will have at their discretion for program production and experimentation. The present 200 stations would be able, under our plan, to aggregate about $50,000 each for services beyond the purely local activities that constitute their core activity. Combined with the initial $6 million recommended production support from the Program Services Endowment, the radio system would have about twice the present level of funds for national and regional programming, interconnection, and promotion.

The radio system's long-range goal of 450 to 500 stations could be reached by about 1985 under our projections. Assuming an average budget at that point of about $430,000 per station, the stations would be capable of pooling $22 to $25 million for common purposes, assuming an average of about $50,000 per station (see Appendix D for details). Our recommendation would set a goal of $18 million annually for radio support at the Endowment, which would mean that radio's more-than-local services in 1985 would reach the $40 million to $43 million level, assuming steady growth in the number of stations and their ability to generate nonfederal financial support.

System Expansion

Under the overall leadership of the Public Telecommunications Trust, we recommend the development and activation of an additional 250 to 300 public radio stations. The addition of new stations will result in improved national coverage for the public radio system, greater diversity among licensees, and broader local programming choice in many markets through multiple outlets.

The expansion of the public radio system to the unserved portions of the nation and the improvement of radio service to those already able to receive a signal will be a major responsibility of the Public Telecommunications Trust. The radio division of the Trust will coordinate all grants to existing and developing radio stations, including those for facilities. It will seek out available frequencies and develop a set of priorities for activating and developing stations. It will seek to stimulate ownership of new radio stations by community groups, particularly among minorities, and make information available to them. The Trust will be able to offer consulting services to provide assistance in starting new stations and to solve ongoing management problems.

The goal of activating or building 250 to 300 new public radio stations is a massive job for the leaders of the Trust. To expand the size of the radio system by more than 100 percent, particularly in areas that have not yet been able to support a station, will require considerable technical skill and political finesse. Three general principles should guide the Trust in this effort.

National Coverage. The immediate first priority, as we have stated, is the achievement of coverage by at least a single public radio outlet over virtually the entire U.S. population. The present coverage of about 50 percent of the population is inequitable and weakens the rationale for federal support of the system. By failing to reach millions of potential listeners, public radio limits its financial and political base and reduces the efficiency of its national promotional and public awareness efforts. Most importantly, it deprives a large segment of the American public of valuable cultural and journalistic resources.

Multiple Coverage. Our estimates indicate that approximately 150 additional full service stations are needed to achieve virtual nationwide public radio coverage. The second priority, after full national coverage, should be to upgrade or activate the 100 to 150 other stations in metropolitan areas that are now already served by at least one or more public radio stations.

A single radio channel is insufficient service for many metropolitan areas where the listening habits are conditioned by stations that compete for listeners by creating a format that can attract an identifiable portion of the total audience. Listeners expect each radio station to be consistently formatted—they tune in for a "sound," not a particular program. Radio listeners tune in the all-news station when they want the headlines, a rock or country music station for a particular style of music, or another station for a particular announcer or radio personality. In this way stations attract loyal, regular listeners, some of whom listen continuously, but many of whom tune in and out as the mood strikes them, with the assurance that the service will be there when they return.

A single public radio station in a major market is inhibited from developing a "sound" or a format that can be promoted and can attract audiences and generate listener support. Moreover, the broad variety of national and more-than-local radio productions that we envision would swamp the capacity of a single station.

We are persuaded that many of the larger markets would be better served by multiple outlets so that a wider diversity of program choices might be made available to the larger number of available listeners. The multiple-station approach has enjoyed considerable success, notably in Washington, D.C., and Boston.

We do not believe that it is necessarily in the public interest for public stations to format their offerings as rigidly as many commercial stations do. However, we are convinced that consistent and regular program schedules are necessary for these stations to attract regular listeners from a broad segment of the public and build strong local followings.

In smaller markets where the listening audience is less accustomed to formatted radio, a greater variety of programs in any one station is more tolerable to the listener. The largest markets, however—where audience interests and cultural activity are more diverse, and where stations have greater access to the best of American and world cultures—require a number of outlets, each clearly focused. For example, there might be a jazz or eclectic music station and a station devoted to specific ethnic minorities, as well as one devoted to the fine arts and one to news and public affairs.

Multichannel satellite distribution and a variety of national program services to supplement local production make it possible to establish services of superior quality relatively economically in urban areas. As demonstrated by their commercial brethren, these more narrowly focused stations will each develop larger audiences than if each tried to serve the whole spectrum of audience interests. Thus multiple stations tend to enlarge the support base available in the community, rather than to divide a limited pool of listeners and funds.

We believe that the creation of multiple outlets in major markets is a cost-efficient expenditure of development funds, and the system's highest priority after first-service coverage expansion. However, we urge the Trust to develop policies that will discourage new stations from duplicating services offered by other public stations.

Several factors give us confidence that such duplication will not occur. Stations offering duplicative services must compete directly for the same community support. A new station will usually do better by offering an alternative service, rather than trying to compete directly. While we do not believe that content judgments are appropriate in determining whether a station qualifies for general support, we believe that a judgment of whether a station provides an alternative service is appropriate in consideration of assistance grants to new or upgrading stations. We are impressed with the efforts of some public stations in the same market to cooperate in counter programming, cross-promotion, and sharing of facilities, as has been successfully carried out in Boston, and urge their continuation to the extent legally permitted.

Licensee Diversity. In extending both first-service and multiple-service coverage, the Trust should encourage licensee diversity. As we have noted, the predominant owners of public radio stations are educational institutions. A major expansion of the system by 250 to 300 stations will provide the opportunity for public radio to broaden the type of ownership entities involved in the system, with the result that programming and policies will be derived from a broader portion of the population.

We believe that two types of licensees particularly deserve special encouragement and attention by the Trustees. First, members of minority groups and women, traditionally excluded from management and control of broadcasting facilities in the United States, will have a unique opportunity to enter the system, as new licenses become available in the next few years.

Second, the concept of community-owned, listener-sponsored radio stations responsive to their local listening publics is an important form of ownership capable of broad application in public radio. These stations must develop specialized fund-raising and management skills in order to establish and maintain public radio stations in their communities. The Trust can supply major support in developing such expertness among potential licensee groups.

Methods for Expansion of the System

The Trust, in cooperation with other elements of the public radio system, will develop a strategy of system expansion that includes regulatory reform activities, and a radio development program that will assist in upgrading existing stations, activating new stations, and the purchase of existing commercial or underutilized noncommercial stations.

Accomplishing the mandate of the Trust to activate 250 to 300 new stations will not be simply a matter of providing adequate funds. Deep-seated historical and regulatory problems present continuing barriers to the full use of the spectrum, recommended by the 1976 Public Broadcasting Act and extended in this report.

We see no easy solutions to such problems. The Trust must design a rather sophisticated strategy that combines regulatory reform, upgrading of existing stations, activation of new stations, and purchase of commercial and underutilized noncommercial stations if it is to be successful in substantially improving first-service and multiple-outlet coverage to many parts of the country.

Regulation. The single most fruitful course of action involves regulatory reform. Recent FCC actions[21] require 10-watt stations to increase their power or move, when necessary, to make room for new or upgraded higher-powered stations. This reform will help to provide spectrum space for activating stations and increasing the power of others, but will be inadequate for full expansion of the system. Other provisions, mandating minimum operating schedules and requiring that underutilized frequences be shared, are positive steps. In addition, we are encouraged that the FCC has again taken up the question of a table of allocations for the noncommercial FM band. We hope the matter will be resolved swiftly. If a table is to be adopted, extended delay will only diminish its potential impact. If there is to be no table (some have argued that it is already too late), other measures can and should be taken to redress some of the worst outcomes of the present "demand" system of allocations.

The United States is seeking an expansion of the standard AM broadcast band in the 1979 World Administrative Radio Conference. If this effort is successful, we urge the reservation of a substantial number of these new frequencies for public radio.

Regulatory reform can also improve the reach of current public stations, because most public stations are found on the FM band. While FM radio now captures 49 percent of the listening audience, and FM or AM/FM receivers now account for 65 percent of all new sales, the possibility remains that marketplace forces alone are not sufficient to ensure that public radio's service will be fully available to the American public. In particular, the relatively low proportion of FM radios in automobiles (35 percent) is a major concern. Should FM growth falter, we urge the Congress to consider the enactment of all-channel radio legislation that would require all radio sets sold in the United States to be capable of receiving both AM and FM broadcasts. We believe that the all-channel television

[21]*Second Report and Order on Noncommercial Educational FM Stations* (Docket #20735)—FCC2d—44 RR2d 235 (1978).

legislation in 1962 was instrumental in the growth of public television. It provides a model for simulation in public radio. The cost to consumers will not be a significant factor.

As encouraging as these possibilities are, we believe that the FCC must take further steps to ensure public radio growth. The pressing demands for spectrum space require priorities for the noncommercial service. Distinctions should be made between licensees that operate their stations for the primary mission of service to the public and those for which public service is incidental to more restricted goals, i.e., student training. As noted above, the FCC now treats 10-watt stations on a secondary, space-available basis. We believe there may be other objective standards that can guide an expanded primary/secondary regulatory scheme. Similarly, the FCC's new minimum-hours standards should be but a first step in establishing a threshold performance expected of all noncommercial licensees.

Such action would have a dual effect on licensees receiving only secondary protection. They would feel pressure to upgrade their operations sufficiently to make broadcasting to the public their primary responsibility. These stations will be able to take advantage of development assistance programs sponsored by the Trust and should then become active members of the public radio system.

On the other hand, some stations may not wish to make this transition. In this case, when a full service licensee wishes to make service available, either by the establishment of a new station, or by increasing power of an existing station, the original station should be required to make room.

FCC regulatory action is a necessary prerequisite for the Trust's principal effort in expanding the public radio system by 250 to 300 stations. Uncluttered channels are necessary for both the activation of new stations, or the upgrading of existing stations.

A Plan for Upgrading and Activating Stations. We estimate that of the approximately 300 noncommercial nonpublic radio stations with more than 10 watts of power, only a third have sufficient power and the financial competence to make further development realistic.

The present policy of requiring radio stations to meet strict standards in order to qualify for ongoing CPB support has built a core of professional public radio stations for a limited pool of federal funds.[22] We endorse the continuation of the qualifications standards, since our goal is to increase the number of qualified licensees in public radio. We believe that standards will assist in the completion of a professionally operated, well-financed radio system.

We do urge the Public Telecommunications Trust to exercise some degree of flexibility in applying qualifications criteria, however. Today, for instance, radio stations jointly operated with television stations are not permitted to count shared personnel toward their CPB qualification. In certain instances, stations that fall below CPB power criteria could not significantly increase their population coverage by increasing wattage.

We recognize the serious policy considerations motivating these rules in the first place, and endorse their intention. However, where these intentions have not been violated, administrative inflexibility can unfairly limit support to stations that serve their communities well.

Because we believe that the qualifications standards, in general, represent the minimum basis for professional operation, the Trust will need to establish a major assistance effort to finance the upgrading of existing stations so that they can meet these standards. With some initial assistance and sufficient time to build stable audiences and community support, these stations will be capable of maintaining service

---

[22]The current criteria include 18-hour-per-day, 365-day-per-year operation, a staff of five full-time members paid at least the federal minimum wage, a budget that includes at least $80,000 of non-federal income (including in-kind support), and effective radiated power equivalent to 3000 watts at 500 feet height above average terrain for FM (or 250 watts for AM).

above qualification standards, thereby earning eligibility for the increased operating-support match from the Trust.

Assistance grants might range from as little as $50,000 to as much as $1 million. Grants at the lower end of this range will typically be made to stations requiring assistance to reach a particular provision of the qualifications standards in order to become eligible for federal support. Common hurdles include the achievement of sufficient power and the payment of staff from nonfederal sources. Larger grants are necessary for stations in major markets wishing to convert from low-power, student-run operations to major high-power, full service stations operating well above minimum standards. Such grants have been made in recent years, and prove to be a successful way to provide public radio for unserved markets.

We expect that approximately 150 stations should receive assistance from the Trust, with an average grant of $300,000. We estimate the cost of the Trust's total assistance program at $45 million.

This budget would include assistance to new stations in addition to the existing nonqualified stations that require upgrading. Only a handful of these currently nonqualified stations are located in the major markets unserved by public radio. Upgrading these stations, therefore, will result in multiple services rather than expansion of coverage. Thus, in order to complete a nationwide radio development plan, many more new stations will need to be activated. Our budget estimate includes assistance for these new stations, which would be eligible for initial planning grants as well as longer-term development assistance. We urge the Trust to study this situation and to stimulate development in unserved communities accordingly.

The radio assistance program at the Trust will be more than simple grant-making activity. Its staff will be required to develop an overall plan for national radio coverage, to stimulate development of new radio stations in communities that are unserved, and to finance technical and management assistance to licensees when such help furthers these policy goals.

Purchasing New Stations. Even with regulatory reform there will continue to be an inadequate number of frequencies, both to extend first-service coverage, and to create multiple-service coverage in many major markets. The only possible solution for some communities lies in the purchase of commercial or underutilized noncommercial frequencies by nonprofit groups. We believe it is essential that such groups be given access to the broadcasting marketplace. One suggested mechanism would be for the FCC to grant the right of first refusal to qualified public groups at the negotiated price for the transfer of any license. We note that some form of limited Trust assistance in the purchase of these stations might be appropriate, although we recognize the risk in having a federally funded entity entering into—and perhaps inflating—transfer prices. We, therefore, urge the interested parties—National Public Radio, the Trust, the FCC, and Congress—to explore this complex issue and to set workable rules and guidelines.

In addition, we believe that a particular priority should be given by the Trust to minority-controlled groups and institutions in developing new radio stations. This is both consistent with the overall policy of encouraging diversity within the system and with the affirmative obligation of the Trust and the public telecommunications system to give special emphasis to serving minority needs.

The Trust's program for special assistance to upgrade existing stations and to activate or purchase new stations is an extremely delicate responsibility, one which the Trustees should treat carefully. Such a funding plan must strike a careful balance between overfunding and underfunding, and be sensitive as well to local community concerns. Criteria for special assistance grants should be sufficiently strict to prove substantial community interest and support before federal funds are made available. Only strong and stable licensees can continue to attract an audience and a management able to raise operating support from the community. Station managers need to be as expert in institutional management as they are in programming.

Such competence should be demonstrable before federal funds are provided to the station.

On the other hand, we do not believe that eligibility requirements for assistance grants should be so severe that no risks are taken. We believe a diverse system to be an important goal, and this will necessarily involve support for stations that cannot be guaranteed to survive.

The Trust's program for development assistance in radio—including upgrading, activation, purchase, and minority ownership—is a significant part of its overall responsibility as the system's chief planning and fiduciary agent. Because the Trust will administer the system's development, as well as provide for station operating and facilities support, the Trustees can coordinate overall system growth and operation. A greatly expanded facilities program in concert with a wide-scale development program should enable public radio rapidly to expand in order to serve a much larger portion of the American public.

Diversity and Growth: The Effects of Our Recommendations

The preceding recommendations to build and fund the public radio system have a dual purpose: growth and diversity. We believe an expanded system serving all Americans and having a strengthened funding base will be capable of providing better programs and services. In addition, by creating incentives for diversity as the system grows, we hope that public radio will involve and serve many who have heretofore been outside the system.

The impact of our funding recommendations will be strongly felt in the system's programming efforts and organizational structure, as well as in a broader and more heterogeneous constituency of stations. Upon adoption, our proposal would have immediate and substantial impact on the existing stations. As the Trust accelerates the addition of new stations into the public radio family, the relationships among stations and the national organizations they sponsor will necessarily require reevaluation.

This section examines the potential impact of our proposal on the system's programming and organizational arrangements. The principal impact upon the stations will be:

- Stations will have more money, attributable to a larger match of foderal funds, thus enhancing the stations' ability to raise funds locally. This will enable stations to pay reasonable salaries, equip their operations, provide better local production and services, increase promotion and public awareness, and undertake more ambitious and diversified cooperative programming efforts on national and regional bases.
- Stations, rather than central organizations, will have a greater share of the total radio funding, with a correspondingly greater degree of involvement in national programming decisions. Because we are recommending that the principal responsibility to determine and finance greater-than-local programming should be vested in the stations, we expect a greater diversity of programs to develop. This ensures that groups of stations can support national and regional organizations serving a wide range of interests and gives incentives to those organizations to be responsive to member stations.
- The number of stations will increase dramatically, as the Trust develops additional outlets in small communities and multiple service in larger metropolitan areas. This will permit stations to develop a better definition of their own special identity to audiences. Adding stations will increase the critical mass of support for special audience programming, as well.
- Our plan, in addition to setting forth eligibility standards for operating funds from the Trust, would provide special support to stations attempting to upgrade.
- Stations would also enjoy new opportunities for production support from the Endowment, and support services from the Trust. With grants for special production centers and programs, public radio would be able to hire producers, independent radio artists and journalists to create new and exciting radio programming.

The effect of our recommendations on National Public Radio and other national organizations will be equally significant. While NPR is today the preeminent national organization within the public radio system, its relation with a growing constituency of qualified stations, as well as with other station groupings and national organizations, will inevitably change under the impact of our proposals.

- The most obvious change is our recommendation for the financing of national membership organizations. We have proposed a transition grant from the Endowment to assure no disruption in NPR's excellent programming division. The Endowment's ultimate role in radio however, should be program innovation, not maintenance of a core schedule. NPR and other production centers, and independents will all be able to draw on greater program funding in the future. The core services for the radio system, just as in television, should be determined by the licensees, as should the configuration of member services and representation.
- A greater number of better-financed licensees will provide an opportunity for NPR and other station groupings to develop more ambitious, diversified programming and multiple, simultaneous radio services to meet different system needs. With federal matching funds going to stations, competition between NPR and its own members for allocation of federal funds will disappear.
- The specified roles for the Trust and the Endowment will mean that station organizations will derive primary fiscal and governing authority from members, not statutory institutions. This will increase their accountability to the stations and reduce their dependence on central bodies.

We have thereby placed an implicit challenge before NPR and the other entities serving the public radio community. Our plan does not include the assured, lump-sum support that has been NPR's mainstay since its inception. Instead, NPR and others face a more open, competitive environment in which it will be necessary to plan for, seek, and justify support from several quarters: first and foremost, the audiences being served, and secondarily the Endowment, and the Trust. Further, national organizations will have a direct incentive to add new stations to their membership, because doing so will enlarge their operating resources.

Our recommendations provide great flexibility to stations and to the national organizations that serve them. The emerging configuration of the system will depend in good measure on the initiative and leadership of those within the system, and upon the newcomers expected to more than double the size of today's system.

We have placed strong emphasis on the role of each public radio station in ensuring greater resources, enhanced autonomy, and more authority within the overall system. The individual stations, acting collectively, will shape the dimensions of program services that public radio will offer to the American people.

With the multichannel capability of the satellite interconnection system, stations will be technically capable of exchanging a variety of programs among themselves. Our proposal gives them the discretionary funds that can enable them to produce programs of greater-than-local interest.

We envision a range of program production mechanisms within the overall public radio system. During the immediate transition period NPR will undoubtedly continue to operate the satellite interconnection and produce a core schedule, financed by the Endowment. Additionally, some or all of the stations might assign to NPR further production responsibility in fine arts, special events, or minority programming. The public radio system has an opportunity to develop imaginative and futuristic uses of the medium beyond the current directions.

Consortiums of stations could spring up which would share their own productions among themselves, or could authorize other entities to exercise production authority. Models for such arrangements already exist within public radio. The Eastern Public Radio Network has shared extensive programming among its member stations. The Southeastern Educational Communications Association recently began a radio service. The Pacifica Foundation produces an alternative news program for its stations, and like the National Federation of Community Broadcasters, maintains a tape service.

While both formal and ad hoc relationships will naturally emerge from this plan, we also believe that coordination is an important responsibility that will emerge for NPR. We expect that NPR might operate several distinct program services: a public affairs service, a fine-arts and cultural service, and an eclectic, American cultural service, as well as special events and minority services. Not all of these would need to be centrally produced. We would expect NPR to draw heavily on other producers.[23]

The Program Services Endowment will contribute to this mix by encouraging innovative program development, both within and without the system. We interject two notes of caution, however. First, the record of the radio system in encouraging and using independent production talent is poor, although this is perhaps understandable considering its poverty. We recommend that the stations and NPR address this inadequacy. Second, we urge the radio system not to repeat the mistakes of the television system by enmeshing its creative people in a host of bureaucratic constraints. The creative process is advanced by giving discretion to bright people, and we urge the radio system to adopt administrative mechanisms flexible enough to deal with its producers.

There are also many options for stations in meeting their service and representational needs. Again, we would expect NPR to continue to play a strong leadership role. As the system grows, we believe the best policy would be to encourage NPR to broaden its constituency in order to include all noncommercial stations

---

[23]Whether or not NPR becomes the single national public radio organization, we believe that while it continues to be financed much as it is now, it should provide nondiscriminatory access to its program distribution system.

dedicated to full service radio. There is also the prospect that additional station groups—either newly formed or in existence—may represent the interests of the new stations and would therefore receive station funding to perform various national functions.

Regardless of how the licensees resolve the issue of their representation, the Trust will have a distinct but complementary role in the national system. By administering the development program, the Trust will work toward the completion of the nationwide station structure. Through the qualification program, the Trust will ensure that ongoing operational support is wisely used. With special efforts designed to bring minorities and other groups into station ownership, the Trust will enhance the national goals of diversity and equal opportunity.

Because the Trust will use a wide variety of grant programs to assist in radio development, the qualifications standards should eventually play a less crucial role in determining the character of the public radio system. At present, the standards determine not only the number of stations eligible for CPB operational funding, but eligibility for entry into NPR as well. Consequently, public radio is defined by the qualification standards.

Both uses of the qualification standards have served to limit the system's diversity. Because they have a broader base of funding and because they can include in-kind support as part of their total budget, educational institutions have had an easier time qualifying for CPB funds than community organizations whose only activity is the operation of a radio station. This is particularly true of communities whose population is too small or too poor for effective listener support. The result has been a continuation of the dominance of one type of licensee.

Use of the qualification standards for NPR membership has also excluded some noncommercial radio stations from the benefits of national representation, programming, distribution, and other services. While NPR continues to function as it does today in serving as public radio's principal policy voice and service agency, it should determine the composition of its membership according to criteria other than the compliance standards the Trust establishes for its own purposes. Should NPR, or any such licensee organization, decide to broaden its constituency, use of the qualifications standards will have a more specialized role in the public radio system.

We believe that flexibility and diversity in programming, representation, and station support is the natural outgrowth of expanded station development, a broadened public radio system, and the funding plan we have outlined. The vitality of the station system, combined with the inherent economy of radio production and satellite distribution, will be an impressive combination. This lies at the center of our vision for the system.

VII

Public Broadcasting in the New Telecommunications Environment

America has entered a new era in telecommunications. The range of advances in information and communications technology in the past decade—and their implications for the future—is extraordinary. Increasingly, our work, our leisure, and our capacity to relate to the world are served and shaped by computers, communications satellites, and sophisticated terrestrial transmission systems. Radio and television, reaching into virtually every American home, have an impact on us rivaling the historic impact of printing. And the future tantalizes and unsettles us with the prospect of the wired nation and the home telecommunications center. We are, in short, becoming an information society in which communications is central to our individual and collective experience.

For public broadcasting, this changing telecommunications world raises significant questions. What is, or should be, public broadcasting's posture in this new environment? How should it make use of the new communications technologies? Will public broadcasting become superfluous, or does it have an integral role in a copious information environment?

Our investigation of public broadcasting's role in this expanding telecommunications environment has been guided by several principles. First, our perspective has been a public one. Our orientation to the range of public policy issues and the applications and innovative services available to public broadcasting through new technology has been that of a viewer and a listener, and not that of a provider. Our concern has been to find methods of providing broad and equal access to the products and services of a more significant public broadcasting system in the United States.

It follows, then, that our focus is not simply on technology. Fundamentally, technology is neutral. What is important, we believe, is how technology can help meet human needs. For public broadcasting, what is important is not merely the availability of new communications technologies, but the ways in which public broadcasters apply that technology to meet real public needs. We think this may be the most compelling challenge facing public broadcasting during the next decade.

Finally, we have found it unwise to attempt to construct a detailed navigational chart for public broadcasting's future in the new environment. We have not viewed our task as one of technological forecaster, nor do we deem it generally appropriate to make specific judgments about the efficacy and utility of particular technologies, distribution systems, or services that public broadcasters might employ in the coming decade. The dynamism of the telecommunications marketplace seems to us to preclude any such set of constricting recommendations.

No observer introduced to any of the range of telecommunications scenarios for the next quarter century can fail to be impressed by the pace and scale of technological innovation and the virtually limitless telecommunications options made possible by developing transmission, production, storage, and retrieval technology. Indeed, while we have focused on the telecommunications landscape of the mid-'80s the prospects for more profound change before the end of the century and the threat of technological obsolescence loom large.

Yet these possibilities must be tempered with

the realization that speculation about the future is just that. And while the basic technologies, systems, and techniques that will fill out the dimensions of the next decade seem apparent, there is little doubt that a panoply of economic, political, social, and marketing factors will ultimately control and shape our evolution in this new environment.

We believe that public broadcasting must have both the flexibility and the means to chart its own course in changing seas and in response to public needs and desires. We are persuaded that public broadcasting does have an integral role to play in bringing the benefits of an enriched information environment to the public and in helping to shape that environment in ways that are not dependent on the marketplace. Less constrained by the dictates of commerce, public broadcasting can play a vital role as an innovator and pacesetter in the telecommunications sector.

> To help public broadcasting in fulfilling its innovative role we make three principal recommendations. First, we urge public broadcasting and government to join in a concerted effort to extend public television and radio service to at least 90 percent of the population over the next five to seven years. Second, we recommend that public broadcasting move rapidly to develop a stronger, ongoing, and more fully integrated research and development capability to assist the system in taking advantage of new technology to meet public needs. Third, we believe that public broadcasting must broaden and become more flexible in its approach to the delivery of programs and services to the American public.

The Public Broadcasting System Today

In the mid-'60s public broadcasting was little more than a disparate collection of stations spread about the country, with little in the way of national operations and support activity. By the mid-'70s the number of television and radio stations had more than doubled, and both television and radio had established live full-time national interconnection services. By October 1978 the public television system included 280 stations in 48 states, Puerto Rico, Guam, the Virgin Islands, and American Samoa.[1] National Public Radio's 217 stations provide service in 5 states.[2] Figures 7–1 and 7–2 show, respectively, the locations of the public television stations and the locations of the public radio stations.

Perhaps the most significant development in the evolution of public broadcasting's physical system is public television and radio's conversion to satellite interconnection. Late in 1978 all PBS stations began to receive national programming via the Western Union "Westar" satellite instead of over common carrier terrestrial facilities. Moreover, in five locations around the country, stations are now able to both receive and transmit programming via satellite. With satellite interconnection, stations are able to receive two television programs simultaneously, as well as four additional audio signals. By installing an additional satellite receiver, stations can double their receiving capacity.

Public radio's satellite system, which will also use Western Union's Westar satellite, is now under construction and is scheduled to be operational in early 1980. Initially, 193 NPR stations will be interconnected via satellite. Fifteen stations will both receive and transmit programs.[3] At first public radio will lease suf-

---

[1]Many public television licensees operate more than one station or transmitter. About a third of the 280 stations are actually repeaters which are fed programming from a primary originating station.

[2]In addition, there are another 800 noncommercial radio stations. However, most of these stations operate at very low power and serve limited audiences.

[3]These radio uplinks are located in Seattle, Wash.; Austin, Tex.; Cincinnati, Ohio; New York, N. Y.; Kansas City, Mo.; Columbia, S. C.; St. Paul, Minn.; Boston, Mass.; East Lansing, Mich.; Ames, Iowa; Chicago, Ill.; Atlanta, Ga.; Denver, Colo.; San Francisco, Calif.; and Los Angeles, Calif.

Figure 1
Public Television Stations

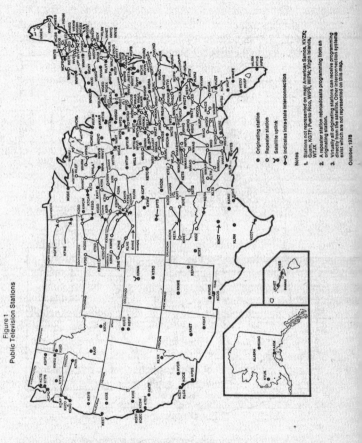

● Originating station
◊ Repeater station
ϒ Satellite uplink
●—◊ Indicates intrastate interconnection

Notes

1. Stations not represented on map: American Samoa, KVZK; Guam, KGTF; Puerto Rico, WIPR, WIPM, Virgin Islands, WTJX

2. A repeater station rebroadcasts programming from an originating station.

3. Virtually all originating stations can receive programming directly from the satellite. Other interconnection systems exist, which are not represented on this map.

October, 1978

Figure 7–1. (See Appendix H, page 387 for listing of stations)

Figure 2
Public Radio Stations

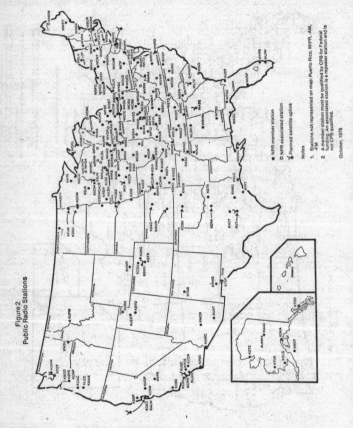

Notes

1. Stations not represented on map: Puerto Rico, WIPR, AM.

2. A member station must be qualified by CPB for Federal funding. An associated station is a repeater station and is not CPB qualified.

● NPR member station
○ NPR associated station
⚡ Planned satellite uplink

October, 1978

Figure 7–2. (See Appendix H, page 387 for listing of stations)

ficient satellite capacity to permit stations to receive four full-time high fidelity channels. Later, this capacity can be increased.

The ramifications of satellite distribution extend far beyond mere relay of programs to stations from a central source. Yet it will be months and perhaps years before the full significance of the satellite is felt by both the system and the public.

Satellite distribution represents a quantum increase in national and regional distribution capability for public television. In the short term satellite interconnection will provide for public television improved transmission quality and reliability, greater ease of interconnecting new stations, full live interconnection of all public stations—including those in the noncontiguous states—and the opportunity to reduce time-zone adjustment problems.

More important, public television's multichannel capability is providing greater autonomy to stations in the selection and scheduling of programs and the opportunity to decentralize program origination. In the long run, multichannel satellite distribution may well create new relationships among stations, and between stations and their national and regional organizations. It can also affect the nature and the number of programs and services distributed, provide for greater access to the television system, reduce costs in national distribution, and even create the opportunity for generating new revenues.

Satellite interconnection will provide many of the same benefits to public radio. Interconnection of new public radio stations will be easier. Simultaneous distribution of four or more programs can strengthen local autonomy, flexibility of scheduling, and format specialization in markets with more than one station. It can also decentralize program production, facilitate "community of interest" program sharing, and provide more timely news and live-event coverage.

Public radio will particularly benefit by the improved quality of satellite transmission. Radio's present 16,000-mile terrestrial distribution system was designed for low-fidelity voice-grade communications. Consequently, virtually all NPR music programs are now taped, duplicated, and mailed to some 200 stations. The process costs $1600 per program hour as compared to less than $30 per hour for satellite transmission. Music programs can be transmitted live, in stereo, or even in quadraphonic sound by satellite.

Unique to broadcasting in this country is public broadcasting's development of full-time regional networks for the acquisition, production, and distribution of programming. Over half of the Eastern Educational Network's (EEN) 53 member stations are interconnected by terrestrial common carrier. The Southern Educational Communications Association (SECA) has experimented with regional delivery of programs via domestic satellite. The capabilities of EEN and SECA, as well as of the Central Educational Network and the Pacific Mountain Network, to distribute programming regionally can be greatly enhanced by satellite delivery, as can the distribution practices of instructional programming organizations such as the Public Television Library, the Agency for Instructional Television, the Great Plains National Instructional Television Library, and the International Instructional Television Cooperative. In addition, the public radio and television system includes a variety of formal and informal networks which give public broadcasting great potential to share programs and services at the state and local levels.

An important and sometimes underestimated aspect of the public system's technical capabilities is the use of portions of the broadcast channel for ancillary signals that can improve present services or provide new ones. Public broadcasting has played a leading role in the United States in tapping the unused capacity of television and radio to convey specialized audio or video information.

In addition to national distribution of open or visible captioned programming, the Public Broadcasting Service, with the support of HEW's Bureau of the Handicapped and CPB, has developed a closed captioning system which will allow hearing-impaired persons to receive captioned programs via their television set. Beginning in 1979 programs will be encaptioned at one of eight PBS captioning centers and distributed via satellite and stations on an unused portion of the television channel; these programs can be received in the home with the aid of a special television set decoder which costs approximately $200.

PBS is also developing an audio transmission system known as DATE (Digital Audio for Television) which will permit satellite transmission of four high-quality audio channels with the standard video signal. Although station facilities and home receivers will have to be adapted to receive the additional transmissions, the DATE system can ultimately be employed for stereo or hi-fi television sound and even for dual-language broadcasts.

Approximately 50 public radio stations have developed alternative or supplemental distribution capabilities via Subsidiary Communications Authorizations (SCA). Through a process known as multiplexing, radio stations are able to broadcast additional programs at the same time and on the same frequency as standard public radio offerings. As in television captioning, reception of SCA signals requires use of a home receiver equipped with a special decoder (costing about $55). To date, most SCA involves reading services for the blind. However, radio subcarrier channels may also have significant instructional and other applications when public radio's satellite system becomes fully operational.

In sum, public broadcasting is today an integral part of the nation's telecommunications structure. In particular, public television and radio's national, regional, and state systems offer enormous potential for significantly increasing the American public's access to quality television and radio programming and new information services. What remains, however, is the challenge of developing comparably flexible and efficient distribution modes at the local level.

The Telecommunications Environment[4]

The present public broadcasting system is only one part of a remarkably sophisticated and diverse national and worldwide telecommunications structure now undergoing great change.

Communications satellite systems are already supplementing, and to an extent supplanting, terrestrial transmission systems as the infrastructure of worldwide and domestic telecommunications. The Intelsat and Intersputnik global satellite systems provide nearly 130 nations with telephone, telex, data, or television services. In some cases satellites have been the means of introducing basic communications services long taken for granted in the more developed nations. Independently, or through these two systems, some twenty nations as diverse as Indonesia, the Philippines, Zaire, and Canada have domestic satellite systems. Regional systems are being developed in Africa, the Arab nations, Europe, and South America.

Worldwide telecommunications development is not confined to satellite communications. In Great Britain the British Broadcasting Corporation (BBC) and Independent Television (ITV) are now providing teletext services which allow viewers to call up news, weather, and other consumer information from a central computer via the television set. Prestel, another teletext service, which uses the existing telephone network to link individuals with the source of information, is now being developed by the British Post Office. Teletext services are in development in Germany, France, Japan, Scandinavia, and the United States.

In Japan, telecommunications innovation is moving along rapidly. In March 1978 the Japanese Broadcasting Corporation (NHK) and the Ministry of Posts and Telecommunications began experimental, direct satellite-to-home broadcasting. NHK is testing satellite receivers costing less than $400. As early as

---

[4]Appendix F contains a more detailed description of the technologies and services of particular significance to public broadcasting.

1972 the Japanese Ministry of Posts and Telecommunications was testing facsimile newspaper service via coaxial cable, and last year Japan launched a trial computerized home information service featuring two-way video communications via an optical fiber system. Japan is also experimenting with stereophonic television.

In America, too, the cost efficiencies and technical capacities of satellite communications are creating new services. Already domestic satellites relay a wide range of data and voice communications, as well as television and radio programs. Newspapers are, in effect, printed via satellite, new special-interest television services are proliferating, and before long "teleconferencing" via satellite may well move from the experimental to the commonplace. Through satellite interconnection, remote communities in the Alaskan bush receive medical and educational services. Information is relayed from offshore drilling sites via satellite.

Our nation's sophisticated and pervasive network of terrestrial common carrier systems, themselves increasingly linked to and employing satellites, are expanding the opportunities for new business and consumer services. Spurred by changing regulatory policies and advanced computer and digital transmission technology, innovative common carrier services have mushroomed in recent years. Virtually all Americans, including over 90 percent of the nation's rural homes, are linked by national and local telephone systems which are technically capable of providing information and telecommunications services far beyond the telephone services routinely available today. A range of data and voice communications, security and facsimile services offered by the telephone companies, private line, and other specialized communications common carriers have emerged stimulated by new technology and techniques, and in turn stimulating even newer services.

In addition to local distribution of information and services via telephone company facilities and ancillary broadcast signals, new high-capacity microwave and cable distribution systems are proliferating, offering the potential for even more specialized telecommunications delivery. Cable television, with its multichannel capacity and potential for two-way communications, now reaches one out of every five American homes with a range of entertainment, information, and educational services. Microwave distribution services—Instructional Television Fixed Service (ITFS), Multipoint Distribution Service (MDS), and other specialized services authorized by the FCC—are further expanding the potential for delivery of audio and video information services to homes, schools, and institutions.

The dimensions of our telecommunications landscape are increasingly expanded by technology which can liberate us from the passivity of traditional communications experience. The minicomputer has reached beyond the office to the home, and through teleprocessing is rapidly becoming capable of reaching back out again. Despite significant marketplace barriers, videocassette systems that allow consumers to record and play back, and even produce their own television programs are entering the home at a faster rate than did color television. After decades of development, the videodisc system, a kind of long-playing video record with enormous information storage capacity, is expanding our communications options. The television receiver itself has already become a vehicle for video games in millions of American homes. Wide-screen, high-resolution television sets with greatly improved audio characteristics are now under development. And tied to interactive distribution systems such as cable television, the home television set is becoming a kind of electronic hearth.

In the long run, beyond the midpoint of the next decade, the future becomes less clear. Yet it appears reasonable to conclude that we will have entered an extraordinarily rich communications environment, one characterized by an abundance of information sources and alternatives for the consumer, with at least an opportunity for a much higher degree of individual selectivity, and with the potential for altering the homogeneity of communications experience. For example, assuming a hospitable attitude on the part of government toward innovation and market entry, our tele-

communications landscape is likely to include a highly
sophisticated satellite communications system, with a
new generation of advanced satellites and literally thousands of receiving terminals—as well as hundreds of
originating "uplinks"—employed by both commercial
and public service enterprises. We can envision fiber-
optic local distribution systems coming into wider use
which will enormously expand the capacity for conveying information.[5] Likewise, broader application of
digital transmission and production techniques will
greatly enhance transmission quality and capacity. The
rapidly growing consumer market for communications
storage and display equipment and the increasing availability of interactive or two-way systems portend new
and more efficient means of communicating in and
among homes, offices, and institutions. The continued
integration of information-processing, transmission,
storage, and retrieval technology appears inevitable, as
does a gradual altering of our traditional forms of mass
communication.

In the main, this rich information environment
will be shaped by the commercial sector. Yet we believe that commerce alone should not be the deter-
minant of our national telecommunications experience.
Public broadcasting has already played an important
role in this experience, and its place in our future
telecommunications scheme is even more vital.

Extending Television and Radio Service
We recommend that public broadcasting and the government join in a concerted effort to extend public broadcasting

---

[5]Fiber optics refers to a form of communications in which light
waves are sent by laser beam through hollow glass threads slightly
thicker than a human hair. The glass fibers, bundled in a cable not
much larger than a finger, have vast information-conveying capacity.
For example, a cable containing 144 fibers can transmit about
50,000 two-way voice conversations. Fiber-optic systems are already
in limited use by telephone companies, cable television operators,
and at least one public broadcaster.

service to at least 90 percent of the population over the next five to seven years.

We have already stressed that a fundamental objective of the Commission is to provide the public
wide and more equal access to the programs and
services of the public system. A primary objective of
the Public Broadcasting Act was to extend "educational television and radio to all of the citizens of the
United States." Despite the significant increase in the
number of television and radio stations since 1967,
this objective has not been attained. We consider this
a significant shortcoming of the American public broadcasting system today.

We are aware that telecommunications advances
will eventually result in the development of new nonbroadcast telecommunciations systems, and we believe
that public broadcasting's development plans must take
cognizance of these trends. At the same time, we cannot ignore the need to extend public broadcasting service over the short term.

It seems to us axiomatic that the benefits of a
public system supported in significant part by federal
tax dollars should be available to all citizens. Most
foreign public broadcasting systems have deemed it
essential to provide nationwide access to the product of
their systems, and have, in fact, substantially achieved
that goal.[6] In Great Britain, for example, the BBC
television and radio services, and services provided
through the IBA generally, are capable of reaching
more than 90 percent of the population. Japan's public system serves 97 percent of the population. The
Canadian Broadcasting Corporation (CBC) has recently embarked on a program to extend service to the
entire population.

We believe that the American public's limited
access to the services and product of its noncommercial

---

[6]We note too that each of the three U.S. commercial networks,
through owned stations or affiliates, reach in excess of 95 percent of
American homes. Commercial radio's coverage is equally extensive.

broadcasting system is a major barrier to the realization of a stronger, more integral role for public broadcasting in our society. There are serious practical consequences of public broadcasting's inability to serve all of the public. A system incapable of serving a significant portion of the citizenry can lay little claim to that citizenry's financial and political support. At the same time the efficiencies possible in creating general audience awareness and in the promotion and ancillary use of national programs are diminished when only a partial national audience base exists. And the impact and value of the significant new, high-quality television and radio programs we envision will not be realized.

Public television's coverage has increased significantly over the past decade, and today it is capable of reaching nearly 87 percent of the population.[7] The fact remains that the nation's access to public television is still incomplete, particularly in hard-to-serve rural areas. Figure 7–3 shows the broadcast signal coverage areas of public television stations. Two states, Montana and Wyoming, are without any public television stations, and there are ten states where 40 percent or more of the population cannot receive a public television signal over the air. Public radio is even less accessible to the American public.

There are many reasons for this uneven coverage pattern in television and radio. Federal funds available through the Educational Broadcasting Facilities Program to activate new stations and extend coverage

---

[7]A recent Area Population (AREAPOP) study performed for the Public Broadcasting Service shows that 87 percent of the population is within the reach of grade B VHF signals and grade A UHF signals. About 82 percent of the population is within reach of grade A UHF and VHF signals. (Within a station's total service area, grade A signals can be received satisfactorily 90 percent of the time at 70 percent of the homes, while grade B signals can be received satisfactorily 90 percent of the time at 50 percent of the homes.) The study also shows that about 50 percent of the population is capable of receiving two or more public television signals. The AREAPOP data are based on broadcast coverage of 273 public television stations and do not include coverage made possible by translators and cable television carriage of public television signals.

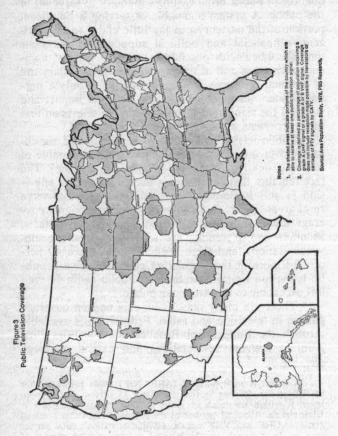

Figure 3
Public Television Coverage

Notes

1. The shaded areas indicate portions of the country which are able to receive at least one public television signal.

2. Coverage is defined as percentage of population receiving a Grade A and/or a Grade B VHF signal. Coverage does not include reception made possible by translators or carriage of PTV signals by CATV.

Source: Area Population Study, 1978, PBS Research.

Figure 7–3.

have been limited and subject to a variety of competing pressures and needs. Individual communities and some states have aggressively pursued establishment of public broadcasting service and provided significant funding support over the years; other communities and states have not. Government policies, technical considerations, and marketplace factors have also slowed the extension of public broadcasting service.

In short, while the number of public television and radio stations has grown appreciably since 1967, important coverage gaps still exist. The extension of public broadcasting service to the nation, an objective of the first Carnegie Commission and established as federal policy by the Public Broadcasting Act, has not been uniform nor can it be said to have been carefully planned.

A Plan to Extend Coverage

We believe that the Trust, in concert with other public broadcasting organizations and the appropriate agencies of the federal and state governments, must develop and articulate a clear and comprehensive long-term plan for extending public broadcasting service to the entire nation. We recommend that a specific plan be developed to extend at least minimum service to 90 percent of the population over the next five to seven years.

We do not envision massive capital expenditures to achieve this level of coverage, although it will require, for the next five to seven years, higher levels of funding than have previously been available. Precisely how coverage should be extended to those areas of the country now inadequately served should await the Trust's development of a comprehensive long-term plan for the extension of public broadcasting service to the entire nation. We think that several general principles should, however, guide development of such a plan.

New Stations

We encourage a cautious—even conservative—approach to the establishment of new conventional broad-

casting stations, particularly in television. We have seen
estimates from public broadcasting organizations of
the need for as many as 500 television stations by
1990 and over 800 such stations by the year 2000.
Public radio projects a need for a system of 1000 or
more radio stations. We are reluctant to support such
contentions for several reasons. The capital costs of
such an undertaking would be well above the $1 bil-
lion level. At the same time, although we possess no
crystal ball, we are persuaded that the local distribution
of many video information services will become more
dependent on nonbroadcast systems over the next two
decades. We note, too, that a major portion of public
television's coverage gap is in sparsely populated rural
and semirural areas where, particularly under our proposed funding plan, it may be difficult to generate
the necessary local funding to maintain viable conventional broadcasting stations.[8]

New public television and radio stations are necessary. PBS has identified some 60 stations in various
states of development which could be activated
over the next five years. The majority of those proposed stations would serve areas of the country presently without any public television station and would
extend broadcast coverage to well over 90 percent of
the population. Qualified public radio stations are now
being added at the rate of 10–15 a year and we estimate
that a total of 480 stations would extend public radio
service to the bulk of the population and provide multiple service in a great many cities as well. Chapter
VI describes in greater detail our recommendations for
public radio development. In general, our posture regarding activation of new television and radio stations
is to place the highest priority on the extension of initial service to the unserved areas of the country.
However, such a policy must be administered with
some flexibility, particularly in the case of public radio

---

[8]We are aware that several states with large rural populations
have done an excellent job of extending public broadcasting service
to most of the population through broadcasting even though the
costs of these efforts have been high. We are not inflexible on this
point, only cautious.

where the establishment of multiple service in communities is more justified. At the same time, we believe it would be wrong to deny a community the right to its own television or radio station where local initiative and support for the service is strong.

UHF Improvement

Another important element of any comprehensive development plan for public broadcasting is a serious effort to achieve maximum coverage and service efficiency from existing radio and television stations. We believe this objective should have a high priority in future system development programs. Coverage efficiency is particularly important in television, since a major factor in the gap between public television's theoretical and actual reach are the inadequacies of UHF television.[9] While true UHF/VHF parity may never be possible, we believe that a prudent approach to extending public television service demands an effort to achieve substantial improvement in UHF operations.

Two-thirds of all PBS stations operate in the UHF band, three-fourths of all public television stations activated since 1967 are UHF, and virtually all new public television stations will be UHF. It is estimated that if UHF television were to reach comparability with VHF, another 5 percent of the public might be reached by existing public television stations.

We are persuaded that there is no quick-fix, one-step solution to the UHF problem. Nor, in fact, can UHF improvement be viewed apart from significant national and international spectrum policy issues and the impact of government standards on manufacturers and the consumer. What is necessary is a sustained and multipronged effort aimed at improving all elements of the UHF television transmission/reception system.

---

[9] The chief shortcomings of UHF compared to VHF television are that UHF transmitters require much greater power and are less efficient. UHF propagation loss due to the presence of obstructions is more severe, UHF receiving antennas are generally less efficient, and the standard television set, particularly the tuner, is less efficient for UHF.

The responsibility for this effort lies with all parties concerned—the FCC, commercial and public broadcasters, and equipment manufacturers.

The FCC has taken a number of steps to promote UHF/VHF comparability. It has required a permanent UHF antenna on any set equipped with a permanent VHF antenna and has also ordered detent, or click-stop, tuners on all sets. The FCC recently ordered a phased reduction in the maximum allowable noise figures in UHF tuners, an action which could help reduce the "snow" commonly associated with UHF, and has also opened a new proceeding aimed at improving other aspects of UHF performance. Manufacturers have engineered improvements in UHF tuners and transmitting equipment which are enhancing overall UHF performance. New and more efficient receiver designs, such as the FCC's experimental "receiver of the future," may greatly increase receiver efficiency and consequently create incentives for manufacturers to engineer more efficient UHF equipment.

To a certain extent improvements associated with UHF transmission, receiving, set performance, and design involve cost and technical trade-offs which must be carefully weighed. For example, while increased UHF transmitting power clearly improves UHF reception, the increased energy costs can pose serious problems. Improvements in set design can result in higher costs for consumers and may affect other important operating characteristics. These factors must be taken into consideration.

Nevertheless, given our strong desire for enhancing the public's access to public broadcasting and minimizing capital investment in new conventional television stations, we are persuaded that a sustained and carefully planned effort to bring UHF television into relative parity deserves high priority.

Alternative Delivery

We believe that the Trust should consider use of alternative broadcast and nonbroadcast systems as a means of extending service to the public. The cost of extending public television and radio service to the last

10 percent of the population by means of conventional broadcasting will in all likelihood be prohibitively high. We conclude that far more attention must be given to the prospects for extending public television and public radio coverage through cable television, translators, and low-power broadcasting.

The cable television industry is developing an extensive network of satellite earth stations and it is estimated that as many as 1500 earth stations may be in operation by late 1980. Although there are technical and programming rights questions to be resolved, it is entirely possible that some cable systems may receive public broadcasting programs from a satellite and distribute them locally.

In recent years Congress and the FCC have shown a willingness to reduce regulatory restrictions on translator operation, and the FCC currently has under study a number of additional changes in regulations affecting translator operations. We think translators, in concert with satellite distribution, offer additional possibilities for coverage extension that should be explored. With satellite distribution of programming, it is possible to contemplate development of a class of low-power broadcast stations intermediate between translators and broadcast stations, with modest program origination capabilities, able to serve rural areas or to distribute special programming in urban areas.

The FCC has recently launched a wide-ranging study of the future role of low-power television, including translators, to increase diversity of service in both rural and urban areas. The results of this proceeding may well suggest additional approaches, and we urge the FCC to give specific consideration to the importance of creating broader public access to public broadcasting.

We recognize that our objective of rapid extension of coverage is ambitious and that financial, regulatory, and marketplace hurdles will have to be cleared to achieve this goal. The notion of anything less than full local broadcast service for all communities of a certain size, for example, was once considered a radical departure from our fundamental policies for broadcasting. Yet as important as the localism principle is, it has also served to deny some members of the public access to any public broadcasting service, service in part made possible by tax dollars.

We suggest that while our primary objective is the extension of both local and national service to *all* of the public, the addition of even partial service via cable television, satellite, translators, or low-power broadcasting is also a valid objective and may well ultimately stimulate development of full service.

We conclude that all public broadcasting organizations—and the appropriate governmental bodies—must work together to develop a plan for the rapid extension of service to the American public. We recommend that the prime responsibility for developing this program be that of the Trust. We believe, that with appropriate legislative guidance and direction to extend public broadcasting service to all of the American people through the most efficient and effective means available, the Trust is the most appropriate organization to direct a public broadcasting development program.

We believe that annual matching funds of $50 million over a five- to seven-year period would, in substantial part, complete establishment of the television and radio systems and extend service to over 90 percent of the population. That level of funding, in conjunction with increased station operating funds, would also provide for the necessary general improvement of existing public broadcasting stations. Once the basic coverage objective is achieved, we believe that the Educational Broadcasting Facilities Program should be eliminated and replaced by either a special maintenance and upgrade program administered by the Trust or through increased station operating grants.

As important as the Educational Broadcasting Facilities Program has been to public broadcasting's development, it was never intended to be a program in perpetuity. After basic service extension objectives have been achieved, we believe that expenditure of funds for improved facilities should mainly come from station operating funds, thus forcing stations to make the hard, but healthy, choices of allocating funds between competing needs.

Research and Development

> We recommend that public broadcasting develop a stronger, ongoing, and more fully integrated research and development capability to assist the system in taking advantage of new technology to meet public needs.

During the past decade public broadcasting has played a modest but significant role in developing and applying new communications technologies and techniques to improve traditional broadcasting service and to create new services aimed at meeting public needs. We believe that such activities are an essential component of the public system's broad mandate for public service. We are convinced that public broadcasting must strengthen its ability to operate on the frontiers of new technology if it is to fully serve the American people.

To assist in carrying out this function, we recommend creation of a small, flexible, adequately funded division within the Program Services Endowment to act as a catalyst to the development of new services and the application of technology in ways appropriate to public broadcasting's mission and objectives. The Endowment should conduct research, encourage demonstration projects, and assist in the implementation of new services and techniques. The accelerating rate of technological innovation and development in the telecommunications sector makes imperative constant monitoring and overseeing of telecommunications. In both private and public sectors the range of telecommunications experimentation, research, and new product development is impressive. Likewise, long-standing regulatory policies in the telecommunications sphere are now under scrutiny, offering the possibility of even more widespread innovation.

We believe that a decentralized public broadcasting system with a high degree of local autonomy will benefit greatly from this centralized research and monitoring capacity. As licensees face the complexities and challenges of telecommunications development in the 1980s, this strengthened capacity will be an essential resource and guide. Public broadcasters must be aware of and plan for innovations in both broadcast and non-broadcast technologies. They cannot ignore developments in the commercial sector. Public broadcasters must constantly be alert to opportunities to apply and reshape technological advances in new and unique ways.

Second, we recommend that this research and development division of the Endowment act as a catalyst to telecommunications development and service innovation through a program of grants to stations and other public telecommunications entities. In general, we envision two areas of funding activity. We think the division should reserve a portion of its funds for encouraging demonstration programs and experiments by individual stations or groups of stations. Grants can be used to encourage development of teletext or interactive educational services. Such grants may be awarded periodically on a competitive basis. Additionally, the largest portion of funds would be reserved for matching grants to implement or make operational services or techniques of an innovative nature. These grants would be awarded to individual stations to develop local services or to groups of licensees for services of a regional or national scope.

A Research Strategy

We wish to stress several guiding principles for this strengthened and more integrated research and development capability. The capability we seek is not one of basic or primary high-risk research and development. Even at the increased funding levels we recommend, public broadcasting could not hope to devote the funds necessary to carry out such technological development. Nor would it be an appropriate use of tax dollars. We have no doubt that the commercial sector will continue to play the major role in basic research and development in telecommunications, particularly with respect to production, and transmission equipment and systems. Yet just as clearly our history demonstrates that marketplace considerations sometimes do not encourage the full development and application of techniques and innovations which benefit all sectors of the public. Removed from the dictates of the marketplace, public broadcasting can play an important leadership role in bringing the benefits of new technology to the public. We see the Endowment and public broadcasting, alert to new applications made possible by developing technology, offering alternatives, acting with flexibility and speed, to shape and apply telecommunications to meet human needs which the marketplace ignores.

We believe public broadcasting's orientation in this area should be toward information and software, not hardware. We think the primary concern of the research and development division is the relationship between developing technology and programming and services. It seems clear that over time there will be a closer connection between the hardware and transmission systems made possible by new technology, and the video and audio material delivered through those systems. Just as the line between data processing and telecommunications is becoming blurred, so are new production techniques and distribution systems converging.

It is in this area that we believe public broadcasting, with its orientation toward programming and services, can make a vital contribution over the next decade. The technology which makes possible teletext services, interactive systems, and wide-band multichannel delivery, for example, is only one part of the service equation. What programs and services are to be delivered with these new technologies? What standards of quality are to be maintained? How will these programs and services benefit people? We suggest that these are not only appropriate concerns for the public system; they are essential concerns.

Finally, we do not mean to imply that all technological research and development in public broadcasting will or should flow solely from the Endowment. While we believe there is great benefit to be derived from a centralized research and development activity within public broadcasting, we expect that individual licensees and their national and regional organizations will continue research and development activities. We urge the Endowment to coordinate its funding activities with public broadcasting organizations and the appropriate government agencies to avoid unnecessary duplication. We anticipate that programs for telecommunications demonstrations and experiments, administered by such agencies as the Department of Commerce, the Department of Health, Education, and Welfare, and the National Science Foundation will continue and that the Endowment's programs, more broadly directed to public uses of telecommunications, will be an appropriate supplement to those efforts.

Funding Research and Development

We recommend that at the full funding level described in Chapter IV the Endowment allocate approximately $10 million annually for research and development. Approximately 10–15 percent of the budget could be reserved for demonstration and experimental projects, awarded on a competitive basis. The remaining funds would be distributed annually in implementation and development grants. Under such an approach the Endowment would be capable of supporting a number of local initiatives as well as one or two large projects on a regional or national scale each year.[10]

We recommend that development grants be awarded on a matching basis in order to ensure that prospective projects have community support and a strong chance of continued funding.

---

[10]An example of a national project is implementation of a nationwide closed captioning system for hearing impaired viewers. The Public Broadcasting Service captioning system, which is expected to be in operation in 1979, has been under development since 1973 and has been supported principally by HEW funds.

However, we think the Endowment should have the flexibility to make grants for the full cost of the project if circumstances so warrant. We also believe that eligibility for grants should be broadly defined so long as the project has a direct relationship to development of a service or program to be delivered by a public broadcasting entity.

In sum we find that the creation of a new and more effective public broadcasting research and development capability will be vital if public broadcasting is to play a central role in the new telecommunications environment. Public broadcasting can be justifiably proud of its past initiatives in this area, and we in no way minimize those accomplishments. Much remains to be done, and we believe a more formalized and coordinated, and better-financed research and development capability can be a vital force for both public broadcasting and the American people.

Telecommunications Development

> We recommend that public broadcasting develop a more flexible approach to the delivery of programs and services to the public.

Public broadcasting, as the name implies, is today primarily a broadcast production and distribution system. We believe that if public broadcasting is to play the necessary role in the American telecommunications system we envision, it must move beyond conventional broadcasting distribution. We foresee many public broadcasting stations evolving into community or public telecommunications centers employing a range of distribution means to deliver various programs and services.

Broadcasting cannot ignore the inexorable march of technology. Broadcasting as a distribution technology is a profoundly powerful and vital instrument in our society. Over the next decade the broadcast mode of delivery will continue to be the primary means for distributing programs and services. But just as clearly broadcasting has its limitations. We are persuaded that in time the major thrust of telecommunications development will be away from passive, one-way, mass audience distribution and toward specialization, individual control and selectivity, and interaction.

Public broadcasting's responsibilities are far more complex than those of commercial broadcasting, with its drive for the mass audience. The new technologies and developing distribution alternatives, such as cable television, videodiscs, and cassettes, seem particularly well suited to helping public broadcasting meet its manifold objectives. This broadened and more flexible approach to the delivery of programs and services to the home, the school, and other institutions will benefit the public. A more flexible delivery capacity can expand audience programming options, provide for greater listener and viewer convenience, and make possible programming and services aimed at smaller audiences with specialized interests and tastes.

Public broadcasting has shown imagination and foresight in developing a multichannel national distribution capability via domestic satellite. Yet without a flexible and efficient local distribution capability the public may not realize the full benefit of this enhanced national distribution capacity.

A Developmental Policy

We recognize the significance of a telecommunications development policy for public broadcasting. However, we do not suggest that in the near future all public broadcasting stations can or should be transformed into fully developed community telecommunications centers. Indeed, we have difficulty with representations made to us that all public broadcasting stations *must* become telecommunications centers for the design and delivery of a broad range of information, education, social, medical, or government services.

Such an arbitrary and all-encompassing recommendation would strain the human and financial capacities of even the largest and most well-developed public broadcasting stations or state systems, inevitably detracting from the station's paramount programming role. Likewise, such a policy would, in most cases, require new and substantial planning and coordination to deal with the myriad problems associated with social service delivery and regulation.

It is not at all clear at this point that public broadcasting is the most appropriate vehicle for the delivery of a wide range of government services. Nor is it apparent what roles the commercial telecommunications sector and developing nonprofit public-service organizations will play in these areas. With respect to the delivery of government services, for example, while the Commission is supportive of efforts to provide the public necessary and useful services, we would be concerned about a role for public broadcasting which, in the eyes of the public, cast the system as a governmental telecommunications system.

While we advocate and underscore the importance of public telecommunications development, we also urge public broadcasters to approach such development carefully, with well-defined objectives and rigorous planning.

We expect that the extent of each licensee's evolution toward a more flexible telecommunications role will depend on many factors. Of primary concern will be the community's need and support for the programs and services to be delivered by nonbroadcast means. The availability of services through other private or public systems, such as cable television, closed-circuit broadcasting, and developing nonprofit service organizations will also be of consequence. Clearly, a station's funding base will influence the extent to which this broadened role is possible.

We are not recommending a major new investment by public broadcasting in distribution systems and facilities in order to take advantage of the developing technologies. Rather we anticipate more cooperative use of existing and developing public and private distribution systems and facilities wherever possible. A variety of lease and sharing arrangements already exist within public broadcasting and between public broadcasters and segments of both the commercial and nonprofit sectors. We believe that, carefully planned, such arrangements can result in a minimum investment in hardware, preserving funds for needed programming.

The application of alternative distribution systems such as cable television, cassettes and videodiscs, Instructional Television Fixed Service, and other microwave and common carrier systems seems particularly well suited to public broadcasting's responsibilities in the area of instruction and education. In varying degrees these distribution and storage systems offer distinct advantages over broadcasting. Instructional and educational services can be targeted to users in the home, school, and office. Teachers and students can make more flexible use of educational programs and materials. Two-way audio and even video interaction between teacher and student becomes possible. At the same time, alternative delivery of limited audience educational material can make available more broadcast time for programs aimed at a general audience, a function more suited to the broadcast mode of distribution.

We are well aware that significant barriers exist to the full application of new broadcast and nonbroadcast technologies by public broadcasters. For example, it would be a mistake to assume that utilization of new technologies will necessarily be less expensive than broadcast distribution, particularly in the short term. Further, the availability of a particular technology does not necessarily mean that it is the most effective means to deliver the services envisioned. We expect that careful planning, research, and experimentation will be necessary before the most appropriate distribution configurations are realized. Demonstration projects and experiments funded by the Endowment should help provide information upon which to make such judgments. Likewise, the full availability of media such as cable television, videodisc, videocassette, and microwave does and will vary greatly and will depend significantly on a combination of regulatory, marketing, and software factors generally beyond the control of public broadcasting.[11] Planning and flexibility will be essential in such a fluid telecommunications environment.

Extended Program Availability

A serious barrier to the wider and more effective exposure and use of public television programs that become possible through more flexible dissemination approaches is the complex contractual and copyright limitations presently placed on the use of such programs. In general, use of national public television programming is limited by union contracts with producers, stipulations in individual talent contracts, and copyright restrictions if traditional copyright exemptions are not applicable.

Typically a public television producer obtains broadcast distribution rights for up to four releases within a three-year period. In addition, limited off-air recording and use of public television programs by schools and colleges are permitted. For additional payment, public broadcasters usually obtain audiovisual rights (distribution of programs on cassette or film for institutional use by libraries, schools, etc.) and foreign distribution rights. Depending upon a variety of factors, rights to employ cable television distribution, direct nonbroadcast distribution to the home, and other nonbroadcast means are not obtained because of the cost of securing such rights and the administrative difficulties involved in obtaining copyright clearances.

It is necessary to balance the rights of creators and performers to fair recompense for their work with the broad public interest considerations of wider and more effective distribution of public broadcasting programs. We are persuaded that in order for the public to benefit fully from the programs and services of the public system, public broadcasters will have to devote great-

---

[11]The issue of cable television's responsibility to provide access to public, educational, and other users is now before the courts. Whether or not cable television is ultimately required by law or regulation to provide such access, we express the strong hope that the marriage of cable's distribution capability and public broadcasting's programming resources will be pursued by both, through contract, franchise agreement, or other appropriate arrangements.

er attention and resources to these issues. It may be necessary to create new administrative mechanisms and to more clearly focus responsibility for efforts to obtain broader availability of programming. We think that the Endowment should launch this effort with a study of current and developing contractual arrangements and practices, the impact of the new copyright law, and the adequacy of existing mechanisms in facilitating the widest possible availability of public broadcasting programming to the public.

Public Telecommunication Models

The expanding public telecommunications role for public broadcasting over the next decade is, we think, a logical extension of developments now taking place. About a third of all public television licensees distribute program material by videocassettes directly to schools and other educational institutions. Stations in San Diego, Spokane, Toledo, Cleveland, and many other places supplement broadcast offerings with Instructional Television Fixed Service or cable television distribution. These are important first steps by public broadcasting in broadening its approach to the delivery of programs, and we think the experiences of such stations can offer valuable guidance to public broadcasters.

Several public broadcasting operations in particular offer good models for public telecommunications development. With strong support from the state, the South Carolina ETV Network has developed one of the nation's most sophisticated and extensive telecommunications system. South Carolina ETV produces and delivers public television and radio programming to virtually the entire state. It also employs multichannel closed-circuit television to interconnect 250 secondary schools as well as 130 hospitals, police departments, universities, and technical centers. The radio network provides both general and instructional programming as well as SCA services for the blind. South Carolina ETV is also exploring integration of commercial cable television operations into the total system to expand audience viewing options.

A different public telecommunications model is the West Central Illinois Educational Telecommunications Corporation, also known as Convocom, headquartered in Springfield and not yet operational. Convocom, a consortium of community-licensed public television stations and educational institutions, is arranging a multifaceted production and distribution system employing television, radio, Instructional Television Fixed Service, common carrier microwave, cable television, and videocassette. Scheduled to begin operating in late 1979, Convocom is funded by diverse private and public sources. Of particular interest in the Convocom system is its regional approach, the extensive public/private sharing of production and distribution resources, and the establishment of a public nonprofit planning, coordinating, and administrative infrastructure to integrate existing production modes and to facilitate development and use of new production and distribution technologies.

In conclusion, it is essential that public broadcasters begin to develop a more flexible approach to the dissemination of their product and services. While we are fully cognizant of the difficulties involved in developing a more versatile local distribution capability, our attention to these difficulties is not and should not be seen as a reason for delaying this effort. Policies are being developed, distribution systems are emerging, and patterns are being established which will to a significant degree determine the future availability of and application of telecommunications facilities and services. Public radio and television should be centrally involved in this development, playing a major role in tapping the unique capabilities of such systems to benefit the public.

We do not minimize the importance of broadcast distribution. The issue is not one of broadcast delivery as opposed to nonbroadcast distribution. Rather, we think public broadcasting's responsibility is to develop a distribution configuration which makes wider, more effective, and more efficient access to its product possible for all segments of the public.

VIII

Telecommunications and Learning

Television and radio have a singular impact upon us. Broadcasting's reach and sensory immediacy—the form and nature of its engagement—render it an intrinsically powerful instrument for learning. The statistics are familiar. Sixty-four percent of Americans rely on television as their principal source of news. The average high-school graduate has spent nearly 50 percent more time in front of the television set than in the classroom. On a winter Saturday morning, when most programming is targeted to children, the television set is on in a quarter of the nation's homes.

We witness history on television and radio—the celebration of our bicentennial, a President resigning, the war in Vietnam. Broadcasting's capacity to instruct and influence is used daily by politicians, religious groups, and advertisers. And yet, despite the power and ubiquity of the broadcast media, a troubling doubt persists of their realized effectiveness as educational tools. In spite of several notable successes in educational television, we have grown increasingly uneasy about the ability of our children to think and write clearly. Is there some connection between the vast amounts of time young people spend watching television or listening to radio and the conceptual fuzziness that their teachers seem to have identified during the last decade?

There are many reasons why America has not yet

fully enlisted television and radio to assist in instructing our children, in broadening educational opportunity, and in stimulating the habit of lifelong learning. Commercial broadcasters have not viewed education as more than peripherally interesting, and the economics of commercial broadcasting reinforce such attitudes. Our educational system has become exceedingly complex as it has attempted to stay abreast of the explosion of knowledge. Bureaucracies have sprung up that tend to suppress innovation, or at least to assure that it is bungled. Broadcast instruction is easily ensnared in such bureaucratic arrangements. Moreover, American schools are constructed on a tradition of local control, while media by their nature tend toward centralized management. Funding for educational and instructional television from local government and private sources has been very uneven; some localities have committed large resources, others nothing. Some educators resist the idea that television or radio can be a valuable tool in learning. A few consider television as a competitive threat. Many teachers have not been trained to use these media as part of their professional equipment.

However valid or understandable may be these and other factors that have limited the role of broadcasting in education, two facts remain clear. Television and radio have great unused potential for learning, and new technologies are on the verge of greatly enhancing this potential.

We believe it is time to take a fresh look at the role of television and radio in American education. The link between public broadcasting and education is strong. One-third of teachers nationwide use television regularly in their classrooms. The typical public television station devotes about 40 percent of its broadcast schedule to instructional programs and the two major children's series, *Sesame Street* and *The Electric Company,* and countless additional hours to programs of broader educational appeal. Much of the funding for public broadcasting comes from states and other sources —for broadly educational purposes. A majority of the public radio and television stations are licensed to universities, school boards, or states.

We believe it is time to launch new efforts to tap the power of broadcasting and the new telecommunications media for learning. Our investigation during the past year persuades us that public telecommunications will play a major role in education. To us, the question is not whether television and radio can teach, but how they are to be best used for learning. The issue is not whether public broadcasting has a responsibility in education, but how best to carry out that responsibility.

Our proposals for a strengthened and adequately funded public telecommunications system are based upon this significant role for education. We believe that stations should have the prime responsibility for the effort, through their own local programs and services, and especially by pooling funds for regional and national activities. The linkage between stations and educators at the local and regional levels is important in ensuring responsiveness to local educational needs and local control over curricula. At the same time, we believe it to be essential that the system build a strong national component that will finance serious research on the functional characteristics of television and radio as instructional tools and will also finance programs to test and demonstrate this potential.

Educational Television and Radio in Perspective

To suggest that America has not fully exploited broadcasting's potential for education is not to argue that this potential has been ignored. First with radio and later television, broadcasters, educators, and government officials have attempted to capitalize on the power of the media to enlighten. As early as the 1950s a variety of studies demonstrated that students could learn as well from television as from conventional classroom instruction. The shortage of teachers at that time, as well as fascination with the power of the new medium, spurred interest in television's ability to teach. Among the first concerns of proponents of educational television was the identification and development of methods for distributing instructional programming. Initially this involved the use of closed-circuit television.

Later it was extended to broadcasting, or open-circuit television, through such pioneering efforts as the Chicago Television College. During the 1950s and 1960s universities, states, school boards, and other educational institutions obtained noncommercial broadcasting licenses. Thus began educational programming for in-school use and university outreach. Since television was expensive and the number of stations available was limited, other educators embraced special distribution systems such as Instructional Television Fixed Service (ITFS), a private microwave service. More recently, cable television and even communications satellites have been used to distribute educational programming.

During these early years, educational authorities invested large sums in educational hardware—television and radio stations, ITFS systems, and classroom equipment. Not until much later was the problem of software, the quality of the educational programs actually transmitted, seriously confronted.

The appearance and success of *Sesame Street* in 1968 had a profound impact on educational television. To date, *Sesame Street* is perhaps the most successful program designed for children's learning. It uses the production techniques of quality commercial television to create appealing programs that meet instructional goals. Before a single program was produced, a detailed curriculum was developed, including a well-defined set of educational objectives. Before any production segment was accepted as part of a finished program, it was tested on a group of children from the target audience. For the first time, educational researchers and professional producers worked closely together in creating a television series that was both instructive and entertaining. Today *Sesame Street* is entering its tenth season, has won numerous awards, and is watched so extensively that its per-viewer cost is only about 1¢ per episode, an extraordinary bargain.

Before *Sesame Street,* most educational television programs involved inexpensive production techniques, talking heads, and little imagination. These programs were designed to meet specific curricular objectives, but there was no research base to guide the production art.

This new program for preschoolers became a standard of excellence and a point of departure for subsequent work. One important result was that the professional and financial resources required to produce programs like *Sesame Street* forced the production of comparable educational and instructional television programs to become more and more centralized. In 1964 about 56 percent of all instructional television programs were produced locally, whereas in 1976 the figure had dropped to 20 percent. Highly professional production organizations like Children's Television Workshop, the originator of *Sesame Street,* appeared and the federal government, which had supported the program, became more heavily involved in funding children's television programs.[1]

In the eyes of some educators not all of this material was ideal for in-school instruction. Moreover, they could not develop alternatives of comparable quality for local use because economies of scale, possible in spreading high production costs over many viewers, were unachievable at the local level. One response to this problem was the creation of the Agency for Instructional Television (AIT). Composed of state and Canadian provincial educational officials, AIT, through consortium ventures, has produced a number of high-quality instructional television series, including *Ripples, Inside/Out,* and *All About You.* One factor contributing to the success of the AIT series is that programs are created in direct response to curriculum needs identified by states and provinces that fund the production. This involvement of educators in program development appears to be crucial to the ultimate success of any instructional radio or television series, because broadcast instruction is not an end in itself but a component of an educational process that also encompasses both the classroom and the library.

At local, state, and regional levels, other success-

---

[1]Under authority of the Special Projects Act and the Emergency School Aid Act, the U. S. Office of Education has spent some $70 million on children's television programming, most of it distributed on public television.

ful instructional series have been created—some for local use only, but most intended for wider distribution.[2]

The Children's Television Workshop, the independent production center that originated *Sesame Street,* also created *The Electric Company,* a series designed to teach reading skills to primary-grade children. First broadcast in 1971, it continues to be the instructional program most used by the classroom teacher. Its wide use has been based, in part, on its acknowledged effectiveness. For example, after extensive use of the series by every teacher in a Lincoln Heights, Ohio, elementary school for one year, third graders scored five months higher in vocabulary than comparative scores in the third grade the year before. The mean score in comprehension was three months higher than the previous year's record, and second graders at the school made equally large gains. Such data are limited in applicability, and rather weak by the highest standards of educational research. But they constitute a precious form of empirical analysis suggesting how production decisions can be made on the basis of knowledge not preconception.

Other efforts to produce quality instructional programming have been led by state networks, funded by some states as part of their commitment to education. In Mississippi, for example, there is a network of eight television stations reaching every corner of the state. Mississippi Educational Television broadcasts over 100 hours weekly. About 40 hours are instructional lessons, principally for primary-grade classrooms. There is also a wide range of self-help programs dealing with such diverse topics as professional training, cooking skills, Mississippi history, and motivating children to

---

[2]The commercial networks and individual stations have periodically created noteworthy educational programs including such valuable series as *Call It Macaroni*, produced by Westinghouse Broadcasting, and ABC's *After School Specials.* Unfortunately, high-quality educational programs appear infrequently on commercial broadcasting and the system as a whole is unwilling or unable to devote significant resources to exploiting television's potential for learning.

write. Similar networks exist in about fifteen other states, most notably Kentucky, Maryland, Nebraska, and South Carolina.

Television is also an important instructional tool in adult education. Using state and regional funds, in 1972 the Kentucky Authority for Educational Television designed and produced a series to aid adults preparing for the high-school equivalency examination. Now in use in 40 states, the series is intended chiefly for adults studying independently at home.

Television has also been used for formal instruction at the post secondary-school level. Since the fall of 1970, for example, over 225,000 people have enrolled in college courses on television as part of an outreach effort by 35 community colleges in southern California. Broadcast courses include consumer law, child development, psychology, and personal finance. Students have come from the diverse age groups and cultural backgrounds that characterize the interested general public in the Los Angeles metropolitan area served by the community colleges. A public television station, KOCE, licensed to community colleges in Orange County, has taken a leading role in developing programs for this effort. It has produced several programs, including a major series on child development. It has also led the effort to use general interest programs distributed nationwide by PBS as vehicles for formal learning. Programs such as *Ascent of Man* and *The Adams Chronicles* have now been used by scores of educational institutions as the centerpieces for credit courses in the history of science and American history. Approximately 50,000 students throughout the nation received course credits in conjunction with *The Adams Chronicles*. KOCE is currently working with the producers of a new series on man and space to see that this program can be used for formal education as well as general enlightenment.

Television also has a wide variety of instructional applications for other specialized groups within communities. A satellite networking experiment in Washington, Alaska, Montana, and Idaho (WAMI) has offered a solution to a lack of facilities for medical education in the Northwest. The WAMI demonstration was designed to test whether television transmitted via satellite could be used to train medical students by substituting for face-to-face contact in clinical counseling activities. The experiment seems to have been successful.

A wide spectrum of programs for adults is provided by the South Carolina Educational Television Authority. Along with extensive service to children in schools, the authority provides a full course of instruction leading to a master's degree in business, and programs for teachers, doctors, managers, and industrial workers to develop their skills and expertise.

Public radio's role in education has been less significant, but successful educational radio programs have been developed. Begun in 1972 at WGBH radio in Boston, *The Spider's Web,* a series of 30-minute programs of stories, interviews, poetry, and folk songs, is now heard on over a hundred noncommercial stations. The content of each program is broad enough to appeal to children and adults. There have been numerous efforts to develop special programs for the aged and the blind on public radio. Books, poetry, newspapers, and other reading materials are offered for listening.

The creation of successful instructional radio and television series has taught the industry several important lessons. It has demonstrated that television and radio can be used successfully to teach certain skills and concepts. Further, successes have occurred most often when educational researchers and professional producers work closely together from the inception of a program idea until it has been produced and evaluated for effectiveness. Experience has also taught that most programs designed for wide-scale use must be expertly produced and of high quality if they are to capture and hold the attention of the viewer.

But despite this catalog of successes, there is an evident shortage of quality instructional programming. Most telling is that the flagship programs, *Sesame Street* and *The Electric Company,* are now several years old. Since the introduction of *Sesame Street,* there have been few new innovative instructional programs to continue the analysis of programming concepts attractive to preschool and primary-school children. Of even greater concern is the fact that no programs capable of replacing these important pioneering efforts are being planned for public broadcasting. Adolescents and adults are still waiting for a *Sesame Street*-type breakthrough.

Significantly greater resources—both financial and creative—must be devoted to producing innovative and conceptually sophisticated instructional programming. The role of the broadcast media in continuing education and lifelong learning must be developed. And new technologies offering the potential greatly to aid or greatly to simplify the learning process must be exploited. For instance, it is not clear to the Commission that broadcast technology will continue to prevail over alternative means such as videocassette and videodisc equipment in delivering educational programming to tomorrow's schools and homes. The new technology appears to be far more flexible and perhaps less expensive, but appropriate delivery systems must be developed and tested.

A Commitment to Telecommunications for Learning

We recommend that public broadcasting renew its commitment to provide programs and services which help fulfill the promise of telecommunications to aid in the education of all Americans throughout their lives. The major responsibility for this effort rests with the stations.

Throughout our investigation of public broadcasting—and as we contemplate the role of the public system during the next decade—we have been acutely conscious of the growing tension within the system between those who perceive its mission as narrowly "educational" and those who see it as a means of enhancing the public culture. Public radio and television, of course, began as an educational outreach, and even today the majority of noncommercial licenses are held by educational institutions and organizations. During the past ten years, in major part because of the recommendations of the first Carnegie Commission, public broadcasting has moved strongly toward a more public role. Nonetheless, educational and instructional programs and services are a significant part of public broadcasting. Televised lessons designed for formal classroom instruction are a significant element of most public television stations' schedules. The typical station devotes 21 percent of its air time to instructional programs for classroom use, another 16 percent to *Sesame Street* and *The Electric Company,* and many additional hours to such broadly educational programs as *Nova, National Geographic Specials,* and *Theater in America,* as well as cooking, gardening, and sports instruction. Public radio has traditionally devoted far less of its air time to instruction.

Whatever tension exists within public broadcasting over its instructional role has resulted from the system's inability to generate the resources necessary to meet both educational and cultural objectives. We believe that the substantially increased funding we have recommended for public broadcasting will go a long way toward resolving this dilemma. We believe that the ultimate decision about the mix of educational, instructional, and more broadly public services provided by public broadcasting is a decision which can only be made at the local level. This is true, of course, about all programming and service decisions in public broadcasting, but we believe it to be especially true of instruction and education. We harbor, in this country, an acute sensitivity about local control of education. Educational and instructional needs vary greatly and are often unique from community to community and state to state. The Commission believes that the stations and the communities they serve are the only qualified judges of local educational needs. They should, however, be able to choose from a variety of high-quality, nationally produced, thoroughly researched educational programming ideas to meet such needs.

Fundamentally, we believe that just as it is not

possible to contemplate a public telecommunications system that is solely an instructional enterprise, so it is not possible to argue for a public system that does not take seriously a responsibility to develop telecommunications for learning. We regard each station as having the responsibility to carve out for itself an appropriate role in this area. Today it may be by providing in-school instructional programs during the daytime hours, although surely during the next decade it will be possible and perhaps necessary to employ more efficient and effective methods to assist in the education of our children. Or it may be through a more serious effort to apply telecommunications to meet the rapidly increasing appetite for lifelong learning. Or it may be in the provision of general enrichment programming which can be utilized in formal or informal education settings. The approach taken by stations may involve the use of FM subchannels for educational programs directed to smaller audiences, the use of cable television channels, or ITFS microwave service, and perhaps ultimately teletext services.

Thus we expect that stations will develop a wide range of educational and instructional services that fulfill the needs of their communities. Many of these needs will also face other stations, so they will often band together to finance program production, thus providing more effective, more carefully researched programs at a significantly lower cost per station.

We also expect that a significant number of stations will be able to produce local programs fulfilling unique instructional needs in their communities. Despite the experience of *Sesame Street* and other national programs, it is not certain that all educational programming must be costly. Experiments at Stanford University with tutored videotape instruction (TVI) for graduate students suggest that low-cost, small-format programs, when presented in an atmosphere that maximizes student interaction in the learning process, can be successful. Other experiments, in which teacher/student interaction was achieved via two-way cable television, have yielded similar results and deserve further exploration.

Another major step to increasing effectiveness while achieving economy is to maintain a library of quality instructional programs. As a station encounters a special need, it may find useful programs already produced and available through such a library service.

The increased flexibility afforded public television and radio by multichannel satellite delivery also makes possible greater sharing of resources to produce and distribute educational programming on a state or regional basis. Increased funds for stations will permit greater pooling of resources for such regional and national efforts.

Our emphasis on the importance of strong local determination in shaping a station's educational and instructional mission requires strong support. State and local governments must pursue this mission by providing not only hardware but also resources for programming. Telecommunications configurations such as those developed in South Carolina, Nebraska, and other states are vehicles through which important educational and instructional services—in-school instruction, continuing education, at-home learning—can be delivered.

A renewed and serious effort to realize the potential of television and radio for learning is thus primarily a matter of local initiative. Yet there are several areas which we think can benefit greatly by the direct involvement of the Program Services Endowment.

How Can Radio and Television Teach Best?

We recommend that the Program Services Endowment initiate research aimed at identifying and developing how and what television and radio can teach best.

Government agencies, universities, and foundations have supported significant research on the use of radio and television for learning. Hundreds of studies on subjects ranging from the use of television to television's role in lifelong learning have been completed during the last decade. Although this research has been important in demonstrating some of the potential of radio and television for learning, it has also raised basic questions about the effectiveness of these media and their role in learning, in the classroom and in other settings by persons of all ages.

The apparent relation between the use of television and radio and the declining literacy in young people is of the utmost consequence. The average score on the Scholastic Aptitude Test, taken by high-school students seeking admission to college, has declined over the last 14 years. A similar decline in the ability of children between 13 and 17 to write acceptable English has been noted. On the other hand, a recent upturn in measured reading ability among elementary-school children has been seen by some as attributable to widespread viewing of *Sesame Street* and other high-quality children's programming. The presumptive relation between substantial television and radio usage and the ability to read and write needs serious study and careful analysis. It suggests a sociological phenomenon of major importance in which the conceptual skills of a population are altered or eroded over a period of years in the manner of the sea working on shore-based rocks. Does it happen? If it happens, is it due primarily to the passivity of the medium, or the nature of the programs viewed? There are many unanswered questions.

Research suggests that television does not adjust well to individual differences among viewers and tends to encourage passive forms of learning. The circumstances under which educational programming is received by an intended audience is a vital matter that needs far greater understanding. This area is particularly important in view of the development of new technologies such as two-way cable television, providing the feedback essential to all forms of learning. Videocassettes and videodiscs can further enhance flexibility and interaction in televised learning.

We have been impressed by some preliminary efforts to isolate the special strengths of television for learning. In the past, proponents of televised instruction have emphasized the richness of information television can communicate in history or science, where reading conveys little of the color or detail provided by visual images. Completed research has demonstrated that television can teach. The question we must address now is: How and what can television teach best?

Researchers have already identified a number of television's special attributes. Remarkably, it can teach processes by clever use of slow motion or fast motion techniques. This can be used to reveal the functioning of an internal-combustion engine, or the processes of growth in plants. Television's concreteness aids in establishing definitions and in illustrating specific forms of problem solving. It is effective as a teacher of values and attitudes. The nonpunitive, nonjudgmental character of television can enhance casual learning, and can help individuals with learning difficulties.

Television also has great capacity to take the viewer to places he could never visit in reality. The television program *The Incredible Machine* takes the camera inside the human body and examines the functions of various organs. The *Nova* series has excelled for a number of years in bringing intriguing scientific concepts to American television audiences by using close-ups, magnification, time sequencing, juxtaposition of sight and sound, and other sophisticated forms of editing.

Using the techniques of slow motion, freeze frame, and instant replay, television has excellent potential for teaching most abstract concepts.

One of the most fundamental research questions needing explanation is what differences exist between learning from the linear, symbolic patterns of print and the spoken word, and the simultaneous, iconic, observational patterns of the visual media. Greater understanding of these differences will enable educational researchers and producers to maximize the instructional effectiveness of television in new program development.

While research on these and other fundamental

questions will necessarily be expensive and slow, effective programs can be made before all questions have been answered conclusively. Producers and researchers must work together closely to design and test components of programs in order to assure that they achieve their objectives.

Radio is also well suited to teaching, although there appears to be considerably less research on the subject. Like print, it can create an environment in which the imagination has great play. And, like television, radio can illustrate a variety of concepts and attitudes exceedingly well. At least one study has indicated that radio and television, when used properly, may be equally effective teaching devices. However, neither a radio nor a televised program can be fully effective in isolation. Each program must be carefully researched and produced as part of an integrated learning situation. The teacher must use the program to stimulate, provoke, and motivate the students, and to illuminate ancillary reading materials. Television and radio can never be more than invited guests in the classroom—the challenge is to make these visits more regular, more welcome, and a more intimate part of the entire classroom experience.

The Endowment's Role in Educational Programming

We recommend that the Endowment and agencies of the federal government support the research necessary to identify and develop the capabilities of radio and television for learning.

We believe national leadership is essential and appropriate, both because the results will be beneficial to all of society and because state and local authorities are unlikely to be able to finance such an extensive undertaking.

We encourage wide dissemination of the results of Endowment-funded study, and particularly recommend that research information and other findings be shared with commercial broadcasting.

In addition, we believe that the Endowment should join with other funders in supporting the synthesis of major research and evaluation findings, and their distribution to educators, laymen, researchers, programmers, broadcasters, and other interested groups. This activity is essential, and has often been neglected in the past.

We recommend, further, that Endowment funds be used to stimulate studies of the effectiveness of programs once they are in use. Techniques should be developed that will aid in determining whether or not a program has achieved its objectives, and whether unintended effects occur.

The cost of an extensive evaluation of every program would be prohibitive. Accordingly, some major programs should be thoroughly evaluated while others would receive more cursory review.

The Program Services Endowment will be deeply involved in supporting these research efforts. Much of the work will be done in educational institutions or perhaps in specially constructed centers supported by the Endowment. We expect that other groups, such as NSF, HEW, foundations, and universities will also want to continue their studies of radio and television in learning. The object of all such endeavor should be a cross-fertilization process yielding a rich body of theory and empirical evidence.

New Programs and Services

We recommend that the Program Services Endowment finance and stimulate the development of high-quality instructional and educational programs that

test and demonstrate the potential of telecommunications for learning.

We have emphasized the need for strong local
action to improve the quality and quantity of instructional and educational programs available to serve
public broadcasting's diverse audience. We expect that
with an increasing flow of funds directly to the stations,
public broadcasters will at last be able to find sufficient
resources to meet the educational needs of their communities. These increased funds will assist those stations and state networks which now produce educational programs. By the same token, schools, state
departments of education, and licensees relying on organizations such as the Agency for Instructional Television to produce programs for in-school use will no
doubt allocate increased funds for such activities.

We also expect that one of the major initiatives of
stations will be in lifelong learning. Public broadcasting
must help each of us come closer to reaching our
educational potential by providing programs that bring
us new skills and that help us maintain competence
in our occupations.

Increased funding at the local level will also permit greater opportunity to aggregate funds regionally
and nationally for producing educational programs
aimed at both in-school and general use in television
and radio. Public broadcasting's new satellite interconnection should make it easier for licensees to develop and share instructional programs for intrastate distribution.

At the same time, we believe it is essential for the
Program Services Endowment to play a catalytic role
in developing new educational programming. We anticipate that approximately $15 million will be allo-
cated by the Endowment for research and programs
that demonstrate the potential of television and radio
for learning. Portions of these moneys might be used
outright to fund directly several educational programs
or series each year, or they could be used as risk
capital to speed development of promising initiatives.
While we anticipate that the general funding activities

of the Program Services Endowment will support television and radio programs of a broadly educational nature, we believe that the Endowment should also reserve funds for programs designed with specific educational objectives and intended for use in schools, in colleges, or even in the home.

Just as the Program Services Endowment in its general program-funding activities is charged with seeking out innovation, testing new concepts, and filling gaps, so the Endowment can play the same role with respect to educational and instructional programming. We have already noted our strong concern that virtually no children's programs of the quality and scope of *Sesame Street* and *The Electric Company* appear to be on the horizon. If this situation is not addressed soon, one of public television's major attractions will be lost. At the same time, the development and application of new communications technologies—videodiscs and teletext services as well as the information services they make possible—will demand serious attention during the next five years.

Much of the direct funding presently provided by the federal government for educational and children's programming is tied to specific goals mandated by Congress. At the same time, other important learning objectives may not receive adequate attention because of funding limitations. With the flexibility to respond to new needs and stimulate the development of educational programming in new areas, the Program Services Endowment should be able to play an important catalytic role in suggesting new directions for federal policy.

If the potential for television and radio in learning is to be realized, these new programs and research findings must be widely available and widely used. Our recommendation for extending the reach of public broadcasting is vital to making the program available to homes and schools. Use in the home is dependent on a wide range of factors, including the availability of a receiver, the quality of reception, and the interest of the potential audience. To compete effectively for the available leisure time, programs for at-home use must be of the highest quality, appealing as well as educational.

The classroom use of instructional programs depends on availability, suitable equipment, and the teacher's decision on how best to use the limited hours in the school day. These programs are now used in a minority of American classrooms, primarily because most of them are broadcast at times that fail to fit an instructor's schedule. New technology should provide easy ways to overcome such rigidity. Audio and video tape recorders and closed-circuit telecasts are constantly increasing the teacher's ability to use radio and television in a manner and at a time of his or her own choosing.

If radio and television are to be fully developed for learning, the complex question of the extended availability of programs must be addressed. On the one hand, it is essential that good television and radio programs for learning be available on an extended basis to allow for their integration in school curriculums. Although the appropriate time to use a program may vary from one classroom to the next, current replay rights provide for use only within a few days following broadcast. On the other hand, if recorded programs are to be used extensively, the individuals involved in the production—both performers and production personnel—must be reimbursed fairly to reflect the likely impact the wide availability of recorded programs will have on the demand for live performances. Cooperation and leadership are required at the national level to find planned solutions to the problem. The Trust, with its responsibility to aid in the development of new and expanded instructional services, should begin this process by financing trial efforts to determine the effect of making programs available on an extended basis. Further, as we point out in Chapter VII, the Endowment should undertake a broad study of the entire question, including the possibility of establishing a national clearinghouse or other mechanism to deal with copyright clearance, licensing, and rights questions.

The potential of television and radio for learning is only beginning to be explored and exploited. Technology is advancing so rapidly that it is difficult to predict in what ways it will shape these media. Even now, however, it is clear that with careful planning, skillful execution, and thorough evaluation, telecommunications will play an increasingly fundamental role in the learning processes of Americans of all ages and backgrounds.

IX

Public Accountability

Public broadcasting has special opportunities, as well as obligations, to provide a full service program schedule that entertains and enriches the American public without the shaping influences imposed by commercial success. However, without a bottom line measure such as increased sales volume attributable to broadcast advertising, noncommercial broadcasting must rely upon other mechanisms for determining whether and how the public is being served.

Individual stations are focal points for interaction between noncommercial broadcasting and the public. We find it a quite remarkable measure of community support that nearly 3 million families contribute voluntarily to public broadcasting stations each year. In recognition of such support, stations must provide meaningful opportunities for individuals to participate in and understand the system. Traditional mechanisms for participating in local station planning and development should be continued and strengthened. But these are not enough. There must be a systematic means for determining whether certain well-defined interests and needs of the public are being satisfied. This chapter presents our recommendations for improving public broadcasting's ability to account for itself, both through existing methods such as public participation in station governance, equal opportunity programs, and financial disclosure, and through the use of specialized audience measurement techniques.

The Goal: A Broad and Diverse Audience

"At the end of a concert at Carnegie Hall, Walter Damrosch asked Rachmaninoff what sublime thoughts had passed through his head as he stared out into the audience during the playing of his concerto. 'I was counting the house,' said Rachmaninoff."[1] The principal test of public broadcasting's accountability to the community is whether anybody is listening or watching.

Stations must choose among a variety of locally and nationally produced programs in an effort to serve their communities and attract their audiences. In making programming decisions, stations must have some measure, beyond the development goals of membership drives or the number of letters and phone calls received, for assessing whether they are serving the many different audiences that commercial broadcasting does not and cannot serve adequately.

At present, the stations have only a limited source of such information—the audience rating reports prepared by the Nielsen and Arbitron companies based on their surveys of approximately one thousand households. These are valid and reliable estimates of how many people are receiving a particular program at a given hour of a particular day. They are designed for advertisers, commercial networks, and individual radio and television outlets. On the basis of such audience measurements, advertisers can determine the extent to which they have achieved their goal of the largest possible audience throughout the day. These audience estimates, although well suited to the mass media commercial system, are of little use to public broadcasters because public broadcasting does not aim to reach a mass audience and hold it against compe-

---

[1]Gary Steiner, *The Creative Organization* (Chicago: University of Chicago Press, 1965), p. 207.

tition for several hours each day. Instead, the aim of public broadcasting is to provide a rich blend of cultural, journalistic, intellectual, and entertainment programming which, because of its diversity, cannot be premised upon mass appeal. Thus, although public broadcasting may capture only a small, specialized fraction of the total audience at any given time, during the course of a week or a month that audience may be of crucial importance in fulfilling the public system's mission. The public system seeks to offer something of interest to a variety of specialized audiences—a service that commercial broadcasting cannot provide. In order to evaluate how well the system is fulfilling this mission, public broadcasting needs to analyze in a different way the basic audience estimates generated by the commercial ratings services.

How Large an Audience?

We recommend that public television seek to serve all Americans, developing programs of such compelling interest that ultimately 100 percent of the potential audience will be served on a regular basis.

We believe that the public television system must aim to serve on a regular basis 100 percent of the individuals with receivers. At first the system should seek to reach each individual at least once a month, with a potential goal of at least once a week. Rather than focus on the share of the audience reached at a given point in the broadcast day as an indication of station service to the community, stations should rely on cumulative audience estimates as a measure of success. The cumulative audience is the number or percent of *different* individuals served over a period of time, generally a week or a month. Only a 1 percent cumulative audience would be generated by programs viewed every day by the same 1 percent of the public. However, if 100 different programs broadcast in a month each attracted a different 1 percent of the audience, the cumulative audience would be 100 percent for that month.

The public television system already gathers information on its cumulative audience. For example, 49 percent of the potential nationwide audience viewed noncommercial television at least once during a typical month in 1975; by 1978 that figure had climbed to' 63 percent. These estimates indicate that public television has already made significant progress toward the 100 percent goal. However, because these estimates are derived from the Nielsen and Arbitron monthly samples of only 1000 households,[2] they do not allow public broadcasters to discover how diverse an audience is being reached. For example, the 1000-household survey, while useful to commercial broadcasters in measuring the mass audience, does not enable the public television system to determine whether and the extent to which children, minorities, the elderly, and low-income groups comprise each program's audience. Such indicators are essential to a system that is premised upon providing a wide scope of program services tailored to the needs and interests of many small audiences.

How Diverse an Audience?
We recommend that available cumulative audience data be analyzed on a per program basis according to demographic group, variety, and frequency of viewing.

Progress toward the goal of a large total cumulative audience is measured by accumulating statistics on the size of the audiences for each program. The cumulative audience will increase to the extent that each additional program attracts a new and different audience. Thus specialized and unique programs will contribute to the cumulative audience measure viewers

---

[2]Nielsen meters 1200 homes in its national sample, but due to sampling errors and other factors, approximately 1000 households are used for the national sample.

who are otherwise not reached by the noncommercial system. To select and schedule programs, public broadcasters need to analyze the characteristics and dimensions of the audience for every program. This analysis will not only enable stations to improve service to their communities by increasing their cumulative audience, but it will also indicate the extent to which a particular program is achieving its goals.

Some programs will and should reach large audiences. For such programs, the national sample of over 1000 homes equipped with Nielsen meters will provide an estimate of total viewing. However, this small number of homes is unacceptable for analysis of demographic characteristics of smaller audiences such as race, age, education, income level, and location. For example, since only 12 percent of the nation's households are black, they represent only about 120 of the 1000 homes used in the Nielsen survey—a sample too small to yield statistically reliable data for any but the most popular programs. Taking the example one step further, by today's standards a relatively successful public television program reaches approximately 5 percent of the national audience, for which the Nielsen survey would include data on only 6 black households, too unreliable an indication of program acceptability to black audiences to be useful to public broadcasters.

One method for obtaining measures of small segments of the audience is by aggregating an alternative set of audience estimates already collected by Nielsen and Arbitron. Several times a year both firms conduct a survey of the viewing habits of a large number of households, about 100,000 nationwide. This larger sample can be aggregated at the national level to yield characteristics of the national audience for most public television programs, even when the audience is small, specialized, concentrated among minority groups, or insufficient to analyze with any reliability in some individual markets. This is essential for measuring viewership of black, Latino, Asian, and other minority groups that are unevenly dispersed throughout the country.

The aggregation of these data would also allow public broadcasters to analyze the degree of overlap and duplication in program audiences so that the programs that bring new and different audiences to public broadcasting can be identified. This is a critical factor in determining which programs form the best building blocks for the total cumulative audience objective. For example, is the audience that watches *Masterpiece Theater* the same or different from the audience that watches *Nova?*

Such aggregated information will provide individual stations with a helpful tool for selecting and scheduling programs. Although each community differs, the overall national figures will offer an important guide for stations making programming decisions when audience figures for their own communities are limited. In addition, local market data from the 100,000-household survey can be compiled for several consecutive periods to yield a larger sample of viewers for analysis.[3] In this way programmers can determine the variety and frequency of their local viewer involvement over time.

As the system provides increased services to new audience subgroups, it should strive to make those individuals dedicated viewers as well. As a by-product of analyzing audience overlap in programming, the system can determine audience interest by examining the frequency with which individuals return to programs or series.

The cumulative measurement approach to determining how well the public is served is also applicable to public radio. On the national level the cumulative audience will be an essential gauge of the success of the public radio system. The components of that audience will need to be understood with a depth of analysis comparable to that achievable in television so that improvements in public radio's national

---

[3]For example, if from the 100,000 sample a local market survey of 4000 households is inadequate for the detailed analysis required by a public television station in that market, it can obtain a larger sample by adding the local survey data from another 4000 persons polled in a previous period.

services can be made. However, there may be limitations on the usefulness of cumulative audience measures by individual public radio stations. Radio listeners generally do not listen to specific programs. They listen to radio stations which distinguish themselves by their sound or format. Because of their great number and varied formats, radio stations typically seek a specialized segment of the general listening audience. However, measures of audience are essential for every public radio station. Where several stations serve a single community, the cumulative audience of the group will reveal whether services are sufficiently diversified to attract a broad segment of the listening public on a regular basis. Individual stations, assuming they can overcome the high cost of obtaining audience estimates with detailed demographic breakdowns, will find audience data a useful tool in improving service. As each station charts the growth of its audience, its cumulative audience should reach an acceptable level, balancing the format of the station and the needs of its community.

The proposed use of audience measurement data provides an important means through which programs can be selected and scheduled in the interest of the public. We believe that analysis of such data is an essential means for individual stations, the public broadcasting system, and its supporters to evaluate regularly how well they are serving the public. However, it is by no means the only method that should be used by public broadcasting to measure the adequacy of its public service.

Strengthening Traditional Methods of Accountability

America and the world have witnessed a decade of extraordinary change since the first Carnegie Commission report of 1967. It has been a period marked by a decline of public confidence in government, the American dream of equality, and the prestige of institutions such as the presidency, universities, and the media. This skeptical decade has spawned an era in which there is great emphasis upon the accountability of public institutions. The indicators are apparent: the demand for fiscal controls; a well-established concern for racial and sexual parity; and a new congressional dynamic, with more independence, greater responsiveness to organized constituencies, and less party loyalty. A decade of special-interest movements has led to more effective public interest groups, and as a result, greater citizen input into public policy.

All of these factors have converged on the communications field, and public broadcasting in particular, during the 1970s. There has been an increasing demand for public participation in policy and programming decisions, and for improved accountability in the expenditure of funds.

Public broadcasting is a major cultural institution that can play a decisive role in bringing together the pluralistic voices and interests of the American community. The creative resources and distribution facilities at the disposal of public broadcasters allow the system to develop program services that speak to the needs of specialized audiences, while channeling the concerns and talents of minorities and special interests into the mainstream of American thought.

To realize its potential as a vehicle for social communication and change, public broadcasting must strengthen public participation while preserving its independence from domination by isolated special interest groups. How may this be accomplished? The answer varies from issue to issue, from station to station, from national organization to national organization. In some settings extraordinarily effective solutions have been found. In other situations extreme polarization has resulted from localized unwillingness even to open dialogue with aggressive citizens' groups. In yet others the result can only be described as a form of co-optation, leading to temporary truces without substantial reduction of grievances.

Although we recognize the efforts of the system to involve and represent the public, there is a widespread and growing perception among many groups on the periphery of public broadcasting that it is a system which is closed, unwilling to change, and afraid of criticism and controversy. The testimony we have heard from representatives of minority constituencies, independent producers, and avant-garde innovators was filled with such assertions.

Public broadcasting must see accountability and public participation as opportunities, not burdens. We offer the following recommendations for strengthening the existing mechanisms.

Financial Accounting

We recommend that there be a complete and regular disclosure of overall station finances, and that the sole objective of full financial disclosure be to assure the fair and efficient use of system funds.

In 1977 the public broadcasting system spent $135 million of federal funds and $347 million of private support. As we observed in Chapter IV, the degree to which Congress imposes conditions upon the receipt of its funds is less a function of the source— dedicated taxes or general revenues—than of the structure of the disbursal mechanism.

In Chapter III, we recommended that stations receive their funds through a Public Telecommunications Trust as a means of balancing the editorial and programming integrity of stations with the obvious requirement for fiscal responsibility in the expenditure of public funds. The Trust would be the principal agency reporting to Congress about the progress of the system; it would report compliance with congressionally mandated policies, and certify the system's income for the purpose of computing the annual appropriation. The Trust would also have the authority to audit station finances, with a particular view to guarding against waste or fraud and assuring compliance with public policy. However, it is essential that such audits not be converted to politically slanted evaluations of programming decisions. The public has a right to know how its money has been spent, but government funders of public broadcasting should restrain their zeal to protect the public interest by dictating the character of a station's programming. The use of accounting as a form of subtle, or occasionally not so subtle, political influence on institutions dependent on public funds is a modern device offering great opportunity for misuse. One of the important roles of the Public Telecommunications Trust will be to protect stations from such predatory intrusions.

The money that stations receive from the Trust is discretionary and will generally be added to moneys received from nonfederal sources to determine the stations' budgets for general operating purposes. We emphasize the right of the Congress and the Trust to be assured that public money is being spent responsibly and in accord with public policy. We do not feel, however, that it is appropriate for either the Trust or Congress to audit the expenditure of station funds raised from private sources. This is an extremely subtle question for which the Trust must develop suitable and effective guidelines. We recommend that audit procedures be developed that respect this distinction. Stations should be sensitive to the need of the Congress and the Trust to know how public money is being spent, and should, to the extent possible, keep their books so as to segregate public funds from their private income. The Trust and the Congress, on the other hand, must not use station commingling of funds as a reason to demand public control of station expenditures, nor should the diversity of all public broadcasting's financial support blur the important distinction between private and governmental institutions.

Nongovernmental contributors have also demanded the disclosure of station budgets and financial data. This is standard practice of publicly held corporations and many nonprofit organizations, after the close of each business year. To the extent that the contributor-subscriber of a station is a "shareholder," he has a right to an accounting of station income and expenditures. We believe that such financial disclosures should be made to both governmental sponsors and the public at large on a regular basis. In sum, it is important that stations, government, and the public regard financial accounting as a method of ensuring that station funds are spent effectively and efficiently, and not as a tool for influencing programming decisions. The Trust should take the lead in developing reasonable accounting procedures and disclosure requirements.

Equal Opportunity

We recommend that the increased funding available to broadcasting stations and production organizations be used to further the system's commitment to equal opportunity in all facets of operation.

Whether as a condition of receiving federal funds or as an independent system-wide goal, the employment of women and members of minority groups must be fully achieved by the system as rapidly as possible. To date, emphasis at the federal level has been on requiring equal opportunity compliance as an eligibility condition for federal funding programs.

Affirmative action and equal employment opportunity have played important roles in the growth and development of both public and private institutions. Public broadcasting must make a positive and public commitment to these objectives. Equal opportunity is in itself a worthy objective, but for public broadcasting it has the added importance of serving to sensitize the system to its role in dramatizing the attractions and strengths of American pluralism. This system goal is most easily met by making minorities and women major participants in the development and operation of the system as a matter of self-determined policy, rather than as a reaction to governmental threat.

Public broadcasting has already made considerable progress towards equal opportunity. However, we believe much greater progress can be achieved in the immediate future as a result of two factors.

First, the proposed reorganization of the system

will carry with it a considerable increase in funds available directly to stations. Although we have recommended that stations aggregate a major portion of that money for programming, we expect that a reasonable amount of growth in personnel will take place at the local level. This will, among other things, provide the opportunity to hire substantially more women and minorities. In addition, increased funds in the stations' hands should result in increased expenditures for training and professional development programs to assist existing jobholders. Furthermore, increased system funding should yield an increase in the number of programs produced each year. More productions, in turn, will provide more job opportunities, thereby enabling stations to meet their equal employment goals more easily.

Second, we anticipate that full implementation by stations of audience measurement techniques will result in the production of a greater number of programs designed for specialized and minority audiences. These productions will provide added opportunities for minorities to serve as producers, assembling staffs with specialized backgrounds and interests. Increased station funds and expanded minority programming will affect not only the larger producing stations, but many of the smaller stations with more limited funds.

In addition, we recommend that Congress and the Trust continue to support training projects to help create a sufficient talent pool of minorities and women to meet the increased demands of the system. Training activities should be targeted at assisting existing minority and female employees to achieve positions of greater leadership and decision-making authority. As of 1978 women represented 34.6 percent of public broadcasting employees—nearly the proportion of women in the national work force—while minorities composed 13.7 percent of public broadcasting employees.[4] Although these statistics are encouraging, they must be viewed in light of the relative importance of positions held by minority employees in the system. For exam-

---

[4] Data from CPB Management Information Systems.

ple, there are few minorities serving as key decision makers (that is, chief executive officer, program or production manager, chief engineer, or chief financial officer) in public broadcasting stations. Of the 583 total key decision makers in public television stations in 1978, 16 (or 2.7 percent) are representatives of minority groups. Of the 328 total key decision makers in public radio, 18 (or 5.5 percent) are minorities.[5]

Adequate support for nationally sponsored training programs can assist the system in building a skilled talent pool of minorities and women and in assisting minorities to achieve leadership positions. Employment training programs should be operated by the Trust and should be subject to periodic evaluation. Without congressional support for training programs, compliance with equal opportunity goals will be difficult and legalistic. Moreover, the provision of earmarked training grants is a more immediate and positive way of achieving employment parity than the law enforcement approach associated with the compliance mechanism.

An additional facet of equal opportunity, insufficiently emphasized by the public broadcasting system, is minority control and ownership of stations. There are very few minority-controlled public broadcasting stations today. Of the 195 radio and 276 television stations in the United States in 1977, only 18 had 51 percent or more minority members on their board of directors. Eleven of these stations are located outside the continental United States (Alaska, Guam, Hawaii, Puerto Rico, and the Virgin Islands).[6]

We recommend that the Trust explore opportunities for assisting minorities in establishing second public television channels in markets with substantial minority populations and for assisting minorities in establishing radio services.

---

[5]Data from "A Formula for Change: The Report of the Task Force on Minorities in Public Broadcasting," (Washington, D. C.: The Corporation for Public Broadcasting, 1978), p. 78. Mimeographed.

[6]*Ibid.*, p. 264.

While opportunities for second television channels are limited, priorities should be established within the facilities and expansion programs of the Trust to assist and support such efforts where the potential and the need are greatest.

As for radio facilities, upgrading and expansion programs of the Trust should also provide assistance to minorities seeking to establish specialized station formats for minority audiences—particularly in areas where there are multiple stations. Radio formats are particularly suited to reaching specialized and distinct audiences. Minority groups seeking to upgrade existing facilities to qualify for federal assistance or those seeking to establish new radio stations should be given special assistance.

The involvement of the public broadcasting system in new approaches to telecommunications services should also focus on the needs of minority audiences and minority producers. Where minority audiences are not sufficiently concentrated for the support of full-time broadcasting formats, alternative modes of distribution and program development such as cable, satellite, and videocassettes should be fostered with the support of both the Endowment and the Trust. By supporting such efforts, the Trust can maximize program services to specialized audiences and increase the availability of quality programs on minority interests for distribution to the mainstream of public broadcasting's viewers.

Station Governance

We recommend public involvement in station governance through the use of any of a wide variety of participation mechanisms including elected governing boards, citizen advisory committees, open board meetings, and volunteerism.

The hallmark of the 1970s has been the almost universal demand for openness in government, from legislatures and state agencies to various private institutions which receive tax funds. Indeed, in many states public broadcasting has provided the major vehicle for letting "sunshine" into the decision-making processes of public institutions. City councils, school boards, and state legislatures have all come into the home via public radio and television. The national telecast of the Watergate hearings and the radio broadcast of the Panama Canal hearings were historic turning points for our national legislature, offering to many citizens scattered across the country their first opportunity to hear and see their elected officials at work.

Citizens have also demanded that public broadcasters enlighten the public about their own operations, through both financial disclosure and open board meetings. The public broadcasting organizations have responded in a variety of ways, depending on circumstances in their localities. Some stations now hold all meetings publicly, even broadcasting certain meetings; others have turned to partly open governance and consultative decision making. But still others have remained strongly opposed, contending that their trustee role precludes any extensive public involvement. The local licensee does not exercise simple trusteeship for the system in its community. It is also the focus of interaction between the public broadcasting system as a whole and its public. As the most direct point of contact between the system and the public, local stations must acknowledge both their trusteeship responsibility to preserve independence in decision making and their responsibility as operators of a publicly funded system to encourage the utmost public participation in station policymaking. It should be a fundamental principle and objective of every public broadcasting licensee to ensure that its governance reflects these understandings, conveying not just independence of action, but also responsiveness to constituencies within its community of service.

Both of these responsibilities can be fulfilled in many ways. There is no convincing evidence that stations governed via entirely elective processes are necessarily more responsive to community interests than those governed by appointed trustee panels. In fact, in some communities there is evidence that stations governed by elected boards have seen themselves as more independent of the public than some stations where governing boards were appointed. In many communities a combined process has evolved in an attempt to strike a better balance. For example, one licensee has found that throughout its history its membership election procedure has been an important avenue for new ideas and constituencies, but that appointment procedures were still necessary to ensure representation of minorities and other groups who were not elected by the contributing members. Furthermore, unlike community stations which can more easily experiment with alternative governing arrangements, many university and state licensees are unable to alter their structure. And yet we have seen a number of examples of such stations which have made enormous strides in achieving responsiveness through the use of community advisory groups and volunteers who function as an integral part of the station staff.

The ultimate objective of a governance mechanism is to foster the improvement of the institution and its ability to assess the needs of its community. The governing board is the anchor for the institution. We believe that the best boards are those that restrain themselves from involvement in day-to-day management, particularly in programming areas. Station governing boards should set broad policies, hire and fire management, and protect the institution.

Because of the wide variety of institutional and community settings, we recommend that stations involve the public through a variety of possible election methods, appointment processes, advisory boards, volunteerism, and public meetings and hearings. Indeed, the great variation among institutional and community licensees and their governing structures makes it imperative that these procedures be adapted to unique local circumstances if they are to be effective. Each community and its licensees must decide precisely what mix of public participation tools seems appropriate and effective. More important than the method chosen are the principles which must underlie it. Public broadcasters must take the initiative actively to involve members of the public in station policy formation in substantial and meaningful ways. The most democratic mechanisms fail in the absence of a strong conviction on the part of station managers that public involvement is a vital resource in station governance.

In addition to a spirit of openness, the most successful partnerships have been achieved in situations in which, whatever the mechanism chosen, both station managers and interested citizens understand their clearly defined roles in the decision-making process. In defining a role for public participants, it is important that station managers look toward actual results, not merely cosmetic changes. Some of the demands made on a station may lack merit or the backing of an informed and supportive constituency. On the other hand, the ways stations respond even to legitimate demands can sometimes be phony and artificial. A station must be tough-minded in differentiating legitimate demands from self-serving pressures, and responding to both in appropriate ways.

Many public groups and organized constituencies go before state and federal legislative agencies to win support for special services in their interest. In this context, specialized public broadcasting services are often sought. Captioning for the deaf, special subcarrier radio services for the homebound, bilingual services, and aid for the handicapped are some of the many existing and potential services the system can provide.

Public broadcasting is developing these capabilities with its own resources, as well as with the assistance of Congress and federal and state agencies. It is the responsibility of the Trust to assess the needs of such special-interest constituencies and to provide incentive funding when appropriate to develop these services. The Trust must ensure that the changing interests and needs are recognized and acted upon.

Ascertainment

We recommend that stations use community surveys to ascertain local interests and needs as a general guide in program development.

As another variation of community involvement, stations perform survey research, known as ascertainment. Apart from stations' interest in collecting such data, they are currently required to do so by the FCC. Many community groups have come to regard these exercises as window dressing, or a way to co-opt community leaders. However, some stations have transformed the ascertainment interviewing process into a real resource for program ideas, station support, and actual on-air programming. Television and radio call-in programs, allowing viewers and listeners to add their opinions to those of featured community leaders, are often stimulating and provocative. We urge stations to regard this tool, like other audience measurement and evaluation techniques, as another method of building a better and more effective service.

The difficulty with ascertainment and certain qualitative audience analysis techniques, however, is their limited usefulness as predictors of program appeal. While a producer may learn that a majority of interviewees are "worried about crime," this is far removed from creating a program about crime that will be interesting and informative. Although nothing can replace the creative process of program development, ascertainment should be used as a general guide highlighting program areas of interest to the local community. Ascertainment should be seen by stations as an opportunity to take the pulse of the community in an effort to learn how well the station is serving its public, rather than a ritualistic activity.

Accountability—The Means to a Creative Partnership

A balance must be struck between a station's responsibility to maintain editorial freedom and its responsibility to be accountable to the public.

Equal opportunity, openness in governance, financial accountability, and ascertainment are fundamental practices and principles which inform the activities of most public institutions. We believe it is essential for public broadcasting to incorporate these broad national policy objectives into its processes in order to realize its potential for leadership in American society.

However, although the public broadcasting system is a major social and cultural institution with clear public responsibilities, it is also a component of our free press. The receipt by private public broadcasting licensees of federal financial support creates obligations for station conformity to the broad institutional and social objectives of equal opportunity, openness, and financial accountability. However, federal support often brings with it the possibility of governmental interference. Furthermore, devices to encourage broader public participation in station governance also carry with them the opportunity for special-interest group domination of station decision making. Such government and special-interest group pressures are most dangerous when they impinge upon programming.

We believe that public broadcasters must maintain a free editorial voice in making programming decisions. Demands that stations and the system set aside fixed portions of their budgets for use by particular constituencies seem to us to be at variance with sound administration and inconsistent with the First Amendment. Demands for more and better programming for underserved minorities have enormous merit. But the wisest course is for the system to serve minorities and women by including them as members of the editorial process itself through hiring and training opportunities.

A delicate balance must be struck between a station's responsibility to insist upon the freedom of its programming decisions and yet to be accountable to the public. Both elements of this balance must be clearly understood, clearly exercised, and clearly defended. This balance will yield a public system in which no commercial voice, no single funder voice, no committee voice, no special-interest voice can dominate. A diversity of voices will be heard and many interests may be served.

Conclusion

In developing a system of accountability for public broadcasting, no single mechanism can reflect the ultimate variety of public interests, just as no single individual or constituency can express the full range of audience concerns. Rather, public broadcasting must choose elements of many approaches in guiding its work and composing its audiences.

Reasonable financial disclosure provides public assurance that tax dollars are being administered efficiently and in accord with the requirements of public policy. Affirmative action, equal employment opportunity, and openness in governance allow public broadcasting to incorporate broad social policy objectives into its role as a leading public institution. Carefully applied audience measurement techniques also allow the system to understand and account for the degree to which the many elements of its public are reached and served by its program service. Such variety is encouraged by training activities that allow public broadcasting to draw on the talents of minorities and women in developing its leadership for program production and decision making. Public participation mechanisms adapted to local station governance and suitable ascertainment strategies will ensure that public needs and concerns can be brought to the attention of system leadership. All these approaches can and should be addressed in a manner that allows the public broadcasting system to safeguard its artistic and editorial freedom, while being accountable and responsive to the needs of the American public.

Finally, it must be recognized that it is in the public interest to allow the system to safeguard a reasonably free and inventive environment for creative talent in the system. A free and original creative voice is also a public voice. We are all served by the artistic and journalistic insights of a system that has as its basic goals a commitment to a broad and diverse audience, and a desire to unify rather than to divide its audience.

X

The Social Dividend of the Electronic Media

The institution we now call public broadcasting has reached an unprecedented intersection of the dynamics of American democracy with advanced communications technology as we are drawn inexorably toward the uncharted configurations of the 21st century.

Each human epoch is profoundly influenced by the ways in which members of society communicate with one another, or in the worst outcome, fail to communicate at all. Whether the dominant form is primitive speech without orthography, carvings on the walls of caves, hieroglyphics, illuminated manuscripts, movable type, or electronic media, our view of ourselves and our ideas of history are inevitably determined by the means by which we communicate with each other.

Since the 1920s America has moved from a mechanical to an electronic epoch. Our activity is increasingly affected by a proliferating array of electronic devices so numerous and ingenious that we can scarcely comprehend their operation, much less the future they portend. These developments point to a great problem peculiar to our own times. The electronic media provide an immediacy and intimacy that can bring Americans together, teach us, and inspire us. They give us the tools to lead the world out of ignorance and misery. But the electronic media also offer an opportunity for despotic power and mind control beyond the wildest dreams of history's tyrants.

Observing the growing degradation of America's commercial communications media—radio and television—in a competition for mass audiences, the Carnegie Commission seeks in this report to point out another way. These magnificent electronic extensions of ourselves can teach, and heal, and inspire, if we use them not for the ruthless pursuit of the least common denominator but for their highest human potential.

Inevitably, the introduction of a new invention is accompanied by ballyhoo promising untold benefits to mankind. But, as we have seen repeatedly, services that meet human needs and that benefit society are readily expendable in a thoroughly exploited market. American radio and television are not just instruments of the marketplace; they are social tools of revolutionary importance. If these media are permitted to assume a wholly commercial character, the entire cultural and social apparatus of the nation will become transformed by what may already have become the dominant mode of the electronic media in the United States: the merchandising of consciousness.

Similar choices have been faced at earlier points of America's industrial growth. Confounding the predictions of simplistic ideology, the merchants became benefactors. Alongside the profit-making enterprises of American industrialists, there grew another tradition that has made a major contribution to the betterment of our people. Universal education, public libraries and universities, and philanthropic support of cultural and voluntary institutions of all kinds presented the means through which the progeny of the poor and the illiterate could better their own lives, largely as a result of the largess of early industrial titans. But now technological development is swift and massive. The traditions of public duty and public service in the electronic media are weak, the stakes for the future very large.

America's nonprofit entities were chartered to

preserve and extend our culture and our philosophy according to inner rhythms resonating to ideas of service that transcend the profit and loss column. It is no great secret that these institutions, universities, hospitals, and symphonies, have come under acute fiscal stress not dissimilar to that suffered by public broadcasting during the last decade. The stress has been caused in part by changing societal demands and rising public clamor for constituency participation. And yet, with all their struggles for better financial management and some approximation of balanced budgets, the nonprofit sector—in education, public service, and the arts —has a different bottom line from the business community. In an ultimate sense, its contributions to human betterment constitute its "profit." This is a unique form of social dividend that Western society has devised as a counterweight to the implacable economic laws of the marketplace. In a historical sense, it was the institutionalization of public education and the goal of mass literacy that brought the invention of the printing press to its full development. It took hundreds of years to realize the social dividend of that technology.

The outcome we envision can be best understood as the social dividend of telecommunications technology. How do we use this technology to build a better society? America might well be asked to believe that the product of commercial radio and television is, in and of itself, a beneficial and desirable contribution to society, a claim that is invariably buttressed by the fact that people consume so much of the stuff. Yet we have discovered from a decade of chronically underfunded public broadcasting in America that there is a magnificent vision of societal benefit beyond the reach of the commercial networks. The Carnegie Commission has seen that dedication by creators and communicators of genius can occasionally lift the medium out of the banal and into the sublime. As television and radio are transformed in the next decades, we expect that public broadcasters will play a major and creative role in the change, particularly in the explosion of innovative noncommercial programming that we believe to be realizable in the proper balancing of publicly oriented and commercially oriented broadcasting activities.

These, however, are social dividends long overdue, benefits for citizens who have suffered too long from the distortions of radio and television attributable to programming designed to maximize audiences for advertisers. Had radio and television evolved in this country with a fuller definition of public service, the need for an alternative institution would have been less critical. The enormous profitability of the commercial electronic media mandates the development of a viable institution operating in the public interest.

As for the newer technologies, few of us would venture absolute predictions. Fewer still will even be correct. Public telecommunications is unlikely to attract the investment capital necessary to accomplish massive projects such as the cabling or glass-fibering of America, the launching of new high-powered satellites, the widespread use of videodisc and videocassette technology. These outcomes are clearly possible, and in many instances highly desirable, but they are very costly in the present state of the art.

What public telecommunications can perform, nonetheless, is an essential role as the future unfolds. As a force for the broader public interest, the institution can stimulate the development of new services and technology above and beyond what can be supported commercially. The Public Telecommunications Trust we have proposed can influence policymakers to incorporate new technology into the fabric of American society in a way that will broaden the opportunities for public service to future generations. With the proper leadership and vision, this new institution can assist the nation in reducing the lag between the introduction of new communications technology and its widespread social benefit.

We recognize the dangers of lapsing into fuzzy-minded ecstasy over the unlimited social potential of the new electronic technology. Indeed, it is unlikely that our generation will ever see the full impact of providing wide-band information and communication services to every American home. There is no major technological problem. The problem is in deciding what is needed and what is wise. More immediately, public telecommunications will probably be the vehicle for America to realize its social dividend from the well-entrenched and already powerful media. As a necessary contribution to the nation's need for self-knowledge and healing, public broadcasters—and soon, public telecommunicators—have the obligation and opportunity to bring together a fragmented and wounded society. We have momentarily lost touch with one another as we react to a decade of terrorism, guerrilla war, racial discontent, and economic danger. Present traumas have evolved despite or perhaps because of the all-pervasive methods by which Americans communicate with one another in the commercial media. The opportunity is at hand to bring us together through the teaching and inspiration possible in a noncommercial telecommunications alternative.

This achievement will come not from the imposition of a new conformity, derived either from government or public opinion polls, but from the careful cultivation of a public discourse in its most expansive and profound sense. Somehow we must build a constituency and a means by which America can again develop consensual agreement about the democratic heritage we all hold in common: history, family, art, science, love of nature and tolerance for differences. We have faltered, and are in danger of losing the will to try again. The growth of the commercial electronic media has perhaps not coincidentally accompanied this loss of mutual grace, and this leads us to conjecture that the sociological impact of radio and television is cumulative. We therefore express both concern and optimism for the impact of the electronic media on our children and their children's children. This power can be used in ways that society has barely begun to try, in the revelation of an ethos of mutual respect. The true greatness of America lies in strength that emerges from a diversity of religious, racial, and cultural heritages. We must come to know ourselves as we really are, not as advertising would have us be.

The Commission is obviously not advocating the establishment of any kind of ministry of culture or propaganda machine that seeks "consensus" by the imposition of ideological orthodoxy. Our vision of an independent and innovative public telecommunications institution is the antithesis of the monolithic outlook of all forms of totalitarianism.

We see, instead, the reverent and the rude, the disciplined and the rambunctious—a celebration of American freedom in all its unpredictable varieties. This revelation of diversity will not please some, notably the book burners and the dogmatists among us. It will startle and anger others, as well it should. But we have found in our own lives that anger yields to understanding. America needs, perhaps even more than healing, a sense of understanding, something that is impossible if we each continue to wall ourselves within the corner of society that we find safe, appealing, and comfortable.

Unless we grasp the means to broaden our conversation to include the diverse interests of the entire society, in ways that both illuminate our differences and distill our mutual hopes, more will be lost than the public broadcasting system.

Americans have rarely been closer to one another than in the isolation of their living rooms as they witnessed in tears the funeral of a martyred president, or took pride in the first tentative steps of our astronauts on the moon. These fundamental events of an electronic age were rare intrusions on a commercially oriented system built to serve other purposes. It must not always be so. Americans have the capacity to rebuild their local communities, their regions, and indeed their country, with tools no more formidable than transistors and television tubes. They need only to want to do so intensely enough to create a public telecommunications system that will bring it about.

We remember the Egyptians for the pyramids, and the Greeks for their graceful stone temples. How shall Americans be remembered? As exporters of sensationalism and salaciousness? Or as builders of magical electronic tabernacles that can in an instant erase the limitations of time and geography, and make us into one people?

The choice is in our hands and the time is now.

Bibliography

Annan, Lord Noel, et al. *Report of the Committee on the Future of Broadcasting.* London: Her Majesty's Stationery Office, 1977.

Arlen, Michael J. *The View from Highway 1.* New York: Ballantine Books, 1977.

Aspen Institute. *Aspen Notebook on Government and the Media.* New York: Praeger Publishers, 1973.

———. *The Future of Public Broadcasting.* New York: Praeger Publishers, 1976.

Barnouw, Erik. *A History of Broadcasting in the United States.* New York: Oxford University Press. Vol. 1, A Tower in Babel, 1966; vol. 2, The Golden Web, 1968; vol. 3, The Image Empire, 1970.

———. *Tube of Plenty: The Evolution of American Television.* New York: Oxford University Press, 1975.

Bower, Robert T. *Television and the Public.* New York: Holt, Rinehart and Winston, 1973.

Brown, Les. *Televi$ion: The Business Behind the Box.* New York: Harcourt Brace Jovanovich, 1971.

Burns, James MacGregor. *Leadership.* New York: Harper & Row, 1978.

Carnegie Commission on Educational Television. *Public Television: A Program for Action.* New York: Harper & Row, 1967.

Comstock, George, et al. *Television and Human Behavior.* Santa Monica, Calif.: Rand Corporation, 1975. Vol. 1, A Guide to the Pertinent Scientific Literature; vol. 2, *The Key Studies;* vol. 3, The Research Horizon, Future and Present.

302

Conference Board. *Information Technology: Some Critical Implications for Decision Makers*. New York: Conference Board, 1972.

De Mott, Benjamin. "The Trouble with Public TV," *Atlantic Monthly*, February 1979. (Based on an essay prepared for the Carnegie Commission on the Future of Public Broadcasting, 1978.)

Jewkes, John, Sawers, David, and Stillerman, Richard. *The Sources of Invention*. New York: W. W. Norton, 1969.

Macy, John, Jr. *To Irrigate a Wasteland: The Struggle to Shape a Public Television System in the United States*. Berkeley and Los Angeles: University of California Press, 1974.

Mielke, Keith W., Johnson, Rolland C., and Cole, Barry G. "The Federal Role in Funding Children's Television Programming. Vol. I: Final Report." Mimeographed. Bloomington: Indiana University Press, 1975.

Netzer, Dick. *The Subsidized Muse: Public Support for the Arts in the United States*. Cambridge, England: Cambridge University Press, 1978.

Noll, Roger G., Peck, Merton, J., and McGowan, John J. *Economic Aspects of Television Regulation*. Washington, D.C.: Brookings Institution, 1973.

Polsky, Richard M. *Getting to Sesame Street*. New York: Praeger Publishers, 1974.

Seidman, Harold. *Politics, Position and Power: The Dynamics of Federal Organization*. 2d ed. New York: Oxford University Press, 1976.

Steiner, Gary. *The Creative Organization*. Chicago: University of Chicago Press, 1965.

Surgeon General's Scientific Advisory Committee on Television and Social Behavior. *Television and Growing Up: The Impact of Televised Violence*. Report to the Surgeon General, U.S. Public Health Service. Washington, D.C.: Government Printing Office, 1972.

Tribe, Laurence H. *American Constitutional Law*. Mineola, N.Y.: Foundation Press, 1978.

U.S. House of Representatives Committee on Interstate and Foreign Commerce. *Options Papers*. 95th Cong., 1st sess., 1977.

Wheldon, Sir Huw. *The British Experience in Television*. London: British Broadcasting Corp., 1976.

Appendix A

Acknowledgments

During this study, many people from a variety of fields have contributed immeasurably to the Commission's understanding of public broadcasting. We wish to acknowledge those who have so contributed. Their names and their affiliations at the time of their association with the work of the Commission follow.

The Commission wishes to thank those who prepared background papers or other materials which were invaluable in making this report:

Consultants: Robert Avery, Univ. of Utah; John Carey, N.Y. Univ.; Grace Dawson; Benjamin DeMott, Amherst Coll.; Andre DeVerneil; Herbert Dordick, Univ. of Southern Calif.; Fred C. Esplin, Pa. Public Television Network; Judith F. Geller; Larry Josephson; Jill Kneerim; Gale Metzger, Statistical Research; Robert Pepper, Univ. of Iowa; Ben Posner; C. Delos Putz, Jr., Univ. of San Francisco Law School; Jonathan Rice, KQED-TV, San Francisco; Randolph Ross; Willard D. Rowland, Jr., Univ. of Ill. at Champaign-Urbana; Marilynne Rudick; Carolyn Setlow; Rhea Sikes; Thomas A. Troyer, Caplin & Drysdale; Charles Woodard, Charles Woodard Associates.

We are also grateful to Samuel A. Carradine, who spent several months on the staff, but resigned in March 1978.

Interns: Barbara Jaffe, Harvard Univ.; Marjorie Lewis, Harvard Univ.; David T. Maloof, Columbia Univ.

We are equally indebted to the men and women who made formal presentations before the Commission:

Chloe Aaron, PBS; Larry Abrams, Southern Calif. Media Reform Workshop; Edward Allison, Inst. for Communication Policy Development; Kirby Alvy, Center for Improvement of Child Caring; Michael Ambrosino, Public Broadcasting Associates; Gloria L. Anderson, CPB; Patricia Anderson, ZBS Media; Ralph Arlyck, Assn. of Independent Video and Filmmakers (AIVF): Ernest Ballest, National Latino Media Coalition; Ting Barrow, AIVF; John H. Beck, WGBH-FM, Boston; Gene Benjamin; Larry Bensky, formerly of KPFA-FM, Berkeley, Calif.; David Berkman, HEW; Jim Biercher; Frank Blythe, Native

American Public Broadcasting Consortium; Kathy Bonk, National Organization for Women; Ronald C. Bornstein, WHA-TV and AM, Madison, Wis.; Thomas Borrup, San Diego Community Video Center; Lydia Bragger, Gray Panthers; Warren Braren, Consumer Federation of America; Les Brown, *New York Times;* Richard Bunce, Social Research Group; McGeorge Bundy, Ford Foundation; Bill Bush, Univ. of Mid-America; Sue Miller Buske, National Federation of Local Cable Programmers; Charles E. Buzzard, KMCR-FM, Phoenix, Ariz.; Jeff Byrd, AIVF; Patricia Deal Cahill, KMUW-FM, Wichita, Kan.; Diana Calland, CPB; Ricardo Callejo, Spanish Speaking/Surnamed Political Assn.; John Camelio, Portable Channel; Joseph Campanella, actor; Margaret Ann Carpenthall, Calif. Public Broadcasting Commission; Bob Chapman, Nebr. Dept. of Education; Umberto Cintron, National Latino Media Coalition; Matthew B. Coffey, NPR; Maxi Cohen, independent videomaker; Mary Conley, Committee for Children's Television; Donald Connelley, KBFL-FM, Buffalo, Mo.; Joan Ganz Cooney, Children's Television Workshop; Sal Cordova, Mexican-American Political Assn.; Genevieve Cory, Canada Coll.; Bonnie Cronin, WBUR-FM, Boston; Pam Croor, Parents of Hyperactive Children; Marc Cummings, San Francisco State Univ.; W. Bowman Cutter, Office of Management and Budget; Crane Davis, independent producer; David M. Davis, Ford Foundation; Willard Davis, Committee for Children's Television; Joe DeCola, producer; Ellen DeFranco, Early Childhood Education; William Devine III, WEBR-AM, WNED-FM, Buffalo; Maureen Donoff, Committee for Children's Television, National Assn. for Better Broadcasting; Peter Downey, PBS; Patrick Drake, KZUM-FM, Lincoln, Nebr.; Irene Duvall, Feminist Party; George Eckstein, Universal Television; Julian Ely, World Future Society; Ed Emshwiller, independent videomaker; Phillip Essman, Los Angeles Co. Superintendent of Schools; Richard Estell, WKAR-AM and FM, E. Lansing, Mich.; B. L. Faber, Center for the Study of Public Policy and the Arts; Geraldine O. Farber, Calif. Public Broadcasting Commission; James A. Fellows, National Assn. of Educational Broadcasters; Pablo Figueroa, producer; Susan Fireman, American Broadcasting Co.; Charles Firestone, Univ. of Calif. at Los Angeles; Peter Franck, Pacifica Foundation; Cliff Frazier, Institute of New Cinema Artists; David Freudberg, independent radio producer; Selma Friedman, Los Angeles Public Schools, Parent Education Supervisor; Fred W. Friendly, Ford Foundation;

Charles Fries, Charles Fries Productions; Bill Froug, Caucus of Producers, Writers, and Directors; James F. Fryer, Alameda Co. School Dept.; Frank Gillard, consultant, CPB; Dean Gillette, Bell Laboratories; Jack Golodner, Dept. for Professional Employees, AFL-CIO; Manuel Gonzalez, National Federation of Local Community Programmers; Abraham Gottfried, Council on Deafness; David Green, San Francisco Archdiocesan Educational Television Center; Lawrence K. Grossman, PBS; Ron Grossman, Citizens Committee on the Media; Michele Grumet, National Women's Coalition; Felix Gutierrez, Calif. State Univ., Northridge; John Hall, producer; Laurence S. Hall, National Task Force on Public Broadcasting; Dee Dee Halleck, AIVF; Josh Hanig, New Day Films; Susan D. Harmon, WAMU-FM, Washington, D.C.; Ellen Stern Harris; Irving Harris, WTTW-TV, Chicago; Maureen Hathaway, KSPS-TV, Spokane, Wash.; Monica Henreid, Children's Radio; Michael Herman, D. Q. Univ.; Charles Hobson, WETA-FM, Washington, D.C.; Samuel Holt, NPR; Al Hulsen, WGUC-FM, Cincinnati; Annette Hutchinson; Reed Irvine, Accuracy in Media; James H. Erwin, WFSU-FM, Tallahassee, Fla.; John Jay Iselin, WNET-TV, New York; David O. Ives, WGBH Educational Foundation, Boston; Phillip D. Jacklin, San Jose State Univ.; Robert E. Jacobsen, Calif. Friends of Public Broadcasting; Nicholas Johnson, National Citizens' Committee on Broadcasting; Richard Johnson, Irish Coalition for Fairness; Boots Jones, National Women's Coalition; Kanya, Tree of Life Bookstore; Larry Kay, Oakland Cable Access; Flo Kennedy, Black Women United for Political Action; Henry Kimmel, Children's Radio; Dorothea Kinney, Friends of Ireland; Arnie Klein, producer; William H. Kling, Minn. Public Radio; Chris Kobayashi; William Kobin, KTCA/KTCI-TV, St. Paul, Minn.; Anda Korsts, independent video artist; Robert Kotlowitz, WNET-TV, New York; Joel Kugelmas, Pacifica Foundation; Ruth Landy, independent filmmaker; Larry Lee, KSAN-FM, San Francisco; Leo Lee; Geoff Leighton, Cable Access Channel 25, San Francisco; Carol Levene, independent producer; Al Levin, WNET-TV, New York; Charles Levine, AIVF; Charles M. Lichenstein, PBS; Joseph C. R. Licklider, Mass. Inst. of Technology; Mitchell Lieber, Open Media Corp.; Charles Light, Green Mountain Post Films; William F. Little, Univ. of N.C.; Lynne Littman, independent producer; Frank W. Lloyd, FCC; Norman Lloyd, *Hollywood Television Theatre;* Henry Loomis, CPB; James V. Loper, KCET-TV,

Los Angeles; David Loxton, WNET-TV, New York; William Lucas, Rand Corp.; Robert MacNeil, WNET-TV, New York; Frank Mankiewicz, NPR; Pluria Marshall, National Black Media Coalition; Fern McBride, WGBH-TV, Boston; Jack McBride, Nebr. ETV Commission; William J. McCarter, WTTW-TV, Chicago; Edward L. McClarty, Calif. Public Broadcasting Commission; Richard McClear, KAXE-FM, Grand Rapids, Minn.; Robert McCoslin, Boston Film and Video Foundation; Mary McGee, media consultant; Nancy McMahon, American Council for Better Broadcasting; Chester Migden, Screen Actors Guild; Marilyn Miller; Newton N. Minow, PBS; Jose Mirelos, KPBS-FM, San Diego; Miles Mogulescu, Film Fund; Stella Montoya, First American Media Experience; Forrest L. Morris, Miss. Authority for ETV; Robert A. Mott, Public Service Satellite Consortium; Julie Motz, Hard Times Movie Co.; Frank W. Norwood, Joint Council on Educational Telecommunications; Michael Nyhan, Institute for the Future; Brian O'Doherty, National Endowment for the Arts; Robert G. Ottenhoff, Newark Public Radio; William J. Pearce, WXXI-TV and FM, Rochester, N.Y.; Gene Pepi, National Assn. of Broadcasting Engineers and Technicians; Sally Pope, Minn. Public Radio; Archie Purvis, MCA Disco-Vision; Eleanor Raen, H.A.V.E.; Fred J. Rebman, WJCT-TV and FM, Jacksonville, Fla.; Julia Reichert, independent filmmaker; John Reilly, Global Village; Michael Rice, WGBH-TV, Boston; George Riddick, Operation PUSH; David Rintels, Writers Guild of America, West; Sam Roberts, Conference of Motion Picture and Television Unions; Mary Jean Robertson, KPOO-FM, San Francisco; Clyde Robinson, NPR; Les Robinson, KDLG-AM, Dillingham, Alas.; Lee Rockwell, Nebr. ETV Council for Higher Education; Howard Rodman, writer; Ralph B. Rogers, PBS; Clara Rosenthal, PTA; Phil Rubin, CPB; Armand Ruhlman, Center for Veterans Rights; Boris Sagal, director; John Sanborn, video artist; William Schechner, KPIX-TV, San Francisco; Herbert Schmertz, Mobil Oil Corp.; Barbara Schultz, *Visions;* Paul H. Schupbach, Great Plains National Instructional Television Library; Sam Scott, KCUR-FM, Kansas City, Mo.; Harry Seagel, psychiatrist; James Serritella, Friends of Channel 11, Chicago; Diane Shalet, actress; Carol Shany, radio producer; Walter P. Sheppard, WITF-FM, Hershey, Pa.; Joan Shigekawa, independent producer; Mya Shone, independent video producer; William Siemering, Minn. Public Radio; Sharon Skolnick, KPOO-FM, San Francisco; Robert D. Smith, WGTE-

TV and FM, Toledo, Ohio; Robin Souza, Gay and Women's Alliance for Responsive Media; Richard Springer, Media Alliance; Stephen Stamas, Exxon Corp.; Jennifer Sterns, AIVF; George Stoney, N.Y. Univ.; Joel Sucher, Pacific Street Films; Patricia L. Swensen, KBPS-AM, Portland, Ore.; Charles E. Tate, Booker T. Washington Foundation; TedWillam Theodore, Chicago Videomakers Coalition; David Thomas; Robert W. Thomas, KWIT-FM, Sioux City, Iowa; Thomas J. Thomas, National Federation of Community Broadcasters; Tony Tiano, KTEC-TV, St. Louis; George Tressel, National Science Foundation; Gail Waldron, Bay Area Video Coalition; Milan Wall, University of Mid-America; Thomas C. Warnock, NPR; Norman E. Watson, Coast Community Coll. District; Helen Weber, Paulist Productions; Darrell Wheaton, Nebr. ETV Network; Huw Wheldon, BBC; Sally Williams, Committee for Children's Television; Jack Willis, independent producer; Burt Wilson, CAUSE; Ethel Winant, Children's Television Workshop; Donald Wood; Donald Wylie, San Diego State Univ.; Elizabeth L. Young, WOSU-TV and FM, Columbus, Ohio; Bobbie Zacharias, Citizens Committee on the Media; Allan J. Zack, AFL-CIO.

The Commission wishes to thank the following people not previously mentioned who participated in seminars or discussions convened by the Commission:

Charles Allen, KCET-TV, Los Angeles; George E. Bair, Univ. of N.C. Television Network; Lewis Bernstein, Children's Television Workshop; Virginia Biggy, Designs for Education; Mary G. F. Bitterman, Hawaii Public Broadcasting Authority; Henry L. Bonner, Ala. ETV Commission; Frederick Breitenfeld, Jr., Md. Center for Public Broadcasting; Charles Brownstein, National Science Foundation; Don Burgess, WMVS-TV, Milwaukee, Wis.; Fred R. Burgess, KVCR-TV, San Bernardino, Calif.; Julius Cain, Miss. Authority for ETV; Joyce Campbell, WETA-TV, Washington, D.C.; Joanne Cantor, Univ. of Wis.; Robert P. Casey, KIXE-TV, Redding, Calif.; Forrest Chisman, National Telecommunications and Information Administration; James N. Christianson, WTVS-TV, Detroit; Burnill Clark, KCTS-TV, Seattle, Wash.; George Coelho, National Institutes of Mental Health; Edwin G. Cohen, Agency for Instructional Television; George Comstock, Syracuse Univ.; Pat Conner, S.C. ETV Network; Betty Cope, WVIZ-TV, Cleveland; William T. Dale, Education Development Center; Halowell Davis, Washington Univ.; Colin Dougherty, KMTF-TV, Fresno, Calif.; Stanley J. Evans, Me. Public Broadcasting Network Board;

Donley F. Feddersen, WTIU-TV and FM, Bloomington, Ind.; Virginia Fox, Ky. Authority for ETV; Lawrence T. Frymire, NAEB; William A. Furniss, KOCE-TV, Huntington Beach, Calif.; Robert Gagné, Florida State Univ.; Raymond C. Giese, Central Educational Network; Shirley Gillette, WNET-TV, New York; Robert C. Glazier, Southern Educational Communications Assn.; George Hall, West Central Telecommunications; Fred Harner, Southeastern Ohio Council for ETV; Leslie Hart, author; Regina Herzlinger, Harvard Univ.; Richard B. Holcomb, WETV-TV and FM, Atlanta; Pres Holmes, Chicago Metropolitan Higher Education Council; Amos B. Hostetter, Jr., CPB; Peggy Hughes, KAET-TV, Phoenix, Ariz.; Nat Katzman, Research and Programming Services; J. C. Kenaston, KLCS-TV, Los Angeles; William Kessen, Yale Univ.; Ira Koger, WJCT-TV and FM, Jacksonville, Fla.; Michael LaBonia, Iowa Public Broadcasting Network; William Lamb, KCET-TV, Los Angeles; Gerald Lesser, Harvard Univ.; David Liroff, KETC-TV, St. Louis; Jack Lyle, East-West Center; Joseph Martin, WSCI-FM, Charleston, S.C.; Thomas R. McManus, KPBS-FM, San Diego, Calif.; Keith Mielke, Children's Television Workshop; Jack W. Mitchell, WHA-AM, Madison, Wis.; Anton J. Moe, Wis. Educational Communications Board; Florence Monroe, WBHM-FM, Birmingham, Ala.; Douglas Montgomery, KCSM-TV, San Mateo, Calif.; John Morison, WHRO-TV, Norfolk, Va.; Hal Morris, Appalachian Regional Commission; Lloyd Morrisett, John and Mary R. Markle Foundation; Rose Mukerjie, Brooklyn Coll.; Carol R. Nolan, WBEZ-FM, Chicago; Roger Noll, Calif. Inst. of Technology; Saralynn B. Oberdorfer, WGTV-TV, Athens/Atlanta, Ga.; Kenneth O'Bryan, Addiction Research Foundation; Maynard Orme, KTEH-TV, San Jose, Calif.; Richard E. Ottinger, Ga. ETV Network; Arthur Paul, KVIE-TV, Sacramento, Calif.; Joseph Pechman, Brookings Institution; Ronald J. Pedone, National Center for Education Statistics; Ed Pfister, KERA-TV, Dallas; O. Leonard Press, Ky. Educational Television; Karl Pribam, Stanford Univ.; John C. Rahmann, WTTW-TV, Chicago; Herb Reeves, WLTR-FM, Columbia, S.C.; Leon I. Rosenbluth, CPB; Ronald E. Roth, W. Va. Wesleyan Coll.; Eli A. Rubinstein, Univ. of N.C.; Ellen Berland Sachar, Mitchell, Hutchins; Vincent Saele, WNIN-TV, Evansville, Ind.; Gavriel Salomon, Stanford Univ.; Elliot B. Sanderson, WTVI-TV, Charlotte, N. C.; Mary Sceiford, CPB; Otto F. Schlaak, WMVS-TV, Milwaukee, Wis.; Wilbur Schramm, East-West Center; Wallace A.

Smith, KUSC-FM, Los Angeles; B. W. Spiller, WCVE/
WCVW-TV, Richmond, Va.; Paul J. Steen, KPBS-TV,
San Diego, Calif.; Thomas L. Stepp, S.C. ETV Network;
Mark Stevens, WGBH-TV, Boston; Stuart Sucherman,
WNET-TV, New York; Percy Tannenbaum, Univ. of
Calif. at Berkeley; Art Timko, WEMU-FM, Ypsilanti,
Mich.; James H. Turk, KEET-TV, Eureka, Calif.; Charles
W. Vaughn, WCET-TV, Cincinnati; Joseph Welling,
WOUB-TV and FM, Athens, Ohio; John White, Md. Cen-
ter for Public Broadcasting; N. W. Willett, KLRN-TV,
Austin, Tex.; John P. Witherspoon, Public Service Satel-
lite Consortium; Frank Withrow, U.S. Office of Educa-
tion.

We are appreciative of the written contributions received from the following representatives of stations and
organizations who have not been previously mentioned:

Jim Adams, Friends of the Earth; Arthur E. Al-
brecht, WSWP-TV/WVPB-FM, Beckley, W.Va.; James
E. Alexander, United Methodist Church; Peter W. All-
port, Assn. of National Advertisers; Alton J. Ashworth,
Jr., KNCT-TV and FM, Kileen, Tex.; Richard C. Atkin-
son, National Science Foundation; Russ Bufkins, Boy
Scouts of America; Carter L. Burgess, Foreign Policy
Assn.; Donald E. Burton, National Assn. for Hearing
and Speech Action; Martin P. Busch, S.D. Public Tele-
vision Network; David Cohen, Common Cause; Richard
S. Collins, American Bar Assn.; Eileen D. Cooke, Ameri-
can Library Assn.; John C. Crabbe, KTSC-TV, Pueblo,
Colo.; Joseph R. Crowley, U.S. Catholic Conference;
Lloyd H. Davis, National Univ. Extension Assn.; Leon
DelGrande, KALW-FM, San Francisco; George Dooley,
WPBT-TV, Miami, Fla.; Earl Ewald, NPR; George W.
Fellendorf, Alexander Graham Bell Assn. for the Deaf;
William F. Fore, National Council of Churches; Robert
F. Fuzy, KCPT-TV, Kansas City, Mo.; James Gabbert,
National Radio Broadcasters Assn.; Richard Gelgauda,
Intercollegiate Broadcasting System; Edmund J. Glea-
zer, Jr., American Assn. of Community and Junior Col-
leges; Earl T. Groves, National Recreation and Park Assn.;
William S. Hart, WYES-TV, New Orleans; John K. Hill,
KLVX-TV, Las Vegas, Nev.; H. Richard Hiner, Jr.,
WHA-TV, WEX Telecommunications, Madison, Wis.;
William E. Hurt, WIPB-TV, Greeley, Colo.; William R.
Hutton, National Council of Senior Citizens; Timothy S.
Jones, KUMR-TV, Rolla, Mo.; Thomas L. Kimball, Na-
tional Wildlife Federation; Robert G. Lewis, National
Farmers Union; Huey B. Long, Adult Education Assn. of

the USA; William T. Maynard, KOZK-TV, Springfield, Mo.; Susan McClear, KAXE-FM, Northern Community Radio, Grand Rapids, Minn.; Stephen H. McCurley, National Center for Voluntary Action; Lyle Mettler, KWSU-TV and AM, Pullman, Wash.; William G. Mitchell, WUSF-TV, Tampa, Fla.; James R. Needham, WIPB-TV, Muncie, Ind.; Charles M. Northrip, KTOO-TV and FM, Capital Community Broadcasting, Juneau, Alas.; Paul M. Norton, Wis. Educational Communications Board; Tony Pelle, Broadcast Commission, Hawaii Council of Churches; J. W. Peltason, American Council on Education; Lee Reaves, Ark. Educational Television Network; Alan Reitman, ACLU; John Ross, KRAB-FM, Seattle, Wash.; John Ryor, NEA; Walter J. Schaar, KSPS-TV, Spokane, Wash.; Curtis C. Schultz, KTDB-FM, Ramah, N.M.; Leon Shull, ADA; Sheldon P. Siegel, WVLT-TV, Bethlehem, Pa.; Al Simensen, U.S. Jaycees; Bruce L. Smith, WKMS-FM, Murray, Ky.; Stephen M. Steck, WMFE-TV, Orlando, Fla.; Paul K. Taff, Conn. Public Television; Jeff Tellis, Intercollegiate Broadcasting System; W. L. Turner, National Univ. Extension Assn.; Mrs. Harry Wagner, Jr., General Federation of Women's Clubs; Marcus Garvey Wilcher, Community Coalition for Media Change; Eddie N. Williams, Joint Center for Political Studies; Roger Yarrington, American Assn. of Community and Junior Colleges.

The Commission has benefited from consultation, support, and suggestions from more than seven hundred individuals both inside and outside public broadcasting. Our special thanks are extended to the staffs of the three major national public broadcasting entities—CPB, NPR, and PBS—as well as the Assn. of Independent Video and Filmmakers; the BBC; Minn. Public Radio; Nebr. ETV Network; S.C. ETV Network; WGBH, Boston; WNET-TV, New York; and WTTW-TV, Chicago.

We also wish to express especial gratitude to the following individuals for the extraordinary time, energy, and thought that they have contributed to the Commission's work:

Michael Ambrosino, Public Broadcasting Associates; Michael Arlen, *New Yorker;* Les Brown, *New York Times;* David M. Davis, Ford Foundation; James A. Fellows, National Assn. of Educational Broadcasters; William F. Fore, National Council of Churches; Fred W. Friendly, Ford Foundation; Henry Geller, National Telecommunications and Information Administration; John Grist, BBC; Lawrence K. Grossman, PBS; Laurence S.

Hall, National Task Force on Public Broadcasting; Richard Hooper, Mills and Allen Communications; Amos. B. Hostetter, Jr., CPB; Henry Loomis, CPB; Frank Mankiewicz, NPR; Mary Jo Manning, Senate Subcommittee on Communications; Gale Metzger, Statistical Research, Inc., Lloyd Morrisett, John and Mary R. Markle Foundation; Richard M. Neustadt, White House; Michael Rice, WGBH-TV, Boston; Carolyn F. Sachs, House Subcommittee on Communications; Robert Sachs, National Telecommunications and Information Administration; Harold Seidman, Univ. of Connecticut; Harry M. Shooshan, House Subcommittee on Communications; Richard Somerset-Ward, BBC; Thomas J. Thomas, National Federation of Community Broadcasters; James E. Webb, Smithsonian Institution; Stephen White, Sloan Foundation.

Appendix B

Chronology of Public Broadcasting

1922
By end of year over 500 radio stations are on the air, including 74 stations operated by colleges and universities. Approximately 100,000 receivers are manufactured and distributed to retail outlets during year.

1925
Association of College and University Broadcasting Stations formed. In 1934 Association becomes National Association of Educational Broadcasters (NAEB). Purpose is to promote interests of educational broadcasters.

1927
Radio Act passed. The U.S. Government is to maintain control over all radio channels and is to provide for use of them by licensees for limited periods. In granting a license, guiding standard is to be "public interest, convenience, and necessity."

1934
Passage of Communications Act. Senators Robert Wagner (N.Y.) and Henry Hatfield (W.Va.) propose amendment reserving 25 percent of all radio frequencies for educational, nonprofit use. Amendment defeated, and American broadcasting remains predominantly a commercial enterprise.

1939
FCC first reserves FM channels for noncommercial educational broadcasting, establishing frequencies for educational use.

1940
1. Commercial television begins regular broadcasts. Programs consist primarily of movies, cooking demonstrations, puppets, and sporting events. Development of television financed largely through commercial radio profits.
2. By end of year, two commercial television stations are on air.

1945
FCC rearranges FM band and reserves 20 of 100 channels for noncommercial radio.

1946
By end of year 12 commercial television stations are on the air nationwide.

1948
FCC encourages educational radio by authorizing 10-watt noncommercial stations. (Ten-watt stations are extremely weak, generating signals that can carry about two miles.) Result: a proliferation of FM stations operating on meager budgets and providing minimal service.

1948–52
FCC stops processing TV license applications. Freeze allows FCC time to develop coherent policy for future use of TV spectrum.

1949
NAEB establishes permanent Washington, D.C., headquarters, begins audio tape duplicating service, engages in research, publishes reports, awards fellowships, and contributes to industry's increased sense of purpose.

1951–61
Ford Foundation money activates and supports educational television stations. During this decade, Ford Foundation is a major factor in developing ETV system.

1952
1. FCC reserves 242 TV channels for education. (Number subsequently raised to 127 VHFs, 528 UHFs.) UHF channels difficult, or impossible, to receive on most TV sets in operation at time.
2. Existing commercial interests retain their licenses, mostly for VHF channels. Educational broadcasters gain few VHF channels, with no VHFs in 69 of top 100 markets.
3. Ford Foundation establishes Educational Radio and Television Center to finance programs to be shared by stations. Center, in 1959, moves to New York City and becomes National Educational Television (NET).

1953
First ETV station, KUHT (University of Houston, Texas), goes on air. Commercial TV stations have been in

operation for over 13 years, and ETV is essentially an add-on to dominant commercial system.

1954–59
1. ETV stations show slow but steady growth. Ten ETV stations on air in 1954; 17 in 1955; 44 in 1959.[1] Most early ETV stations are licensed to and supported by educational institutions. Noncommercial television in America begins in an educational context.
2. WQED, Pittsburgh, first noncommercial TV station licensed to and supported by community nonprofit organization, begins operation in 1954.
3. During 1950s, 10-watt (low-power) stations continue to be predominant type of noncommercial radio stations.

1955
Station KQED, San Francisco, a community television station, holds first on-air auction. Auctions become a major device through which community stations raise money.

1960
Eastern Educational Network (EEN) formed. First of regional networks established to share programs and develop unified stand when appearing before funding groups.

1961
Creation of Midwest Project on Airborne Televised Instruction (MPATI). Goal is to demonstrate that schools could use effective instructional television programs produced outside their own school districts. Programs are transmitted to schools in a six-state area from a circling airplane.

1962
1. Educational Television Facilities Act is passed. First federal support of ETV. Authorizes $32 million over a five-year period to be used for construction of towers, transmitters, studios, etc. Limited to $1 million per state; funds must be matched 1:1 by a new station.
2. Seventy-five ETV stations are on air; 194 FM educational radio stations are operating.
3. Channel 13, New York City, purchased from commercial groups for $5.75 million, becomes WNDT, a non-

---

[1]All ETV station figures are as of December 31 of each year. Source: PBS.

commercial station. Ultimately Channel 13 becomes largest noncommercial station in nation.
4. By end of year educational television gains foothold,
aided by Ford Foundation, federal government, and community groups.

1963
1. NAEB members form Educational Television Stations
(ETS) Division to present their case before federal government and the Ford Foundation, and also to work with
NET.
2. NET provides ETV stations with ten hours of programming weekly, divided roughly between cultural and
public affairs programs.
3. State and local governments continue to be largest supporters of nationwide ETV efforts.

1964
1. NET reduces production from ten to five hours per
week and raises production standards.
2. NAEB convention recommends creation of presidential
commission to study needs of evolving industry. Johnson
prefers nongovernmental study, and in 1965 Carnegie
Corporation creates Carnegie Commission on Educational
Television, a panel of distinguished citizens. Commission
is asked to recommend lines along which noncommercial
television stations might most usefully develop during the
years ahead. Noncommercial radio is not to be examined.
3. One hundred and one ETV stations on air. Their funding comes primarily from state and local governments,
colleges and foundations. Ford Foundation contributes
$7.6 million.
4. Two hundred thirty-seven noncommercial FM radio
stations are on air.

1966
1. Carnegie Commission undertakes extensive study of
ETV industry. James Killian is Commission chairman.
Ninety-two ETV stations in 38 states are visited, eight
formal Commission meetings are held.
2. December, Ford Foundation creates Public Broadcasting Laboratory (PBL) in New York. Laboratory produces major Sunday evening cultural and public affairs
series which is distributed simultaneously to all ETV stations.
3. Six hundred ten commercial and 126 ETV stations
on air; 268 noncommercial FM radio stations in opera-

tion. Commercial TV's income is 20 times as great as ETV's. ETV's total income is $58.3 million. Local governments contribute $11 million; state governments, $15.7 million; state universities, $6.5 million; federal government, $6.8 million; foundations, $8.4 million; underwriters, $1 million; businesses, $2 million; viewer-subscribers, $3.2 million; and assorted other income is $3.2 million.[2]

1967

1. January, Carnegie Commission issues its report. Coins name "Public Television" for system. Main recommendations:

    a. Increased state and local support for ETV stations, with new program of federal assistance administered by HEW.

    b. Creation of Corporation for Public Television (CPT), a nongovernmental, private corporation to finance programming. CPT also responsible for (1) support of two national production centers; (2) support of productions for greater-than-local use; (3) support of local broadcasting.

CPT is to operate a national network that will connect all PTV stations, enabling them to receive a television broadcast simultaneously. CPT is to be funded by an excise tax on TV sets, and is to work for federal legislation that will fund new stations and improve facilities through HEW support.

2. NET provides 15 live interconnections of ETV stations. First live interconnection carries President Johnson's State of the Union message.

3. Radio: 326 educational radio stations are now on air; 40 more are awaiting permits. Nearly half operate on budgets of less than $10,000 per year. None has federal funding.

4. Radio: Major source of programming is National Educational Radio Network (NERN), outgrowth of NAEB's radio network. Coordinated program service operates only via mail.

5. Radio: April, Ford Foundation-financed study, *The Hidden Medium: A Status Report on Educational Radio in the United States,* appears. Published by National Educational Radio (NER), report indicates:

    a. Educational radio underfinanced, understaffed, and operates with poor facilities;

---

[2]Data from Carnegie I survey of station income.

b. Recommends increased system support, greater research, pursuit of table of allocations for educational FM channels;

c. Capability for national and international coverage; Report helps persuade Congress to include noncommercial radio in 1967 public broadcasting legislation.

6. November, Public Broadcasting Act of 1967 is signed by President Johnson. Among act's chief provisions:

a. Creation of Corporation for Public Broadcasting;

b. Noncommercial radio and television stations would receive operating support from CPB;

c. A presidentially appointed CPB board of 15 members, subject to Senate confirmation;

d. CPB to be financed from annual appropriations;

e. CPB prohibited from running station interconnection;

f. Radio included;

g. Authorizes study of instructional broadcasting.

7. November, PBL programs begin, fed live to PTV stations nationwide. PBL's programs are often controversial.

1968

1. April, CPB board meets for first time and is incorporated. It is given responsibility to facilitate development of public radio and television and protect them from outside control.

2. By end of year CPB awards first grant, to *Black Journal,* and commissions study of public radio.

3. The Children's Television Workshop is formed.

1969

1. February, John Macy is appointed president of CPB.

2. First CPB grants to television stations, a uniform $10,000 to each licensee.

3. Advisory Committee of National Organizations (ACNO) first meets. Comprising 26 professional and voluntary organizations, ACNO is conceived as group to lobby in Washington for federal financing of public broadcasting.

4. CPB radio study indicates public radio grossly underfunded. Establishes priorities for CPB radio department focusing on development of public radio system and on live national public radio service.

5. November, Children's Television Workshop production *Sesame Street* goes on air. Project is funded by con-

sortiums of foundations and federal government. Designed to teach basic cognitive skills to preschool children, series joins educational content with commercial TV production techniques. Series becomes, in single season, most widely viewed PTV program. Credited with putting PTV on map.

6. CPB establishes American Fellowship Abroad program. From 1969 to 1971, 11 fellowships are awarded to public broadcasting producers of unusual ability and promise for a year of foreign study and work. Disbanded in 1971 for lack of funds.

7. November, PBS is incorporated in Washington, D.C.

1970

1. National Public Radio (NPR) is incorporated with 91 charter member stations. NPR functions as both program producer and distributor.

2. National PTV programming is provided by five major production centers: NET, New York; WGBH, Boston; WETA, Washington, D.C.; KQED, San Francisco; and KCET, Los Angeles. Children's Television Workshop is also a major producer for system. Each production center receives grants from CPB and Ford Foundation for productions to be distributed nationally. CPB and PBS are involved in selection of program proposals.

3. PBS develops set of programming standards and practices—an attempt to control content of NET programs, which many licensees continue to find troublesome.

4. Fall, PBS begins interconnection operation. First year of interconnection brings outstanding BBC-produced series including *Forsyte Saga* and *Civilisation,* which was a gift to PTV from Xerox.

5. CPB establishes incentives for growth of local public radio stations through its report, *CPB Policy for Public Radio Station Assistance.* Report lists criteria necessary for CPB assistance to local public radio stations. Criteria include requirements for a station to operate with a certain minimum power, have one full-time staff member receive nonfederal income, and operate at least eight hours a day, six days a week, 48 weeks per year. Criteria are to become incrementally more rigorous so that levels of service can be raised.

6. For year, PTV's total income is $100 million; income of CPB qualified radio stations is $9.4 million.

1971

1. Mobil Oil Corporation underwrites cost of *Masterpiece Theatre,* a highly popular British dramatic series.

2. NET's *Banks and the Poor* lists 133 legislators and government officials with banking connections.

3. PBS expands its role to include the monitoring of national television programming.

4. CPB and PBS agree on grant-making process that designates WNET, WETA, and KCET as major production centers to receive grants. Remaining programming funds are awarded on basis of open competition.

5. The Ford Foundation facilitates merger of NET with New York's Channel 13. Station becomes WNET and assumes many of NET's production responsibilities.

6. First attempts at long-term funding of public broadcasting fail. PTV's income is $140.8 million with 17 percent from federal and public broadcasting agencies, 47 percent from state and local agencies, 11 percent from foundations, 9 percent from viewers and on-air auctions, 7 percent from universities and colleges, and 9 percent from business and industry. Income of CPB-qualified radio stations is $12.1 million.

7. Clay T. Whitehead, director of White House office of Telecommunications Policy, speaks before NAEB convention in Miami. Accuses CPB and PBS of forming a "fourth network" and calls for a return to "bedrock of localism." He indicts present system and warns that business as usual will assure that "permanent financing will always be somewhere off in the distant future."

8. Major target of White House anger is National Public Affairs Center for Television (NPACT) in Washington. NPACT was established by the Ford Foundation and CPB, and attached to WETA. Center produces *Washington Week in Review* and *Thirty Minutes With*, as well as election coverage and documentaries. NPACT is also under fire from some local licensees who charge it with ultraliberalism and being dominated by the Ford Foundation.

9. Continued strife between WNET and PBS over programs such as *Great American Dream Machine* and *The Politics of Woody Allen*. PBS cites its responsibility for programs it distributes as its reason to become judge of acceptable programming; WNET accuses PBS of attempted censorship.

10. Public broadcasting's first experimental satellite transmission: NPR broadcasts to Alaska on experimental ATS-1 satellite.

11. April, NPR begins network transmission with live coverage of Senate Foreign Relations Committee hearings

on Vietnam and, in May, NPR's *All Things Considered* debuts.
12. Between 1969 and 1971, 28 new noncommercial TV stations go on air. Total of 216 public television stations are on air at end of year.

1972

1. PBS and CPB meet frequently and attempt to clarify respective responsibilities and develop a cooperative working relationship.
2. June, President Nixon vetoes two-year public broadcasting funding bill, citing system's lack of localism and fiscal restraint.
3. August, John Macy resigns as president of CPB; his position goes to Henry Loomis. Shortly thereafter, CPB announces its intention to take over many responsibilities currently exercised by PBS.
4. September, Frank Pace declines to stand for reelection as CPB board chairman; newly appointed member Thomas B. Curtis takes the post.
5. November, further conflict on programming control erupts when CPB offers Apollo 17 moon-walk programs directly to stations, bypassing PBS. Offer is ultimately withdrawn. Intense CPB-PBS negotiations on control of interconnection.
6. ACNO meets with CPB officials and accuses them of attempted control of interconnection.
7. Public television's income for year is $157.9 million. CPB-qualified radio stations' income is $15.4 million.

1973

1. CPB board unanimously passes resolution calling for PBS to give all scheduling and programming responsibilities to CPB, leaving PBS with technical role of program transmission. Stations rally around PBS because it is station-governed and many licensees distrust centralized authority of CPB.
2. PBS turns for help to governing board chairmen, group of lay representatives of PTV stations led by Ralph Rogers.
3. Group of station board chairmen, as station representatives, meet with CPB board to work out differences between the two groups.
4. CPB announces intention to cut off funds for several public affairs television programs.
5. PBS, governing board chairmen, and ETS division of

NAEB merge into newly chartered Public Broadcasting Service. Ralph Rogers named chairman of the board. Board has representatives from both station management and boards.

6. April, CPB board meets to consider CPB-PBS compromise agreement. Board defers action; CPB board chairman Curtis resigns, charging White House tampering with CPB board members. James Killian elected CPB board chairman.

7. May, CPB-PBS announce partnership agreement, which provides:

a. Non-CPB-funded programs to have access to interconnection;

b. PBS given diminished role in deciding which programs to be funded by CPB;

c. PBS remains in charge of interconnection;

d. Joint CPB-PBS committee to resolve questions of program balance and objectivity;

e. CPB to pay for interconnection; licensees to pay for services provided them by PBS;

f. Increased percentage of CPB appropriations to be used for station support (increased Community Service Grants).

8. July, Congress passes two-year, $130 million (plus $55 million for facilities) public broadcasting financing bill.

9. Summer, PBS and NPR carry Watergate hearings.

10. August, President Nixon signs two-year financing bill, indicating system has made progress in returning power to local stations.

11. September, CPB, NPR, PBS, and NAEB agree on unified position, issue *Task Force Report on Long-Range Financing of Public Broadcasting*. Report recommends:

a. Five-year federal funding bill;

b. Significant increase in funds to CPB and to broadcast facilities;

c. Ratio of two nonfederal dollars to each federal support dollar.

12. CPB-qualified radio stations form Association of Public Radio Stations (APRS) to represent their interest nationally.

13. CPB funds three projects to test impact of public radio:

a. Six-year experiment with Minnesota Public Radio intended to provide comprehensive public radio service and encourage local support to supplant CPB support;

b. WOSU-AM and FM in Columbus, Ohio, to test

need for multiple stations in major markets. WOSU trip-
ples its audience by programming the two stations separately;

c. Creation of music production center at WGUC in
Cincinnati.

14. By end of year PTV's income is $241.2 million
with 16 percent coming from federal and public broadcasting agencies and 84 percent from nonfederal sources.
There are 144 CPB-qualified radio stations operating with
a total income of $25.3 million. From 1969 to 1973
noncommercial radio stations increase 55 percent. CPB-
qualified stations double.

15. CPB begins awarding Minority Training Grants. Requiring matching funds from recipient public broadcasting
station, program is designed to help members of minority groups move to positions of greater responsibility within public broadcasting.

1974

1. Station Program Cooperative (SPC) is created. Plan
allows television stations to select and fund programs for
national distribution. Initial funding for SPC comes from
CPB, Ford Foundation, and participating stations. SPC
serves dual purpose: creating pool of funds for national
programming, while maintaining stations' responsibility
for selecting the programs.

2. Following creation of SPC, CPB assumes role of ini-
tiator rather than sustainer of national programming. CPB
no longer funds programs beyond a second season, after
which they must be sustained by other funders.

3. Ford Foundation announces it will begin phasing out
its support of public broadcasting. By the time Ford
Foundation concludes the bulk of its support in 1977,
the Foundation has contributed nearly $300 million.

4. Station Independence Program (SIP) is established.
Initially financed by Ford Foundation, project is established as part of PBS, and is designed to assist PTV
stations in increasing nonfederal support through greater
viewer awareness and contributions. SIP three-year project, with Ford Foundation matching grants, increases
viewer support from $24.1 million in 1973 to $57.9 million
in 1977.

5. Summer, President Nixon calls for five-year public
broadcasting funding.

6. Satellite Working Group formed with members of
PBS, CPB, Ford, and later, NPR. Feasibility and en-

gineering studies are begun to determine practicality of using satellites to interconnect public broadcasting licensees.

7. CPB Board opts for another year of allocating 16.7 percent of its funds to public radio, after dispute between public radio and television representatives over shares of CPB budget. Such a formula does not penalize radio for its inability to raise great amounts of nonfederal money. Public radio supporters feel it cannot yet compete with PTV in nonfederal fund raising because public radio is in an earlier stage of development.

8. CPB creates task force to study and report on the status of women in the industry. Task force reports in 1975, indicating a lack of women's programming on PTV and NPR, and that women are underrepresented at the middle and high levels of industry. Task force issues list of recommendations to improve image of women as portrayed in public broadcasting programs.

9. ACNO begins study of relationship between public broadcasting and education. Report, issued in 1975, indicates that CPB has no policy toward education, that a positive policy should be developed, and that CPB should assume leadership role in bridging gap between PTV and education.

10. December, Robert Benjamin succeeds James Killian as CPB board chairman.

11. By end of year PTV's income reaches $266.6 million. Twenty percent of total comes from federal and public broadcasting agencies, 14 percent from viewer contributions and auctions, 35 percent from state and local agencies, and 6 percent from foundations. Roughly 50 percent of all American households view public television at least once a month. Seventeen percent of system's programming is instructional television; *Sesame Street* and *Electric Company* contribute an additional 21 percent; news and public affairs account for 13 percent; information skills, 16 percent; cultural programs, 18 percent; general children's programs, 11 percent; and other programming, 4 percent.

12. There are 155 CPB-qualified radio stations operating. Their total income is $31.4 million. Sixty percent of their schedule is devoted to classical music, 2.5 percent to instruction, 26 percent to public affairs/information, and 10 percent to culture.

1975

1. President Ford signs Public Broadcasting Financing Act of 1975. Bill creates five-year funding authorization.

House Appropriations Committee agrees to recommend a three-year appropriation. By August 1976 a House-Senate Conference Committee agrees to authorize $103 million for fiscal year 1977, $107 million for 1978, and $120 million for 1979. Multiyear funding represents landmark for public broadcasting.

2. Congress demands more equitable employment practices and accountability from industry.

3. Federal funding of system rises from 10 percent in 1969 to 25 percent in 1975. From 1973 to 1976 Emergency School Assistance Act (ESAA) contributes $36 million to system in programming grants. Corporate underwriting moves from $3 million in 1973 to $14 million in 1976. By year's end PTV's total income reaches $276.6 million. Federal government gives 25 percent, colleges and state and local governmental agencies give 14 percent, subscribers, foundations, and viewer auctions account for 31 percent. One hundred sixty-five CPB-qualified radio stations on air; total income: $39.8 million.

4. CPB originates its Coverage Expansion Grant program, designed to aid groups interested in establishing new noncommercial radio stations.

5. National Federation of Community Broadcasters is formed with 18 member radio stations. Purpose is to represent interests of community broadcasters with national policymakers, provide practical information to stations, and exchange programming and ideas. NFCB membership has grown to 50 in 1978.

1976

1. Continued stress in CPB-PBS relationships. CPB favors funding several new low-budget productions for a year or two and then letting system finance them; PBS wants long-term CPB commitment to major new projects. PBS objects to CPB funding BBC Shakespeare project.

2. In response to its frustration with CPB's programming decisions, PBS board adopts resolution in Kansas City, Missouri, requesting CPB to get out of programming and have 75 percent of their appropriations go directly to PTV stations.

3. March, FCC issues *Notice of Proposed Rule Making* (Docket 20735) proposing noncommercial FM table of allocations, freeze on 10-watt activations, and move of 10-watt stations into commercial portion of the spectrum or into spectrum space to be newly provided under the proposal.

4. March, CPB begins its Women's Training Grant pro-

gram to help women within public broadcasting gain access to positions of greater responsibility within the system.

5. CPB provides grants to upgrade public radio in major population centers. First award is to KUSC, University of Southern California, Los Angeles. Purpose is to convert student-run radio station into full-service alternative classical music station. Grant is for $350,000 in 1976, $375,000 in 1977, and $300,000 in 1978.

6. December, at request of CPB, NPR, James Killian, and other concerned citizens, Carnegie Corporation establishes task force to evaluate need to form second Carnegie Commission.

7. By the year's end public television has a total income of $364.9 million, of which 27 percent came from the federal government, 40.7 percent came from local and state government sources, and 32 percent came from private sources. Public radio's total income is $50.9 million, with sources being the federal government, 32 percent; nonfederal tax sources, 47 percent; and nontax-based income, 20 percent. There are 185 CPB-qualified radio stations on the air. In 1976 (including transition quarter) CPB spends $94.6 million for its activities; PBS, $18 million; and NPR, $5.4 million.

1977

1. January, CPB signs a $25.3 million contract with Rockwell International for the construction of 150 ground terminals that will form the basis of public television's satellite distribution service.

2. February, television licensees vote overwhelmingly in favor of PBS management of satellite interconnection. CPB sets up coordinating office, and finances satellite. Satellite costs approximately $40 million.

3. FCC rules that public broadcasters have obligation to ascertain community needs and interests.

4. Public broadcasters are criticized by House of Representatives for their poor Equal Employment Opportunity record.

5. New copyright law. Law remains basically preferential to public broadcasting's unique status, although requiring public broadcasters to negotiate with BMI, ASCAP, and others.

6. PBS national program schedule costs $67 million, with SPC providing $12.5 million, and federal agencies and corporate underwriters adding $34 million more. Foundations provide $7 million more for national schedule.

7. May, members of NPR and APRS merge into National Public Radio. New organization has two divisions: one to produce and distribute national programs, other to represent station interest before Congress.

8. Planning for satellite interconnection of public television stations nears completion. It calls for main PBS uplink, five regional uplinks, and receive-only facilities at each PBS station. PBS transponder allocation committee to determine use of transponders when not being used by PBS for national schedule.

9. July, NPR board approves basic details of satellite interconnection for radio. Costs in excess of $16 million.

10. September, ACNO votes to dissolve itself, citing lack of effectiveness and confusion over organization's role.

11. CPB study of instructional television reveals less than one-third of American teachers have been trained in use of ITV; one-third of nation's schoolchildren regularly use ITV, and an additional one-third have no access to ITV.

12. October, President Carter proposes Public Broadcasting Financing Act of 1978. Bill provides for:
   a. Increased funding;
   b. Reduced CPB programming role;
   c. Improved EEO enforcement and financial accountability.

13. Fall, second Carnegie Commission begins work. Report due January 1979.

1978

1. Spring, Senate and House introduce their own legislation for redesign and funding of public broadcasting. Members of public broadcasting industry alarmed, in part, at conditions placed on allocation of Community Service Grants (CSGs), requirement of uniform system of accounting for all funds received by licensee, and mandatory community advisory boards.

2. Carnegie Commission continues deliberations. Holds regional meetings, receives testimony from within and outside industry.

3. FCC approves proposals requiring 10-watt stations that do not increase their power to move to other frequencies, setting a minimum operating schedule for FM noncommercial stations, and allocating a new channel on the spectrum for low-powered stations. FCC issues further *Notice of Proposed Rule Making* regarding noncommercial FM table of allocations. In other proceedings, FCC considers revision of criteria for grant of noncommercial

licenses, looks toward new standards for fund-raising activities and underwriter credits, and reexamines practice of allowing one noncommercial licensee to control two television or two radio stations. Chairman Ferris promises to consider seriously the setting aside of any expanded AM spectrum space for noncommercial radio.

4. June, Representatives VanDeerlin and Frey submit proposed rewrite of Communications Act of 1934 to House Communications Subcommittee.

5. The Public Telecommunications Financing Act of 1978 passes Congress and is signed by President Carter. The act imposes tougher regulatory standards on the stations, calls on CPB to give greater emphasis to programming activities, changes the funding match to 2:1, and raises the funding ceiling to $220 million.

Appendix C

Statistical Overview

Public Broadcasting in the Commercial Context

The broadcasting system in this country is overwhelmingly a commercial one.

This section of the appendix illustrates the relative position of public broadcasting within its commercial context through a number of statistical measures. Included are comparisons of number of stations, average audiences, income, expenditures, programming, employment, and availability of service.

Table C–1

Number of Stations Licensed or On Air

	Commercial	Public
Television	728	280
	516 VHF	111 VHF
	212 UHF	169 UHF
Radio	7,582	198
	4,516 AM	23 AM
	3,066 FM	175 FM

Sources: *Commercial television:* FCC listing of stations licensed, or operating on special authorization or construction permits, Sept. 30, 1978. *Public television:* PBS Research, Oct. 30, 1978. *Commercial radio:* FCC listing, less 22 CPB-qualified AM stations listed by FCC as commercial because they operate on commercial licenses, Sept. 30, 1978. *Public radio:* CPB Management Information Systems, Dec. 1978. This total is for CPB-qualified stations only. There are, in addition, approximately 800 noncommercial FM stations that do not meet the CPB requirements for staff, budget size, power, and air time (FCC listings, Sept. 1978).

Table C–2

Audience

	Commercial	Public
Television:		
Prime-time average		
Minute rating/approximate "share"	18.8/30.0[a]	1.5/2.4
Weekly cumulative audience	90.3[a]	33[b]
Radio:		
Average quarter-hour audience	15.6	0.1
Weekly cumulative audience	95.0	2.4

Sources: *Commercial television average ratings:* A. C. Nielsen Co., average rating of prime-time network program, March 1978. *Public television average ratings:* A. C. Nielsen Co., average prime-time rating, all public television stations, March 1978. *Television weekly cumulative audience:* A. C. Nielsen Co., average of network full-week cumulative ratings and public television cumulative rating, week of Sept. 19–25, 1977. *Radio:* Arbitron, April/May 1977. (Copyrighted, used with permission.)

Television data are expressed as percentage of television households. Prime-time average minute rating is defined as the percentage of all households tuned into a program in any particular minute. The corresponding share measures the percentage of households using their television sets at a given minute tuned into the program. Weekly cumulative audience is defined as the percentage of all households tuning in to the specified stations one or more times a week.

Radio data are expressed as a percentage of all persons, age 12 or older, tuned into a program. The entry in the commercial column represents total usage and includes both commercial and noncommercial stations but is close to what the commercial only figures would be. This is because the public radio audience is small and, in the case of cumulative audience, because few people listen to public radio exclusively. The entry in the public column represents CPB-qualified stations only.

[a]One (average) network.

[b]PTV's monthly cumulative audience is substantially larger, 63.2 percent in March 1978. Source: A. C. Nielsen Co.

Table C–3

Revenue (1977)

	Commercial (millions)	Public[a] (millions)
Television	$5,889.0	$416.5
Radio	2,274.5	65.5
	$8,163.5	$482.1[b]

Sources: *Commercial:* Federal Communications Commission. *Public:* CPB Management Information Systems.

[a]Includes in-kind support.

[b]Column does not add due to rounding.

Table C–4

Expenditures (1977)

	Commercial (millions)	Public (millions)
National program expenditure per network (television)	$506	$67.5
Budget per station:		
Television	$ 3.2	$ 2.1
Radio	0.3 (1976)	0.2

Sources: *Commercial expenditure per network:* One-third of total network program expenses as reported to FCC including payments to program producers, and cost of public affairs and for music and other rights. *Public expenditure per network:* PBS Research. Includes costs of original production distributed by PBS in 1977, plus cost of acquisitions and step-ups of local production, which generally reflect only a fraction of the original production costs. *Commercial budget per station:* Calculated by dividing gross expenditures of all stations by number of stations as reported by FCC. *Public television budget per station:* PBS Research (average station nonfederal income + Community Service Grants). *Public radio budget per station:* CPB Management Information Systems (average station nonfederal income + Community Service Grants).

Table C–5

Programming		
	Commercial	Public
Television (% of prime-time hours, 1976):		
Drama	45[a]	23
Comedy	19[b]	3
Feature film	17	5
Variety	11	17[c]
Information and other	8	52
Radio station formats (% of stations):		
Middle-of-the-road	30	2
Country and western	26	1
Top 40	16	1
Beautiful music	7	0
Religious	6	0
News	1	1
Progressive	3	0
Talk	2	2
Classical	1	43
All others	8	51[d]

Sources: *Commercial television:* A. C. Nielsen Co. survey of sponsored network program hours (1976). *Public television:* Katzman survey of all prime-time hours broadcast by stations (1976). *Radio:* Based on format listings as published in *Broadcasting Yearbook,* 1978. Used with permission. Public column adds to 101 due to rounding.

[a]Includes general drama and suspense/mystery.

[b]Situation comedies.

[c]Music, dance, performance programming.

[d]Most public stations in this category are "fine arts" stations combining two or more musical categories, often plus news, public affairs, and special programming.

Table C–6

Employment and Wages in Stations

	TV Commercial	Public	Radio Commercial	Public
Total employment (full-time)	48,212	8,123	64,215	1,615
Average salaries:				
Chief executive/ Station manager	$47,000	$28,000	$35,000	$18,000
Program manager	25,000	21,000	19,000	12,000
News director	25,000	19,000	18,000	10,000

Sources: *Public television and radio:* CPB Management Information Systems, 1977. *Commercial television employment:* FCC, 1977. *Commercial radio employment:* FCC, 1976. *Commercial salaries:* Broadcast Financial Management Association, 1977.

Table C–7

Television Signal Availability

Commercial and Public Stations	Share of TV Households
1–3	4%
4	8
5	11
6	12
7	18
8	9
9	11
10+	27
	100%

Source: A. C. Nielsen Co.

Table C–8

Public Television Coverageª by State

	% of Population		% of Population
Alabama	87.6	Montana	0.0
Alaska	59.3	Nebraska	90.8
Arizona	77.5	Nevada	55.1
Arkansas	92.0	New Hampshire	91.2
California	85.6	New Jersey	98.3
Colorado	79.7	New Mexico	55.5
Connecticut	86.9	New York	86.5
Delaware	91.2	North Carolina	79.5
District of Columbia	100.0	North Dakota	46.8
Florida	90.6	Ohio	80.4
Georgia	88.4	Oklahoma	79.7
Hawaii	82.9	Oregon	75.5
Idaho	48.6	Pennsylvania	84.4
Illinois	91.1	Rhode Island	99.6
Indiana	60.0	South Carolina	70.9
Iowa	85.9	South Dakota	89.3
Kansas	73.2	Tennessee	90.5
Kentucky	78.0	Texas	67.9
Louisiana	65.8	Utah	80.5
Maine	95.8	Vermont	60.0
Maryland	92.7	Virginia	80.3
Massachusetts	96.6	Washington	79.7
Michigan	76.0	West Virginia	55.6
Minnesota	82.1	Wisconsin	77.4
Mississippi	79.9	Wyoming	5.1
Missouri	71.0		

Source: PBS Research, "Areapop Study."

ªCoverage is defined as percent of persons receiving grade A UHF, or grade A or B VHF signals.

The Growth of Public Broadcasting

Although small compared to commercial broadcasting, public broadcasting has achieved an impressive record of growth. This section illustrates this with three statistical measures: growth in the number of stations, growth in the size of the audience, and growth in income.

Table C-9

Growth in Number of Public Broadcasting Stations

	1955	1965	1970	1973	1978
Television	17	114	200	244	280
	13 VHF	66 VHF	88 VHF	95 VHF	111 VHF
	4 UHF	48 UHF	112 UHF	149 UHF	169 UHF
Radio (CPB-qualified)	—	—	86	144	198
			16 AM	19 AM	23 AM
			70 FM	125 FM	175 FM

Sources: *Television:* PBS Research. *Radio:* CPB Management Information Systems.

Table C-10

Public Broadcasting Audience Growth

	1975	1976	1977	1978
Television weekly cumulative rating (March):				
Number of households (millions)	21.5	26.0	27.6	29.8
Percent of households	31	37	39	41
Radio weekly cumulative rating (April/May):				
Number of persons (millions)	3.3	3.4	4.2	N.A.
Percent of persons	1.9	2.0	2.4	N.A.

Sources: *Television:* A. C. Nielsen Co. *Radio:* Arbitron Co. (copyrighted, used with permission).

Table C-11

Public Broadcasting Income Growth

	1973 (millions)	1974 (millions)	1975 (millions)	1976 (millions)	1977 (millions)
Television	$241.2	$266.6	$330.0	$364.9	$416.5
Radio	25.3	31.4	39.8	50.9	65.5
	$266.5	$298.0	$369.8	$415.8	$482.1[a]

Source: CPB Management Information Systems.
[a]Column does not add due to rounding.

Public Broadcasting Today

As the system has grown in size, it has also grown in complexity. This complexity is manifested in the differences among stations, in the audience and programs, and in the sources and levels of funding.

This section attempts to illustrate as full a cross section of the system as possible, drawing on statistical indexes of licensees (by number and type), audience demographics, program content, total income (by source), station income, sources of funding for the PBS schedule, and employment.

Table C-12

Public Broadcasting Licensees, by Number and Type

	Total	Community	University	State Authority	Local Authority
Television:					
Licensees[a]	155	60 (39%)	53 (34%)	24 (15%)	18 (12%)
Stations	280	73 (26%)	76 (27%)	111 (40%)	20 (7%)
Radio stations[a]	198	41 (21%)	127 (64%)	8 (4%)	22 (11%)
Joint radio/television	68				

Sources: *Television: PBS* Research. *Radio:* CPB Management Information Systems.

[a]Includes joint licensees.

Table C–13

Demographics of Weekly Public Broadcasting Audience

TELEVISION:	
Composite	39.6%
Age:[a]	
18–34	47.5%
35–49	39.7
50+	34.7
Race:	
White	39.5%
Nonwhite	40.8
Income:	
$–10,000	29.8%
$10,000–$14,999	36.7
$15,000–$20,000	42.6
$20,000+	52.3
Education:	
Less than 4 years high school	27.3%
4 years high school	39.5
1–3 years college	45.6
4+ years college	52.3
RADIO:	
Composite	7.0%
Age:	
18–29	6.1%
30–44	9.1
45–59	6.6
60+	6.3
Race:	
White	7.2%
Black	5.0
Income:	
$–7,000	5.1%
$7,000–$15,000	6.0
$15,000–$25,000	8.3
$25,000+	9.2
Education:	
College	10.2%
High-school graduate	5.9
Nonhigh-school graduate	4.8

Sources: *Television:* A. C. Nielsen Co., March 20–26, 1978, based on one-week, full-day cume. *Radio: Roper Reports,* March 1978, of people reporting listening to public radio station within past week.

[a]Since data are for households, age shown is of "lady of the house" for each household. Penetration in all households where there is no "lady of the house" is 35.5 percent.

Table C–14

Public Television Program Content, by Program Type

	Station Broadcast Hours	
	Full Day (1976)	Prime Time (1978, preliminary)
News/public affairs	11.9%	16%
History/biography	4.7	7
General information	7.2	12
Science	2.3	6
Skills, how-to-do-it	5.7	1
Children's	10.0	0
Culture/art/reviews	2.5	3
Music/dance/performance	7.7	17
Drama	6.8	23
Feature film	2.7	5
Comedy/satire	.8	3
Sports	2.1	3
All other general	2.1	1
Instructional television	16.6[a]	1
Sesame Street/ Electric Company	17.8	0

Sources: *Full day:* Katzman and Wirt, *Public Television Programming by Category*, 1976, CPB. *Prime time:* Katzman, "Preliminary Results of CPB Public Television Programming Category Survey," July 1978, CPB Management Information Systems.

[a]Includes *Electric Company* (1.6% of total) and *Villa Allegre* (0.2% of total) broadcast during school hours on days when school was in session.

Table C–15

Public Broadcasting Income, by Source (fiscal year 1977)

	TV (thousands)		Radio (thousands)	
Local government sources	$ 30,345	(7.3%)	$ 6,405	(9.8%)
State government sources	95,294	(22.8%)	4,969	(7.6%)
State colleges	35,696	(8.6%)	18,560	(28.3%)
Other colleges	3,554	(0.9%)	3,270	(5.0%)
Foundations	21,840	(5.2%)	787	(1.2%)
Business	37,904	(9.1%)	2,054	(3.1%)
Subscribers	45,298	(10.4%)	4,946	(7.5%)
Auction	12,610	(3.0%)	850	(1.3%)
All others	20,278	(4.9%)	2,165	(3.3%)
Nonfederal	$302,819	(72.7%)[a]	$44,006	(67.1%)
Federal government	113,729	(27.3%)	21,540	(32.9%)
Total	$416,548	(100.0%)	$65,546	(100.0%)

[a]Column does not add due to rounding.

	Public Broadcasting (thousands)	
Local government sources	$ 36,750	(7.6%)
State government sources	100,263	(20.8%)
State colleges	54,256	(11.3%)
Other colleges	6,824	(1.4%)
Foundations	22,627	(4.7%)
Business	39,958	(8.3%)
Subscribers	50,244	(10.4%)
Auction	13,460	(2.8%)
All others	22,443	(4.6%)
Nonfederal	$346,825	(71.9%)
Federal government	135,269	(28.1%)
Total	$482,094	(100.0%)

Source: CPB Information Management Systems

Table C–16

Public Broadcasting Station Income and Community Service
Grants (1977)

	Nonfederal	Community Service Grants	CSG as % of Nonfederal
Television:			
Average station	$ 1,853,417	$ 328,745	15.1
#1	29,782,806	3,772,367	12.7
#5	8,777,147	1,925,973	21.9
#100	855,727	195,385	22.8
#149	293,501	72,523	24.7
Radio:			
Average station	$ 187,783	$ 37,708	20.1
#1	1,047,911	157,174	15.0
#186	75,000	25,000	33.3

Sources: *Television:* PBS Research. *Radio:* CPB Management Information Systems.

Table C–17

Sources of Funding for Original Broadcast Hours Distributed
by Public Broadcasting Service, and Percentage of Hours Fully
or Partly Funded (fiscal year 1977)

	Funding (millions)	% of Hours Funded[a]
Licensees[b]	$14.9 (22.1%)	53.3
Corporation for Public Broadcasting	4.4 (6.5%)	12.5
Agencies of the Federal Government	19.3 (28.6%)	32.0
Foundations	6.7 (10.0%)	28.8
Corporations (Includes $8.4 million for oil companies)[c]	14.5 (21.5%)	41.4
Other	7.7 (11.4%)	
	$67.4[d]	

Source: PBS Research.

[a]Because funding from several sources is often combined to fund a single program, these percentages add to well over 100%.

[b]Includes $12.5 million from SPC for programs aired in this period (includes Ford Foundation/CPB matching funds not counted under CPB or Foundation headings), $2.1 million from the Station Acquisition Market, and $0.3 million from the Station Independence Project.

[c]Oil companies accounted for 12.5% of the total dollars, and fully or partly funded 17.4% of the hours.

[d]Column does not add up due to rounding. Total is correct figure.

Table C–18

Full-Time Employment, Public Broadcasting Licensees
(January 1978)

	TV	Radio
Officials:	776 (100%)	424 (100%)
Female	108 (14%)	83 (20%)
Minority	30 (4%)	29 (7%)
Managers:	868 (100%)	393 (100%)
Female	335 (39%)	121 (31%)
Minority	64 (7%)	46 (12%)
Professional:	2,922 (100%)	636 (100%)
Female	902 (31%)	172 (27%)
Minority	331 (11%)	84 (13%)
Technical:	2,255 (100%)	230 (100%)
Female	330 (15%)	55 (24%)
Minority	273 (12%)	28 (12%)
Support:	1,476 (100%)	155 (100%)
Female	1,215 (82%)	136 (88%)
Minority	390 (26%)	47 (26%)
Trainees:	144 (100%)	42 (100%)
Female	92 (64%)	27 (42%)
Minority	82 (57%)	15 (25%)
Total:	8,441 (100%)	1,880 (100%)
Female	2,982 (35%)	594 (32%)
Minority	1,170 (14%)	249 (13%)

Source: CPB Management Information Systems.

Appendix D

Costs

Introduction

This appendix contains estimates of the spending required for the public telecommunications system to realize the mission and responsibilities we propose for it. It includes the annual operating costs and the capital and development costs to establish such a system.

We believe that a sound estimate of the costs of the public telecommunications system we propose is essential to meaningful consideration of this report. Both the government and the system require cost and spending projections in order to weigh our proposals and to allocate limited resources.

Our estimates and projections are general in some areas for two basic reasons. First, we have attempted to avoid too detailed a description of the programs and services of public telecommunications because we are firmly convinced that only public broadcasting itself can select the programs of the system. We often provide illustrations of the kinds of costs required for certain programs and services, but we strive to avoid crossing the line into appearing to recommend specific programs. All our references to specific programs and services should be understood as illustrations only, and not as prescriptions. Second, our figures are sometimes general because complete and reliable information is not available.

The government and system decision makers will need more detailed spending plans in the future, which we urge the Trust to develop with the stations, the Endowment, and others. Of course, the Trust should not offer detailed plans that would enable Congress and others to approve or reject specific programs proposed for upcoming years. Nonetheless, the Trust should be able to provide a more complete analysis of need and opportunity than we have here.

Required Spending Level

The Commission's estimate of spending required to implement its recommendations for strengthening public telecommunications has several subsections: television;

radio; capital and expansion needs; and special initiatives, including the leadership activities of the Trust.

I. Television
Strengthening National Programming

A public television station broadcasting 18 hours a day provides its community with 126 hours of programs each week and 6552 hours of programs each year. Stations select the programs to broadcast to their communities, with the result that about two-thirds of the typical station's schedule is national programs. This is about 4400 hours each year. Some of these hours are repeat broadcasts of programs aired earlier.

We assume that a national program service, reflecting the diversity and breadth of interest of the public, should offer stations about 70 hours of new programs each week, or about 3600 per year. Such a national service would provide each station the resources to include in its schedule many quality national programs while rejecting other quality programs that may not meet community needs and interests.

We estimate the cost of these 70 hours of new national programs per week on the basis of an assumption of the cost per hour for programs broadcast at different times throughout the day. Table D–1 shows the cost per hours for various public and commercial television programs. Costume dramas like *The Adams Chronicles* and *The Scarlet Letter* cost $500,000 or more per hour, while a public affairs documentary averages about $150,000. As high as those costs seem, program costs in commercial television are much higher. A situation comedy like *Laverne and Shirley* costs $520,000 per hour, a made-for-TV movie averages $600,000 per hour, and an extraordinary drama like *Roots* averages about $1 million an hour.

Public television programs generally cost less than commercial television programs for many reasons. It is difficult to compare similar programs between the two systems because the structures and purposes of the two systems are so different. Since commercial television is a highly profitable business with intense rivalries among the three national networks, program costs tend to be higher. Our study has shown that the differences between costs for programs on the two systems have begun to narrow, and that we can expect this trend to continue. However, in the long run we expect public television programs to cost somewhat less per hour than commercial television programs. This difference will generally result

Table D–1

Examples of Television Program Costs

		Cost per Hour
Public:		
Costume drama	*The Scarlet Letter*	$ 550,000
	Adams Chronicles	500,000
Performance special	*Dance in America*	350,000
	In Performance at Wolf Trap	150,000
Drama	*Visions*	220,000
Public affairs documentary		150,000
Public affairs	*MacNeil/Lehrer Report*	20,000
	Washington Week in Review	10,000
Commercial:		
Situation comedy	*Laverne and Shirley*	$ 520,000
Made-for-TV movie		600,000
Public affairs	*60 Minutes*	170,000
Historical drama	*Roots*	1,000,000
Average prime-time program		460,000

from the profits, higher sales and other administrative costs, and higher talent fees for commercial television programs.

Given this information on the costs of different sorts of programs, we have estimated the number of hours of national programming service for various periods of the day, estimated an average cost per hour, and then calculated a total cost for that time period, each week, and a year. This calculation is shown in Table D–2.

The total cost of the 71 hours per week is $312.5 million annually. Given that these programs are generally high quality productions for a broad audience, these programs account for 25% of the hours and about 60% of the funds. Children's programs represent nearly one-third of the hours and about one-fifth of the dollars so public television can strengthen its service to youth and build on the successes of *Sesame Street* and other programs for this group. Other time periods are funded at lower but, we believe, no less adequate levels.

We recognize that these levels are only rough estimates. However, they can be easily justified. In fact, these funding levels are, in our opinion, barely adequate for the strengthening of public television's national programming that we recommend. To show how these estimates are justified, we have selected prime time to examine further. Table D–3 shows several different programs that have been called for—either by those who have appeared before us or by critics, public broadcasters, and others—that would be appropriate for the prime-time period. This list is only one illustration of how the nearly $190 million in funds for prime-time programs might be spent. Again we repeat our earlier caveat that these illustrations are not meant to limit or prescribe specific programs for public television. What they do indicate is that the $190 million could easily be well spent for appealing, entertaining, and important programs that will benefit the public. Indeed, we believe these illustrations show that more than $190 million could easily be justified and well spent.

Promotion and advertising of public television programs are essential if the public is to be aware of the diverse quality programs available to it. A diverse mix of quality programs will not achieve their purpose—service to the public—unless the public knows when they will be broadcast and chooses to tune some of them in. Thus, as a minimum, we have set the budget for promotion and advertising at 15 percent of the program funds, or nearly $50 million for national programming. We hope this will be adequate to make the national programs known throughout the country, but we also recognize that this promotion budget is a minimum that falls far below comparable advertising expenditures by commercial broadcasters. For example, it is estimated that each commercial network spends $300 million, including the cost of using its own airtime, to promote its schedule.

Thus the estimated cost of a strengthened national program service for public television is $360 million, approximately $310 million for programming and $50 million for promotion and advertising.

Strengthening Regional and Local Production

Local and regional productions and programs acquired from a variety of sources will provide the balance of programs broadcast by a station. Together, we expect these sources will represent about one-third of the hours of the typical station, or about 2200 hours each week.

Regional pooling of resources and production of programs serving common interests will increase in the future because of the satellite interconnection system. We believe that these efforts are important and should be strengthened. To estimate costs, we have assumed that each of four regional groups will produce or acquire 20

Table D–2
Cost Estimate for National Public Television Programming

	Hours per Week	Average Cost per Hour (millions)	Weekly Cost (millions)	Annual Cost (millions)
Prime time	18	$0.2	$3.6	$187.2
Late Evening	10	0.025	0.25	13.0
Children's morning and early evening	21	0.06	1.26	65.5
Weekly daytime	14	0.025	0.35	18.2
Weekend daytime	8	0.040	0.32	16.6
Instructional	a	0.050	—	12.0
	71			$312.5

a Eight series, thirty programs each.

Table D–3

Examples of Possible Prime-Time Programs for
Public Television

	Annual Cost (millions)
A news and public affairs evening program, seven days a week, usually one hour, including discussion, interviews, commentary, film inserts, and minidocumentaries	$20
The best of the performing arts, live and on tape, including dance, opera, and music. Five hours a week at a minimum cost of $200,000 per hour	50
A series of documentaries on major public issues from stations and independent producers around the country. Two hourly programs each week at the modest budget of $200,000	20
A family-oriented science series, including the best science documentaries, special reports, and discussion of important issues. Two hours a week at $200,000 each	20
A major drama series, one hour each week, with the best American artists and performers. Each show at $500,000	25
A weekly series of one-hour and two-hour new dramas written expressly for public television and budgeted at $220,000	20
A series of documentaries and special programs exploring social issues and problems, especially those unique to persons of different groups (including differences of race, sex, and national origin as well as age, region, and occupation). Two hours weekly at $300,000	30
Experimental video work which explores the ever-expanding technologies and how they change our ability to create and communicate. One hour each week at $100,000	5

hours each week, at an average hourly cost of $30,000, for an annual cost of $125 million.

We believe that stations should undertake a serious and professional commitment to local programming. At present, local programs produced by a station represent about 10 percent of its broadcast hours, or nearly two hours each day. Because local program costs are often not separated on a per hour basis from an overall station budget, we have no complete information on these costs per hour. An in-studio program may be charged anywhere from $1000 to $15,000 per hour, exclusive of talent costs. Reported costs of local documentaries range from essentially nothing to over $100,000. Thus, the sort of per hour calculation of costs that we have done above is not possible for local programming.

To estimate a cost for the improvements to local programming that we urge, we have assumed an increase of $500,000 for this activity in the average station's budget. While this means only $10,000 more each week for the typical station, it will be adequate for strengthening local programming in many ways, ranging from new or better in-studio shows to financing film pieces at the standard of $1000 per minute. Assuming 175 licensees, this increase for local programs will total $88 million.

Promotion and advertising for local programs as well as the full schedule selected by each station are, as noted above, important to the future of public television. Accordingly, we believe that each licensee should bolster its local awareness efforts with $100,000, or a total of $17.5 million for the whole system.

Other Improvements to Television Stations

Throughout this report there are many other suggestions for strengthening the public television system. It is essential that stations, if they are to merit the support of the public and funders, make every possible effort to eliminate waste and inefficient activities. Every possible dollar should be focused on programming and promotion; and general management and support functions must be financed at the lowest possible level consistent with good management and professional operation. We believe that this continued vigilance for economy and improvements will help maximize resources that can be made available for programming and promotion.

We estimate that the current operating costs of the stations, exclusive of programming and promotion activities, are about $160 million. New initiatives in fund raising, public participation and research, training and personnel development, use of technological innovations, use of television for learning and instruction, and other areas must come principally from increases in this amount. Table D-4 shows our estimates of the system-wide increases required for these new initiatives as well as for improved national representation and programming leadership on the stations' behalf, and for direct station financing of the costs of the satellite interconnection system. The total for these new costs is $125 million, including $15 million for the satellite interconnection system that has been financed directly with federal funds.

Table D–5 shows our cost projections for the television system—a total of $875 million. This amount represents a dramatic increase over present funding levels ($417 million in 1977). While $875 million is certainly a large amount, it is small when contrasted to the approximately $2 billion spent by any of the three commercial television networks and its affiliated stations.

II. Radio

Our cost estimates for radio are more general than for television, largely because the public radio system is less well developed than television and the financial information available is less specific. Also, costs associated with commercial radio do not provide useful models, since profit-making radio stations operate very differently from public radio stations.

Our plan for strengthening public radio has two principal components: (1) system expansion and development (to make at least one station available to virtually

Table D–4

Estimate of Public Television Station Operating Costs
Excluding Programming and Promotion

	Amount (millions)
Current Costs	$160
Cost of recommended improvements:	
Fund raising	34[a]
Public participation and audience research	17.5[b]
Training and personnel development	13[c]
Technological innovations	17.5[b]
Learning and instruction	17.5[b]
National satellite interconnection	15
National representation and programming leadership	10
	$284.5

[a]Estimated at 25¢ to raise additional $1, with $135 million increase.
[b]Estimated at $100,000 per station.
[c]Estimated at 5% increase in staff with total per person costs of $20,000 and $25,000 increase in professional development funds at each station.

Table D–5

Estimated Annual Public Television Cost

	Annual Cost (millions)
National programming and promotion	$360
Regional programming	125
Local programming improvements	88
Local promotion improvements	18
Station operations:	
Current	160
Improvements	125
	$875[a]

[a]Does not add due to rounding.

all Americans and to increase the number of different alternatives for many) and (2) improvement of programs and promotion at both the local and national levels. This plan is described in Chapter VI.

We project that 480 stations spread throughout the country will achieve the first objective—making public radio widely available with alternatives in most areas. We recommend multiple public radio stations in most areas so each station can focus on a distinctive sound and service (news and public affairs, one type of music, etc.) and thereby mesh with people's listening habits. Table D–6 shows the number of stations projected for each of the 265 market areas, and the budget size, or cost, estimated for each station. In the largest metropolitan areas, there will be two stations each costing $1 million, one station costing $750,000, and one station costing $500,000. The two largest stations are budgeted to have the capacity to produce segments or whole programs for national sharing among stations. The typical budget we have assumed is twice the average of today, but we believe these budgets are in no way excessive. They have been constructed using line-by-line costs of lean, full service public radio stations. The major component of these budgets is the number of staff, since personnel is the major determinant of the diversity and quality of the programs broadcast by a station. Table D–6 shows the total staffing levels (including managerial, technical, public information, development and administrative support positions as well as programming positions) that we estimate for each of the various budget sizes. Large as these budgets may appear, they are barely

Table D-6

Estimated Number and Annual Cost of Public Radio Stations

Market Population (millions)	Station Budgets (millions)[a]	Staffing Level	Typical Market of Given Population		Market Size	All Markets of Given Population	
			No. of Stations	Cost (millions)		No. of Stations	Cost (millions)
2.5+	$1	30					
	1	30					
	0.75	25					
	0.5	18	4	$3.25	1–10	40	$32.5
1–2	0.75	25					
	0.75	25					
	0.5	18					
	0.3	12	4	2.3	11–35	100	57.5
0.5–1	0.7	22					
	0.5	18					
	0.3	12	3	1.5	36–70	105	52.5
0.3–0.5	0.4	15					
	0.25	10	2	0.65	71–110	80	26
—0.3	0.25	10	1	0.25	110–265	155	38.75
						480	207.25

[a]Budget or cost per station includes total operating costs of local stations, including salaries, technical costs, promotion costs, development costs, local program costs, administrative costs, and national services and interconnection. Budget excludes national program costs.

adequate to sustain the level of staff we have associated with them. Also, these budgets are below—and in many cases significantly below—the average budget for a commercial radio station in markets of these sizes, even though commercial radio stations rely more heavily on prerecorded programming than we recommend be the case for public radio.

The total cost for these 480 stations is $207.25 million. This covers all operating costs, including staff, technical, programming and promotion, and administrative costs and each station's share of the costs of the national representation, satellite interconnection, and program leadership activities financed by the stations.

National programming and promotion costs are not included in the station costs. While the economy of radio production and the diversity and local nature of radio services will make public radio less dependent on national programs than public television, we expect a strong and vital national public radio service that stations will use throughout their broadcast schedule. This national service will be multidimensional. We estimate the cost of its news and public affairs component at $12 million; the cost of a series of highest quality performances in music, drama, and other arts at $12 million; and money spent on special-interest programs and for other purposes at $4 million. Promotion and advertising are, in some cases, just as expensive for radio as for television, so we have provided an awareness budget for this national service of $5 million, about the 15 percent rule-of-thumb used for television. This is a bare minimum for this activity. Thus the total cost for the national public radio program service and promotion is $33 million. Table D–7 shows the total annual cost, $240 million, of a complete public radio system. This figure represents just over $1 per year for every person in our country.

III. Initial Costs: Capital and Development

As we discussed in Chapter VII, it is essential that the Trust design and implement a comprehensive plan for extending public broadcasting services throughout the nation. This plan should include significant attention to the alternative means of distribution and new, more efficient technologies.

We believe the establishment of the complete system of 480 public radio stations will require significant funding over the short term for capital equipment and facilities and for developing and upgrading stations to a

Table D–7

Estimated Annual Public Radio Costs

	Cost (millions)
Operations of 480 stations	$207
National programming and promotion:	
News and public affairs	12
Performances	12
Special programs	4
Promotion	5
	$240

minimum operating level. Public television will face capital and development costs for strengthening current stations and adding new stations or other means to distribute programs to those Americans still without service. These costs are one-time-only. Included in the annual operating costs of both public television and radio are some funds for replacement and improvement of facilities and equipment as the system depreciates.

The initial costs of the public radio system proposed by us contain several elements. First, each of the 280 additional stations in the system is assumed to require at least some improvements in facilities and equipment, even if the station currently exists. New stations will cost from about $200,000 to $500,000 to establish, depending on the size of the station and the community and the extent of program production plans. A major-market public radio station that will produce extensive local programming and some programs shared nationally with other stations can be outfitted with state-of-the-art equipment and facilities for about $500,000. We estimate that 140 of the additional stations will be new and require a new facility, beginning with space and a transmitter, which will cost an average of $300,000. The other 140 stations will already exist but they will require improvements to equipment and facilities averaging $200,000. Thus the total cost of this activity is $70 million.

Second, improvements in capital equipment and facilities for the current 200 public radio stations are necessary in many cases. We estimate these expenditures to cost $30 million. Another component of the plan to strengthen public radio is purchasing radio frequencies where spectrum space is unavailable. Commercial radio

stations typically sell for a few million dollars in larger
cities, the areas where public radio will most likely be
lacking stations. We estimate that purchase of 20 stations
at a cost of $40 million will be required. These efforts
to bolster the facilities and equipment of public radio
total $140 million.

In addition to these costs, the competitive development program is assumed to involve 150 stations with
an average cost of $300,000 spread over two or three
years. This would amount to $45 million, and it in-
creases the initial costs to create the public radio system
we propose to $185 million.

In television, our estimate of capital and developmental
costs reflects the more advanced state of the television
system and the need to begin focusing on less costly
alternate methods of distributing programs and services.
The costs of initial improvements in the system include
estimates of $50 million to improve UHF stations so they
are more easily viewed by the public (by such means as
increased power, directional antenna, and improved transmitters); $30 million to complete the physical plants of
the stations already in place; and $85 million to provide
new stations or other, nonbroadcast means for making
public television available to nearly all of the public.
This totals $165 million.

Table D–8 shows a summary of the initial costs to
put the public radio and television systems we recommend
in place. The total is $350 million. These costs will be
spread out over several years. Assuming a seven-year
spread, the costs are about $50 million per year.

IV. Special Initiatives and Other Costs

The Commission's plan for strengthening public telecommunications also includes several new initiatives and
activities that are not part of the mainstream costs of
the system. Essentially, these initiatives have been recommended in areas of special promise and importance,
where the Commission believes a small but wisely used
amount of additional funds will yield benefits way beyond the cost. There are three of these areas.

The first special initiative is the emphasis on the
leadership role for the Public Telecommunications
Trust. This function is essential to the Commission's plan
for an effective system. It has been estimated to cost $20
million annually, including a major effort at system
accounting, research, planning, and evaluation at $10 mil-
lion, a major effort in training and personnel develop-

Table D–8

Estimated Initial Costs for Public Broadcasting
Capital and Development

	Cost (millions)
Television:	
Capital at current stations	$ 30
Capital at additional stations or nonbroadcast facilities	85
UHF improvement	50
	$165
Radio:	
Capital at current stations	$ 30
Capital at additional 280 stations	70
Purchase of frequencies	40
Development and upgrade	45
	$185
Television and Radio:	$350

ment at $5 million, and $5 million in operating costs, principally for travel, meetings, consultants, and other external costs which complement a very small, highly expert staff.

Another special initiative the Commission proposes is a program budgeted at $10 million annually to explore new services made possible by new technology. As described in Chapter VII, the emphasis would be on these new services, not on hardware and technological innovation. This level of funding is adequate for the support of several programs (such as initial development of a teletext system, $2 million; cable distribution of public broadcasting on a special basis to test alternative service strategies, $2 million, interactive health care experiments using radio, television, and satellite and other program distribution means, $2 million; and radio subchannel services in languages and for the blind, $2.5 million). The effort by public television to make television available to the hearing-impaired through a captioning system that does not appear for those without hearing problems is a prime example of this activity.

Television and radio have strong potentials for contributing to instruction and general learning. As described in Chapter VIII, the Commission's plan includes special emphasis on a new initiative in this area to strengthen the use of public radio and television in education. This activity is budgeted at $15 million each year, above and beyond the considerable expenditures included in the costs of the radio and television national and regional program services and the costs of the local stations themselves. It is estimated that this amount will support research and evaluation plus contribute to the funding of programs. With the annual cost of a single program like *Sesame Street* around $8 or $10 million, we believe this budget is the minimum for this special initiative.

Summary

The total annual cost of the public telecommunications system we foresee is $1.16 billion. The one-time-only costs for capital and development are estimated at $350 million, or an annual cost of $50 million for seven years. Table D–9 summarizes the costs.

Table D–9

Total Estimated Costs of Public Broadcasting

	Cost (millions)
Annual costs:	
Television	$ 875
Radio	240
Special initiatives	45[a]
	$1,160
Initial capital plus development:	
Television	$ 165
Radio	185
	$ 350
Annual cost for 7 Years:	$ 50

[a]Trust, $20 million; telecommunications, $10 million; television and radio for learning, $15 million.

Appendix E

The Educational Broadcasting Facilities Program

The Educational Broadcasting Facilities Program (EBFP) was created by Congress in 1962 to provide a means for federal support to local communities to help meet the educational, cultural, and informational needs of Americans through broadcasting. The program does this by awarding matching grants to noncommercial television and radio licensees to activate new broadcast stations or upgrade the facilities of existing stations. A special branch of the Office of Education (HEW) has been responsible for administering the program and since 1963 has made available a total of about $150 million in facilities funds.[1] Eligible applicants may be awarded grants for up to 75 percent of the cost of the planning, acquisition, and installation of facilities such as towers, transmitters, microwave equipment, recording equipment, and monitoring equipment. Operating costs and the cost of constructing or repairing structural housing for such equipment, however, are not covered. The total amount in grants awarded in each state or territory may not exceed 8.5 percent of the program's total appropriation in one year.

In 1967 eligibility for facilities grants was extended to noncommercial radio. Before this only television facilities were covered. And in 1975 the Facilities Act was modified to set forth separate grant criteria for television and radio. It established for television a higher priority on grants that would *improve* the service of existing stations than on grants that would *extend* service coverage through new stations, while the reverse applied to noncommercial radio.

Table E–1 portrays the congressional authorizations and appropriations history of the program. It shows that actual EBFP appropriations have often been considerably below the amounts authorized by Congress.

---

[1]The Public Telecommunications Financing Act of 1978 provides for the transfer of the EBFP to the National Telecommunications and Information Administration in the Department of Commerce.

Table E–2 is a profile of program requests and grant awards. More than 1240 applications for grants totalling $255.4 million have been submitted since 1963; 851 grants totaling $150.2 million have been awarded.

Table E–3 shows the history of grant awards broken down by grants for new station activations and grants for expansion of or improvements in existing stations for both television and radio. In each of the first seven years of the program, most of the funding was awarded for new station activations. Considering the entire history of the program, however, almost twice as much was awarded for upgrading existing stations as for activating new stations.

While the EBFP has been the major factor in the physical development of public broadcasting, the program's financial resources have not nearly been commensurate with demand. A great many requests for funds have been refused because of the limited funds available. In the last three years alone, 189 of the applications considered went unfunded.

Table E–1

Educational Broadcasting Facilities Program:
Authorizations and Appropriations History

Fiscal Year	Authorization (millions)	Appropriation (thousands)
1963	⎫	$ 1,500
1964	⎬	6,500
1965	$ 32	13,000
1966	⎭	8,826
1967	—	3,304
1968	10.5	0
1969	12.5	4,375
1970	15	5,083
1971	15	11,000
1972	15	13,000
1973	25	13,000
1974	25	16,500
1975	30	12,000
1976	30	12,000
1977	30	15,000[a]
1978	30	19,000[a]
	$270	$154,088

Source: Office of Education, Dept. of Health, Education, and Welfare.

[a]Includes $1 million appropriated for telecommunications demonstration grants.

Table E–2

Profile of Public Broadcasting Program Requests

Fiscal Years	Pending Applications		Applications Received	
	No.[a]	Amount (millions)	No.[a]	Amount (millions)
1963–67	—	—	235	$61.0
1968	74	$29.0	0	—
1969	74	29.0	51	8.0
1970	108	30.0	21	5.0
1971	89	25.8	96	19.7
1972	119	30.9	76	11.0
1973	77	18.9	84	17.2
1974	87	21.9	121	26.2
1975	114	25.4	79	18.1
1976	100	31.1	121	18.1
1977	92[b]	21.3[b]	213	40.1
1978	104	24.3	150	31.0

Fiscal Years	Applications Considered		Grant Awards	
	No.[a]	Amount (millions)	No.[a]	Amount (millions)
1963–67	235	$61.0	161	$32.0
1968	0	—	0	—
1969	125	37.0	15	3.2
1970	135	39.0	40	5.4
1971	185	45.5	57	11.0
1972	195	42.2	69	13.0
1973	161	36.1	78	13.0
1974	208	48.1	74	15.7
1975	193	43.5	62	12.0
1976	221	49.2	73	12.9
1977	268	52.9	100	14.0
1978	254	55.3	122	18.0

Source: Office of Education, Dept. of Health, Education, and Welfare.

[a]Does not include applications returned during processing in previous fiscal years.

[b]Of the pending applications, 6 were returned and 31 were not reactivated for consideration this fiscal year.

Table E–3

History of Public Broadcasting Grants

Fiscal Years	Grants	TV Activations Federal Funds (millions)	Average Grant (millions)
1963–67	92	$19.93	$0.22
1968[a]	—	—	—
1969	7	2.01	0.29
1970	11	2.70	0.25
1971	12	4.37	0.36
1972	10	3.30	0.33
1973	8	3.20	0.40
1974	6	2.87	0.48
1975	5	2.19	0.44
1976	6	2.56	0.43
1977	7	2.42	0.35
1978	2	1.20	0.60
	166	$46.80	$0.33

Fiscal Years	Grants	TV Expand/Improve Federal Funds (millions)	Average Grant (millions)
1963–67	69	$11.99	$0.17
1968[a]	—	—	—
1969	6	1.10	0.18
1970	10	1.84	0.18
1971	18	4.96	0.27
1972	33	8.18	0.25
1973	40	7.90	0.20
1974	41	11.08	0.27
1975	36	8.64	0.24
1976	37	8.17	0.22
1977	40	7.89	0.20
1978	61	12.93	0.21
	391	$84.68	$0.21

Fiscal Years	Grants	Radio Activations	
		Federal Funds (millions)	Average Grant (millions)
1963–67	N.A.	—	—
1968[a]	—	—	—
1969	2	$0.10	$0.05
1970	9	0.52	0.06
1971	12	0.81	0.07
1972	7	0.58	0.08
1973	10	0.89	0.09
1974	4	0.34	0.08
1975	10	0.73	0.07
1976	9	0.94	0.10
1977	8	0.99	0.12
1978	9	1.01	0.11
	80	$6.92	$0.08

Fiscal Years	Grants	Radio Expand/Improve	
		Federal Funds (millions)	Average Grant (millions)
1963–67	N.A.	—	—
1968[a]	—	—	—
1969	—	—	—
1970	10	$ 0.34	$0.03
1971	15	0.86	0.06
1972	19	0.94	0.05
1973	20	1.00	0.05
1974	23	1.38	0.06
1975	11	0.43	0.04
1976	21	1.30	0.06
1977	45	2.69	0.06
1978	50	2.87	0.06
	214	$11.81	$0.05

Fiscal Years	Grants	All Radio and TV Federal Funds (millions)
1963–67	161	$31.97
1968[a]	—	—
1969	15	3.21
1970	40	5.40
1971	57	11.00
1972	69	13.00
1973	78	12.10
1974	74	15.68
1975	62	12.00
1976	73	12.98
1977	100	14.00
1978	122	18.01
	851	$149.35

Source: Office of Education, Dept. of Health, Education, and Welfare.

[a]No funds appropriated.

Appendix F

New Technologies and Services

New technology is having a profound impact on established communications systems. Such technological advances as laser/fiber-optic and digital transmission, widespread integrated circuit, computer, and micro-processor development, and the establishment of new satellite and microwave transmission systems are already altering traditional communications service and will, over the next decade, make possible new telecommunications services for the public. Even today, technology has already made possible a range of services and technical systems which appear to have important ramifications for a more fully developed public telecommunications system. Six such services or systems are described here:

Cable Television

Cable television (CATV) is a multifaceted communications system which employs coaxial cable and other sophisticated electronic equipment to deliver a range of programming and information services to the home and other locations. Although CATV is not new—rudimentary systems were operating in the late 1940s—advancing technology, changing regulatory policies, and improved marketing and services have combined to stimulate CATV development in recent years. Today nearly 4000 cable systems in all 50 states serve 14 million subscribers, or one out of every five American homes. Although projections of CATV's future growth typically have been overoptimistic, it remains likely that cable television will serve more than 30 percent of the population by the early to mid-1980s.

CATV began as a means to improve reception of local television signals by delivering those signals to the home via a community antenna and cable, and that function remains one of its basic selling points. However, over time it became clear that the enormous information-carrying capacity of coaxial cable meant that many additional services could be delivered by CATV. The key to cable television's potential is its access to the home with wide-band, multichannel capacity—new systems typically have 30 or 40 channels—and its potential for two-way communications.

Faced with the extraordinary capital cost of laying cable, the opposition of established communications interests, and regulatory policies which slowed its development, cable has been forced to develop additional services to induce consumers to become cable subscribers. Among these services are simple automated information channels devoted to news, weather, financial, and consumer reports. Extra channel capacity has also permitted some systems to make available channels for public access, educational, and other local programming. During the mid-'70s some cable operators moved aggressively to develop additional premium services for which subscribers would be willing to pay extra. Chief among these is pay television, or pay cable, a service primarily devoted to new movies, sporting events, and entertainment specials. Domestic satellite transmission of programs by pay cable services such as Home Box Office and Showtime has significantly aided the development of pay services. Satellites are also used to deliver the signals of independent "superstations" to cable systems across the country, as well as specialized news services. By 1980 it is anticipated that more than a third of all CATV systems will have access to additional programming services distributed via satellite. Prototype cable systems such as Warner Cable's 30-channel QUBE system in Columbus, Ohio, have experimented with a wide range of interactive entertainment, informational, and educational services. A cable system in Irvine, California, by making use of a powerful "Plato" computer and the system's bidirectional capability, has experimented with a range of community, business, educational, and home interactive services. In Reading, Pennsylvania, senior citizens use the two-way CATV system to communicate among themselves and with public officials about a wide range of subjects. These and other advanced cable systems are demonstrating the kinds of telecommunications services that CATV may be able to provide on a larger scale during the next decade.

Although CATV development has been given a boost by the introduction of new programming services, its future is still heavily dependent upon a variety of regulatory and marketing factors and its ability to compete with other broad-band distribution systems and traditional entertainment services. Nevertheless, CATV appears to offer public radio and television important opportunities for improving service to the public. By enhancing reception of television signals, and through the importation of out-of-town signals, CATV can assist in extending public broadcasting service to the public. Some public broadcasters have also made use of CATV channels as a means to distribute specialized programming to schools, institutions, and even the home. Over time, and particularly in areas where CATV serves a large percentage of homes, public broadcasters may be able to make use of cable's multichannel and interactive capability to deliver additional services to the school and the home.

Subsidiary Communications Authority

Subsidiary Communications Authority (SCA) refers to an FM radio multiplexing technique whereby two or more separate signals of information are transmitted on a single broadcast channel. With the permission of the FCC, radio stations may broadcast programs intended for a general audience while at the same time delivering, on an SCA subchannel, programs intended for a closed or limited audience. To receive a subchannel program a listener or subscriber must have a radio equipped with a special decoder. Usually these special receivers are acquired through a broadcast station or government agency.

Since the FCC first authorized the use of SCA by commercial stations in 1955, it has been used to provide subscription services such as background music, detailed weather forecasting, and special telemetry and telecontrol functions. In 1961 the FCC authorized SCA use by educational FM stations, and it was first employed in 1966 by WHA-FM at the University of Wisconsin. Today, approximately fifty noncommercial stations employ SCA for limited audience programs such as information services for the print-handicapped, and continuing education programs for practicing professional groups.

Although use of SCA by noncommercial stations is growing, there are limiting factors. First, capital costs for SCA station equipment can range from $10,000 to $100,000, depending on the size of the planned operation. Home receivers cost at least $55 each. In addition, ongoing programming generally requires a separate staff. Second, transmitting power for SCA signals must be considerably lower than that of main channel signals. Thus SCA signals cover a comparatively restricted area and are more vulnerable to interference. Finally, most SCA receivers currently available are less mobile than regular receivers—listeners are largely restricted to home use.

Nevertheless, the various noncommercial applications of SCA have proven to be increasingly valuable. For example, the University of Wisconsin first used SCA to transmit postgraduate medical programs on the state FM radio network. Since then, additional university extension programs have been set up to serve other practicing professionals. Many other university stations operate similar off-campus continuing education programs. SCA has also been employed to transmit specially prepared programs to bus-riding high-school students en route to and from school. To utilize the otherwise unconstructive time of riding the bus, Ohio University in conjunction with a rural school district provides programs on news, sports, book reviews, teacher interviews, and student affairs. The most widespread noncommercial use of SCA is for delivering information services, or as they are often called Radio Talking Books, to the print-handicapped. This was first done by Minnesota Public Radio in 1969, and now many public stations and state networks offer such services. Programming typically includes readings of newspapers, magazines, and novels, and community forums such as telephone callback shows and interviews with public figures.

Beyond the delivery of various audio services, SCA capability can also be applied to instructional and informational uses via slow-scan television or facsimile services.[1] The use of such material, either in conjunction with or separate from audio programming, greatly broadens the possibilities for SCA service.

The coming public radio satellite interconnection will greatly enhance public radio's capacity for program sharing among stations and state networks. This sharing can help spread out programming costs for stations already engaged in SCA service and allow more stations to begin such operations. The satellite also opens the way for national or regional SCA program services.

SCA, therefore, is a means by which public radio can extend special services to limited audiences without diminishing regular broadcast operations. Because the availability of receiving equipment is controlled, audiences can be precisely defined and their specific needs accurately

[1]Slow-scan is a nonbroadcast technique for delivering still television pictures over a narrow bandwidth transmission system (e.g., SCA) for display on a television screen or a hard-copy facsimile terminal. It is well suited for transmitting materials such as still pictures, alphanumeric data, charts and graphs, and other nonrealtime information.

ascertained. And because SCA transmission channels exist within each FM station's frequency allocation, radio spectrum scarcity generally does not preclude use of SCA.

Videodiscs

Videodisc systems, composed of a long-playing video record and a playback machine attached to the standard television set, are potentially important new means of distributing, storing, and using a broad range of video programming and information in the home, school, or office. Videodiscs are similar in appearance to long-playing phonograph records, but are more durable and sophisticated in their information storage capacity. All disc playback machines can be used with a standard television receiver and most are capable of reverse and variable speeds, freeze frame, random search, or push-button access to individual frames. Several manufacturers have disc systems in premarketing development and the first such system is expected to be available to consumers in 1979. Players are expected to cost $500–$800 and programmed discs, $10–$20.

Disc systems employ one of a number of advanced techniques during playback such as laser scanning or electrocapacitance principles. In general, discs designed for one type of player cannot be used on another. None of the systems can record—users will be largely dependent upon disc manufacturers for programs.

Transferring programming to a disc is a fairly elaborate process and costs about $1000. Actual discs are then "stamped out" much as phonograph records are made. Each stamped copy only costs about 40 cents to make. Because it would cost about $1000 to produce one copy of a program and only $400 more to produce 1000 copies, mass production of individual programs is essential in keeping the retail price of discs low. This means that, initially at least, programs that appeal to a broad range of potential consumers are most likely to be marketed. However, less expensive mastering techniques are being developed.

Home entertainment will be an important use of videodiscs. Most manufacturers currently plan to offer a variety of feature length motion pictures, documentaries, concerts, and other broad-appeal recordings. Discs are also well suited for educational, business, and governmental use. With the versatile playback feature some of the prototype systems offer, in-school instructional programs can be designed to call for ongoing student interaction, i.e., stopping the program in action so one can ponder the material, slowing it down for closer scrutiny, or backing it up for review. For business and government, disc systems can serve as relatively inexpensive and easy to operate electronic data files. Over 100,000 pages (or over 100 billion bits) of information can be accommodated on a one-hour disc.

Despite their promise, videodisc systems face an uncertain future. A major factor influencing their availability and future development will be the consumer market. Once on the market, discs will have to compete with home video cassette recorders. Since home recording is possible on discs, their acceptance is closely tied to the availability of programmed discs. Equipment standardization may be a further complication. By 1980 four or more incompatible systems may be on the market. If no standard emerges, the availability of programming for each system may be limited.

Nevertheless, over time videodiscs may represent an important opportunity for public broadcasting. Because of their versatility and durability, discs may be especially suitable for distributing and using in-school instructional programming. With the development of less expensive mastering techniques, distribution of programs for limited audiences with special needs may be possible. In two separate experimental projects now underway, the Nebraska Educational Television Network is already examining the possible educational use of disc systems for the deaf and hearing-impaired, and for nonhandicapped students at all levels of education. Ultimately it is even conceivable that public broadcasting programs of interest to larger numbers of viewers may be distributed by videodiscs.

Teletext

Teletext is a generic term for information retrieval services which make use of a home television receiver and existing broadcast or nonbroadcast transmission systems. In its simplest form teletext allows the individual user to select information from a central broadcasting source for display on a specially equipped home television set. And by utilizing existing telephone (or cable) lines into the home, the range of information available to the consumer can be greatly increased.

Teletext systems are currently being developed in Europe, Japan, and at a slower pace in the United States. Great Britain is furthest along in developing both broadcast and wired teletext systems. The BBC operates a broadcast teletext system called Ceefax and the ITV companies, one called Oracle. The systems are technically compatible and can be accessed with the same home equipment. Ceefax and Oracle employ a previously unused portion of a television broadcast signal[2] to insert and transmit up to 100 sequential "pages" of information. To call up or "seize" a page of information, the home user must have a television set equipped with a special selector/decoder, which currently costs about $200. The selected pages may be displayed against a blank TV screen or superimposed on the carrier channel's regular programming.

Broadcast teletext services can be used to retrieve and display virtually any information in alphanumeric or graphic form. Since the content of the transmission can be continuously or periodically changed by the broadcaster, these services are well suited for information of a transient nature such as news, weather, sports, and stock-market reports, as well as more enduring information such as timetables and schedules. For the Ceefax and Oracle systems such information is organized in an indexed, magazinelike format. In the home a small digital keyboard is used to select the desired page for display. Normally there is a brief, though variable, waiting time depending upon where the requested page happens to be in the cyclical transmission sequence. In teletext systems transmitting as many as 800 pages, waiting time would be about two minutes.

Because information can be superimposed on regular programming, broadcast teletext can also be used to provide closed-caption subscripts. These might be in English for the benefit of the deaf and hearing-impaired or in a foreign language for the benefit of non-English-speaking members of the audience. (British teletext developers are now experimenting with "near-instant" captioning which employs phonetic symbols and, in effect, is a form of electronic translation.) Further, broadcast teletext can be used to provide read-along supplements to in-school instructional television programs, or to display on command answers to questions asked on regular television programs.

The British Post Office has developed a wired teletext service called Viewdata or Prestel with technical specifications that have already been adopted by other

---

[2]Certain portions of the time and frequency domains of a TV channel are normally unused. The Ceefax/Oracle systems employ the vertical blanking interval of the time domain for transmission.

countries. Such wired teletext services are different from broadcast service not only in the way information is transmitted to the home but also in the amount of information that can be made available. Moreover, a Viewdata-type service is not an information service per se but a communication service that delivers information from a variety of independent sources.

In a Viewdata-type system, an administrative or communications carrier organization, such as the postal service or a telephone company, operates a central computer in which a virtually unlimited number of pages of information are stored. Information providers, such as newspapers, encyclopedias, libraries, or others, lease the blank pages on which any information they wish to market is programmed. Thus the central operator does not gather or edit information but merely delivers it. In the home, the user must have fairly sophisticated and expensive terminal equipment attached to a television set which is interconnected with the central computer via telephone lines. Using a digital keyboard, the user can employ tree-searching techniques to "hunt down" desired information. Accordingly, Viewdata is a fully interactive or two-way service. In addition to the initial cost of the terminal equipment, the user pays monthly charges based on telephone rates and the number of pages accessed. The cost of retrieving a page of information can range from a few pennies to several dollars depending on the type of information selected.

Possible applications for Viewdata-type systems, in addition to information retrieval, include calculator service, simple computer programming, telemetry and telecontrol, and point-of-sale inventory monitoring.

Teletext services are in experimental form in the United States at the present time, and it is not yet clear whether commercial broadcasting at large will embrace teletext. As yet, there is uncertainty about the commercial viability of broadcast teletext in the United States. Moreover, several other questions remain to be resolved; some of which concern consumer interest, the use of common technical standards among broadcasters, who would control the information bases, and whether such services should be commercial or strictly noncommercial.

There are at least three cogent characteristics of teletext services. First, they build on existing electronic distribution systems—new transmission systems do not have to be constructed. Second, they can greatly expand the variety and amount of information available to the home.

And third, teletext provides an interactive service with which the home user can in effect "converse" with a central data processing unit.

Home information retrieval service, in particular broadcast teletext, may represent an additional means for public broadcasting to expand service to the public. Teletext can be used to provide news, sports, financial, community events, and program-scheduling information to the general audience. It can also be used to provide instructional services to students in class or at home. Or it can be used to transmit closed-caption program subscripts to the deaf and hearing-impaired, or non-English-speaking members of the audience. In short, teletext appears to create new opportunities for public broadcasting to better serve both general audiences and the special needs of smaller audiences.

Instructional Television Fixed Service

Instructional Television Fixed Service (ITFS) is a microwave transmission service used to deliver instructional and general educational services, and sometimes in-service training and instruction, in a variety of institutional settings. A private, nonbroadcast service operating in the 2500-2690-MHz band, ITFS must be licensed by the FCC. An ITFS licensee may be assigned as many as four full television channels to transmit programs and services from a central location to nearby fixed locations. In addition, a separate audio channel may be assigned to each television channel permitting receiving locations to interact with the program origination source.

The FCC first authorized ITFS service in 1963 to allow local school districts to operate their own instructional television systems. Since then, a variety of nonprofit institutions such as universities, archdioceses, school districts, and public broadcasting licensees have obtained ITFS licenses. ITFS growth has been limited by the relatively high capital and operating costs associated with the service and the inability of the FCC to lay out a coherent developmental policy for the service. Nevertheless, ITFS has grown gradually and today nearly 200 ITFS systems are in operation around the country.

The various limiting factors associated with ITFS have, in part, led to cooperative arrangements among separate organizations whereby ITFS links are operated by or integrated with a larger telecommunications system. With such arrangements, the costs of equipment, programming, and management can be shared. Since 1968 public television station WVIZ in Cleveland has operated a multi-channel ITFS system in cooperation with other local institutions, through which special programs are transmitted on separate channels to nearby public schools, a university, and a hospital. Similarly, the South Carolina ETV Network operates two ITFS systems to provide instructional programming to elementary and secondary schools. In a demonstration project, KPBS-TV at San Diego State University used an ITFS link to transmit college courses to the local CATV company's head-end for cable distribution. Other possible applications for ITFS include relaying satellite feeds to fixed receiving points, and the interconnection of two or more transmit/receive locations for teleconferencing.

Initially ITFS was intended as a private television system for local school districts; over the years its value as an independent educational service has increased. At the same time, cooperative arrangements among ITFS operators, public broadcasters, and cable television have in a number of instances enhanced the public-service capabilities of all three. As public broadcasting's new satellite distribution capability widens the range of programming and service options at the local level, it may be possible for ITFS operators to play an expanded role in the delivery of instructional services to schools and other limited audiences.

Videocassettes

Videocassettes are compact, easy-to-use devices for storing or distributing television programs. They are designed to be inserted in a videocassette player/recorder (VCR) which attaches to a regular television set. With a home VCR, prerecorded programs can be viewed at the user's convenience, or regular broadcast programs can be recorded on a blank cassette for later viewing. With a video camera, self-produced programming is possible. There are five main kinds of cassettes, each containing magnetic tapes with different technical formats. They cannot be used interchangeably. Cassette recorder/players cost from $800 up, and blank cassettes from $13 up depending on their length.

The first VCR—the ¾-inch "U" tape format type—was developed by the Sony Corporation. It was introduced in the United States in 1971, offering easier operation than the traditional "open-reel" video tape recorders. Initially, VCRs were used mostly by large organizations and institutions for internal purposes such as disseminating administrative information and producing instructional programs for student or employee training. In 1975 Sony introduced a less expensive ½-inch-tape VCR intended for home users. The home VCR market quickly proved successful and three additional types of ½-inch home VCRs were offered by other manufacturers.

Since 1975 sales of home VCRs have risen considerably. There are now over 500,000 units in the United States, most of which are used for home entertainment. A recent market study indicates that by the mid-1980s as much as 10 percent of all homes may have a VCR.

Currently there is a broad variety of prerecorded cassettes available at retail outlets. Programs include full-length motion pictures, documentaries, renowned television series, concerts, self-instruction courses, and even pornography. In addition, several public broadcasting libraries offer programs through cassette rentals and sales. The major drawback in acquiring prerecorded cassettes is that they are rather expensive.

Overshadowing the future of VCRs is a question concerning the legality of recording copyright-protected programs that are broadcast. There is a suit now in federal court to prevent further manufacture and sale of recordable home videocassette machines. Without recording capability, home videocassette machines could suffer in the future consumer market.

For public broadcasting, videocassettes have already become an established method of distributing programs. The obvious advantage in using cassettes is that more programming can be made available than by traditional broadcast distribution. However, the primary use of cassettes in the future is likely to be, as in the past, distributing instructional/educational programs to schools. In-school use of cassettes for instruction—unlike broadcast programs—permits classroom schedules to determine program viewing rather than vice versa. In addition, the instructor or student has complete control over the program, making it possible to design programs that permit viewer interaction.

Appendix G

Memorandum of Law[1]

After reviewing ten years of public broadcasting experience, the Carnegie Commission on the Future of Public Broadcasting has developed a series of proposals to improve noncommercial broadcasting. The Commission proposes that a private, nonprofit corporation, to be known as the Public Telecommunications Trust, be established to perform certain planning and financial functions for noncommercial radio and television. It also proposes that a Program Services Endowment be established to serve as a patron of the arts and skills essential for the production of high-quality programming for television and radio.

The Commission further proposes that the federal government substantially increase its funding of noncommercial broadcasting. It proposes that separate appropriations be made to the Trust for its activities and administrative costs; to the Trust for distribution to noncommercial licensees; and to the Trust for distribution to the Endowment. The appropriation for licensees would be provided as matching funds, in amounts based upon the nonfederal funds that they raised. The appropriation for the Endowment would be measured as a percentage of the federal funds provided to the licensees.

Finally, the Commission proposes the imposition of a fee on licensed users of the electromagnetic spectrum for their use of assigned frequencies.

The Commission's proposals are designed to achieve multiple goals: they are intended to increase the overall commitment of resources to public broadcasting; to protect public broadcasting programming from political influence; and to maintain high standards of financial accountability. All of the proposals depend upon enactment of new legislation. Thus an analysis of the legal issues that they raise must focus upon Congress's power under the Constitution to enact the necessary implementing legislation. Final resolution of these issues depends

---

[1] By Thomas A. Troyer, member of the firm of Caplin & Drysdale, Washington, D.C.

to some degree upon the precise formulation of whatever legislation is ultimately enacted. It is possible, however, to make judgments of a general nature on the approaches suggested by the Commission, and these judgments are discussed in this memorandum.

We have been asked to discuss three distinct legal issues. The first is whether the processes whereby the trustees of the Public Telecommunications Trust and the members of the board of directors of the Program Services Endowment would be appointed are constitutionally permissible. The second issue is whether entitlement funding, based on a match of federal to nonfederal funds, is constitutionally permissible. The third issue is whether assessment of a fee for licensed use of the electromagnetic spectrum is constitutionally permissible.

I. The Appointments Procedures Specified by the Commission Are Constitutional

The Commission proposes that the nine-member Board of Trustees of the Public Telecommunications Trust be appointed by the President of the United States, without confirmation by the Senate. It proposes, further, that there be a statutorily established nominating panel composed of the librarian of Congress, as chairman; the director of the National Science Foundation; the chairman of the National Endowment for the Arts; the chairman of the National Endowment for the Humanities; the secretary of the Smithsonian Institution; a representative from public television; a representative from public radio; and, for the selection of the first Board, the speaker of the House and the president pro tempore of the Senate. This panel would prepare a list of nominees for the President's consideration.

The Commission's proposal for the appointment of the trustees is fully consistent with the constitutional scheme governing presidential appointments. The only constitutional constraints on the President's power to make appointments pursuant to the laws of Congress are set out in Article II, section 2, clause 2 of the Constitution:

> [The President] shall nominate, and by and with the Advice and Consent of the Senate shall appoint . . . all other Officers of the United States, whose Appointments are not herein otherwise provided for,

and which shall be established by Law: But the Congress may by Law vest the Appointment of such inferior Officers, as they think proper, in the President alone, in the Courts of Law, or in the Heads of Departments.

Whether or not Congress would be required to provide for presidential appointment of the board of trustees of the Trust, it is clear that it may properly choose to vest that power in the President alone.[2] Moreover, while a statutorily appointed nominating panel of such stature could be expected to compile a list of highly suitable candidates which would be accorded very serious consideration by the President, the existence of this panel would serve in no way to restrict the President's appointment power.[3]

Congress has on several occasions chosen to grant the President sole appointment power with respect to the governing boards of legislatively established entities, including nonprofit and for-profit corporations. Among those so selected have been the members of the board of directors of the Federal National Mortgage Association,[4] the interim board of directors of the Student Loan Marketing Association,[5] and, until 1976, the National Council on the Humanities and the National Council on the Arts.[6] The Commission's proposal that the President alone ap-

---

[2]There can be little doubt that the trustees are not among the class of "officers of the United States" whose appointment must be made with the advice and consent of the Senate. The general parameters of that requirement were well stated as long ago as 1878 in *Collins* 14 Ct. Cl. 569: "Having specified certain officers, ministers, consuls and judges of the Supreme Court who shall be nominated by the President and appointed by and with the advice and consent of the Senate in all cases, the Constitution leaves it to Congress to vest in the President alone, the courts of law, or the heads of departments the appointment of any officer inferior or subordinate to them respectively, whenever Congress thinks proper to do so."

[3]The principle that the Congress can advise the President by statute, to heed the recommendations of a particular group of citizens is exemplified by the language establishing the National Council on the Humanities. "The President is requested in the making of such appointments to give consideration to such recommendations as may from time to time be submitted to him by leading national organizations concerned with the humanities." 20 U.S.C. §957(b) (1978). See also 20 U.S.C. §955(b) (1978); 47 U.S.C. §396(c) (2) (1978); 42 U.S.C. §1863(c) (1978).

[4]12 U.S.C. §1723 (1978).

[5]20 U.S.C. §1087-2 (1978).

[6]20 U.S.C. §957 (1978).

point the trustees is, therefore, neither unusual nor improper.

The Trust is only one part of the Commission's proposed structure for public broadcasting. Of equal importance is the Program Services Endowment. The Endowment is to be an autonomous division of the Trust charged solely with providing support for the creative activity required to support innovation and excellence in programming. It is to receive funds from the Trust, but is to be insulated from the pressures of the ordinary political process by the method of selection of its 15-member board of governors. The initial board is to be selected by the trustees of the Public Telecommunications Trust from a list of candidates compiled by the permanent nominating panel for the Trust (that is, the panel headed by the librarian of Congress without the addition of the speaker of the House and the president pro tempore of the Senate). Vacancies on the board are to be filled by the trustees, but the board itself is to nominate candidates for the positions. Five board members are to be selected each year, normally for three year terms.

Private corporations, including nonprofit ones, are, in general, empowered to utilize divisions or subsidiaries which are insulated to varying degrees from the principal organization. By virtue of their appointment as trustees of the Public Telecommunications Trust, the trustees would be empowered, in the fullest sense, to manage that corporation in accordance with the governing principles specified by Congress. Included in this mandate would be the duty to appoint the board of the Endowment. Given this type of relationship between the Trust and the Endowment, there should be no constitutional infirmity in conferring such appointment power on the Trustees.

2. The Appropriation of Federal Funds to the Trust Based upon Non-federal Funding of Licensee Stations is Constitutional

The Commission recommends that the funding of the Trust be based principally upon an entitlement concept, whereby Congress would appropriate federal funds to the Public Telecommunications Trust based upon non-federal funding obtained by noncommercial licensees.[7] It

---

[7] The Commission also recommends an annual appropriation directly to the Trust for its operational and administrative costs. Such an approach presents no novel issues; there can no longer be any question that Congress has the power to make such appropria-

proposes that a direct appropriation be made to the Trust; that an appropriation be made to the Trust for distribution to noncommercial licensees in the amount of $1 of federal funds for every $1.50 of nonfederal funds raised by those licensees; and that an additional 50¢ of federal funds be appropriated to the Trust for distribution to the Program Services Endowment for every $1 of federal matching funds provided to the noncommercial licensees. As in any matching fund arrangement, there must be some time lag between the generation of the *matched* funds and the payment of the *matching* funds, and in this case, it is probable that a second-succeeding year approach would be adopted.[8]

This funding arrangement would accomplish several goals. Most importantly, it would substantially insulate the federal funding from the annual congressional appropriation process and the political judgments that affect that process. Having decided that it would match nonfederal funds with appropriated federal funds, Congress would no longer be required to determine periodically the particular level of federal funding for noncommercial public broadcasting.

In addition, the availability of federal matching funds, which would be passed through directly to the licensees which generated the nonfederal funds, would operate to encourage each licensee to improve the services it provides to its local community as a means of expanding its fund-raising base.

Finally, the matching arrangement would produce a predictable, reliable flow of funds that would permit and encourage planning by the licensee stations. At any given time, stations would have substantial assurance of funding for at least the two following years.

The basic constitutional provision governing congressional expenditures is contained in Article I, section 9, clause 7:[9] "No money shall be drawn from the Treasury,

---

tions. See Jennes, "Memorandum of Law," in Carnegie Commission on Educational Television. *Public Television: A Program for Action* (New York: Harper & Row, 1967), pp. 121–28, for a full discussion.

[8]Thus, for example, $1.50 of nonfederal support in fiscal year 1980 would yield $1 of federal funding in 1982 for the licensee and 50¢ for the Endowment.

[9]The only other constitutional provision limiting appropriations is contained in Article I, section 8, clause 12, which imposes a maximum term of two years on appropriations "to raise and support armies."

but in consequence of appropriations made by law. . . ." Because Congress must enact all appropriations, ultimate financial control of federal expenditures must always be retained by Congress.

Nothing in the Commission's proposals would derogate from congressional authority over the appropriations process. Congressional appropriations may be made for multiple years.[10] They may be made in particular amounts, or determined according to a formula.[11] They may be for dollar amounts that are estimated, and supplemented as necessary to complete the funding of a program.[12] Nor is the concept of matching federal funds to nonfederal funds in any way troublesome. Indeed, the present financing of the Corporation for Public Broadcasting is based partly on a matching arrangement.[13]

Under the Commission's proposals, Congress could presumably adopt any of several alternatives. It could make a multiyear appropriation by a formula expressing the matching obligation. If it preferred, it could make a specific dollar appropriation for each fiscal year.[14] If necessary, that specific dollar appropriation could be supplemented during the course of the fiscal year. Even if annual appropriations were made, it can be presumed that, since such appropriations would be to fund matching obligations already incurred, congressional consideration of those items would be subject to less controversy than would be the case absent the prior commitment to matching. The decisive constitutional consideration in determining the validity of this financing proposal is that the entitlements would require congressional appropriation

[10]See, e.g., Departments of Labor and Health, Education, and Welfare, Appropriation Act, P.L. 94–439, 90 Stat. 1418, 1434 (1977). (Multiple-year appropriation for Corporation for Public Broadcasting.)

[11]See, e.g., Land and Water Conservation Act of 1965, P.L. 88–578, §4(b), 78 Stat. 897, 900 (1964).

[12]See, e.g., Supplemental Appropriations Act, P.L. 95–26, 91 Stat. 61, 69 (1977). (Supplemental appropriation for, inter alia, veterans' medical care benefits.)

[13]Public Telecommunications Financing Act of 1978, §307, P.L. 95–567, 92 Stat. 2405, 2415 (1978).

[14]In general, the second succeeding year approach should permit Congress to determine the precise amount of matching funds required by the target date of its second concurrent budget resolution, which date is set by statute for Sept. 15. See 21 U.S.C. §1331(b). In other words, if the nonfederal funds in fiscal year n are known by Sept. 15 of fiscal year $n+1$, then Congress can comfortably make a precise dollar appropriation of matching funds for fiscal year $n+2$.

and would thus be subject to congressional control: Congress could, if it chose to do so, alter the program at any time.[15] The fact that appropriations would, as a practical matter, be nearly self-executing under the Commission's proposals causes no deviation from the dictates of the Constitution, and in no way diminishes the congressional power and responsibility to make appropriations.

Of course, Congress can only enact appropriations which are necessary and proper to accomplish purposes enunciated in the Constitution.[16] All other powers are reserved to the states and the people.[17] However, in view of the long history of federal support of public education in general, and of noncommercial broadcasting in particular, Congress's ability to appropriate funds for this purpose cannot be seriously questioned.

3. Congress May Impose a Fee on the Licensed Use of the Electromagnetic Spectrum

The Commission proposes that a spectrum use fee be charged to all licensed users of the electromagnetic spectrum. The Commission believes that a fee system would promote efficiency in the use of the spectrum, and that the revenue raised by such fees could substantially offset the cost of financing an augmented public broadcasting effort. In addition, the Commission is impressed with the appropriateness of charging the users of a scarce public commodity for that use.

We believe that spectrum use fees—whether in the form of excise taxes or true fees—could be constitutionally valid if properly designed. Congress has broad power to impose excise taxes, provided that such taxes are "uniform throughout the United States."[18] A levy imposed upon a privilege or on the use of property, rather than upon the mere ownership of property, is properly classified as an excise tax, and thus is not subject to the constitutional requirement of apportionment which is applicable to direct taxes.[19] Moreover, Congress routinely

---

[15]Congress could presumably preclude the possibility that any legal claims would be asserted upon termination of the program by simply providing that no vested rights would be created by the entitlement financing.

[16]Article I, §8, cl. 18.

[17]Amendment X.

[18]Article I, §8, cl. 1 of the Constitution.

[19]Article I, §8, cl. 4. See *Pollock v. Farmers Loan and Trust Co.,* 157 U.S. 429 (1895).

imposes fees for many purposes. It imposes charges for services that the government provides,[20] for goods that the government vends,[21] and to compensate for the government's costs in operating regulatory agencies.[22]

There is no clear line which demarcates taxes from fees. It has been held that an exaction for the primary purpose of raising revenue is a tax. However, the Supreme Court has also indicated that a charge may be a fee, rather than a tax, where it is based on the value to the recipient of a benefit conferred by the government.[23] In any event, since the spectrum use fee would be adopted by Congress, we do not believe that the distinction between taxes and fees would be critical.[24]

To a considerable degree, the proposed charges could be justified in terms of the spectrum-related services provided by the government: particularly, its regulation of the airwaves—without which the airwaves would have minimal value. But beyond those services, it is generally recognized that the electromagnetic spectrum belongs to the public. Commercial users of the spectrum have had a valuable factor of their production provided for them at no cost. Historically, this practice arose when the airwaves seemed no more scarce than the air itself.[25]

---

[20]E.g., postal rates. 39 U.S.C. §3621 (1978).

[21]E.g., charges by the Government Printing Office for government publications. 44 U.S.C. §1708 (1978).

[22]The Independent Offices Appropriation Act, 65 Stat. 290 (1952), codified at 31 U.S.C. §483a et seq., authorizes the general principle that the government should require reimbursement for certain services.

[23]*National Cable Television Association, Inc. v. United States*, 415 U.S. 1304 (1974); *Federal Power Commission v. New England Power Co.*, 415 U.S. 345 (1974). In *National Cable Television Association, Inc. v. United States*, supra, the Supreme Court held that a fee schedule established by the FCC for community antenna television systems exceeded the power of the FCC because it was more in the nature of a tax than a fee. Since Congress alone is empowered to levy taxes, the Court narrowly construed the Independent Office Appropriations Act, supra, under which the FCC had acted.

[24]*Rodgers v. United States*, 138 F.2d 992 (6th Cir. 1943). See also *Pace v. Burgess*, 92 U.S. 372 (1875); *Gibbons v. Ogden*, 22 U.S. (9 Wheat.)1 (1824); *Moon v. Freemen*, 379 F.2d 382 (9th Cir. 1967).

[25]For an excellent discussion of the history of the FCC's regulation of the airwaves see Robinson, "The FCC and the First Amendment: Observations on 40 Years of Radio and Television Regulation," *Minn. L. Rev.* 52 (1967): 67.

The scarcity of spectrum space is now well recognized,[26] however, and the government is obviously the only entity that is able to require that spectrum users compensate the public for their preemption of particular portions of the spectrum space.

Since commercial broadcasting inevitably involves considerations of free speech and free press, it is necessary to examine not merely the general power of Congress to regulate and impose fees, but also whether the First Amendment prohibits a fee system which may adversely affect purveyors of information.

The latter inquiry must begin with a recognition of the unique status of broadcast speech for First Amendment purposes. Because of the scarcity of spectrum space, courts have consistently recognized that the rights of broadcasters to speak freely must be balanced against a variety of competing considerations, some of which carry their own First Amendment significance. Broadcasters may not broadcast on frequencies or at times or in places for which they are not licensed.[27] Failure to enforce such prohibitions would undoubtedly do more to abrogate than to encourage free speech.

Even the content of broadcasting is properly subject to extensive regulation. For example, the FCC is empowered to prohibit offensive speech—protected by the First Amendment in nonbroadcast contexts—on the airwaves.[28] Not only can some types of otherwise permissible speech be prohibited in the broadcast context, but the converse is true as well: a broadcaster can be required to open his part of the spectrum to speakers with viewpoints different from his.[29] In approving the constitutionality of the fairness doctrine of the Federal Communications Commission, the Supreme Court, in *Red Lion Broadcasting v. F.C.C.*,[30] made a well-known observation: "It is the right of the viewers and listeners, not the right of the broadcasters, which is paramount."[31] Some First Amendment commentators have gone so far as to maintain that government ownership and operation of all

---

[26]The practical scarcity of the spectrum has been recognized by the Supreme Court in *Red Lion Broadcasting v. F.C.C.*, 395 U.S. 367 (1969).

[27]E.g., 47 U.S.C. §303 (1978).

[28]Compare *Cohen v. California*, 403 U.S. 15 (1971), with *FCC v. Pacifica Foundation*, U.S., 98 S. Ct. 3026 (1978).

[29]E.g., 47 U.S.C. §315 (1978).

[30]395 U.S. 367 (1969).

[31]Ibid. at 390.

broadcast facilities would not necessarily be unconstitutional.[32] Others have suggested that spectrum use be sold to the highest bidder.[33]

The special nature of broadcasting—which essentially results from the scarcity of the spectrum—makes charges imposed on broadcasters easily distinguishable from fees or taxes exacted from other media.[34] This does not mean, however, that Congress may ignore the First Amendment altogether in developing a fee structure. Each particular proposal must be examined to make certain that it does not operate to abridge protected rights.

In that regard, the most significant general characteristic of the Commission's proposal is that it would apply to spectrum users in all parts of the country, with respect to all types of uses. It would create no pernicious incentives to broadcast or to refuse to broadcast particular programs or ideas. It would create no chilling effect on free expression. It would in no way discourage criticism of governmental practices. It would not impinge upon the independence of spectrum users.

In fact, the sole effect of a fee system would be to increase the cost of spectrum use over present levels. The justification for this economic burden would be the appropriation of valuable spectrum space. First Amendment rights do not include the right to consume resources without charge. A newspaper's First Amendment rights do not include the right to obtain free newsprint and ink.

[32]T. Emerson, *The System of Freedom of Expression* (1970), p. 654. Though he notes that First Amendment problems would arise regarding government's use of the monopoly power, and over access by the public to the airwaves, Emerson finds: "To the extent that a physical scarcity of facilities is involved, the First Amendment would probably not have prevented this arrangement [of public ownership and control]."

[33]This suggestion is made in Coase, "Evaluation of Public Policy Relating to Radio and Television Broadcasting: Social and Economic Issues," *J. L. and Econ.* 41 (1965): 161, and commended in Kalven, "Broadcasting, Public Policy and the First Amendment," *J. Law & Econ.* 10 (1967): 15 at 31:

> The point of insight in Professor Coase's analysis is . . . that it was a mistake not to use the traditional pricing mechanism to determine who should get the license. In brief, he asks why we have not awarded licenses to the highest bidder. And before one rushes to answer that it would be unseemly and against public policy to award these valuable resources to the highest bidder, it is well to reflect on how we allocate almost all other valuable resources.

[34]Cf. *Grosjean v. American Press Co.*, 297 U.S. 233 (1936).

Nor can the broadcaster insist upon free spectrum space as a constitutional matter.[35]

We emphasize that any legislation in this area must be carefully drafted to avoid constitutional infirmity. Any opinion on the constitutionality of particular proposed legislation would depend upon close examination of all the relevant details of such a proposal. It is our judgment, nevertheless, that the general ideas embodied in the Commission's proposals contain no inherent constitutional defects, and can be translated into legislation that is appropriate and constitutional.

CAPLIN & DRYSDALE
By: /s/ Thomas A. Troyer

December 14, 1978

Grosjean held that a tax applied only to newspaper revenues was constitutionally invalid. The Supreme Court has subsequently recognized implicitly that broadcasting requires different treatment. See *National Cable Television Association v. FCC*, 415 U.S. 336 (1973), which invalidated certain FCC fees, but only on the ground that the fees were in fact taxes, which could only be levied by Congress (415 U.S. at 340).

[35]Ironically, broadcasters themselves resist the idea that spectrum space is costless when they are asked to contribute it. They have, for example, successfully contested contentions that they should be required under the equal time doctrine to give *free* time to a political candidate merely because the opposing candidate has purchased time. See *Paulsen v. F.C.C.*, 491 F. 2d 887 (9th Cir. 1974).

Appendix H

Public Television Stations[1]

ALABAMA
Birmingham ●WBIQ/10
Cheaha State
Park ○WCIQ/7
Demoplis ○WIIQ/41
Dozier ○WDIQ/2
Florence ○WFIQ/36
Huntsville ○WHIQ/25
Louisville ○WGIQ/43
Mobile ○WEIQ/42
Montgomery ○WAIQ/26

ALASKA
Anchorage ●KAKM/7
Bethel ●KYUK/4
Fairbanks ●KUAC/9

AMERICAN SAMOA
Pago Pago ●KVZK/2

ARIZONA
Phoenix ●KAET/8
Tucson ●KUAT/6

ARKANSAS
Arkadelphia ○KETG/9
Fayetteville ○KAFT/13
Jonesboro ○KTEJ/19
Little Rock ●KETS/2

CALIFORNIA
Eureka ●KEET/13
Fresno ●KMTF/18

Huntington
Beach ●KOCE/50
Los Angeles ●KCET/28
●KLCS/58
Redding ●KIXE/9
Sacramento ●KVIE/6
San
Bernardino ●KVCR/24
San Diego ●KPBS/15
San
Francisco ●KQED/9
○KQEC/32
San Jose ●KTEH/54
San Mateo ●KCSM/14

COLORADO
Denver ●KRMA/6
Pueblo ●KTSC/8

CONNECTICUT
Bridgeport ○WEDW/49
Hartford ●WEDH/24
New Haven ○WEDY/65
Norwich ○WEDN/53

DELAWARE
Wilmington ●WHYY/12

**DISTRICT OF
COLUMBIA**
Washington ●WETA/26

[1]See Figure 7–1 on page 225

FLORIDA
Gainesville   ●WUFT/5
Jacksonville   ●WJCT/7
Miami   ●WLRN/17
   ●WTHS/2
   ●WPBT/2
Orlando   ●WMFE/24
Pensacola   ●WSRE/23
Tallahassee   ●WFSU/11
Tampa   ●WEDU/3
   ●WUSF/16

GEORGIA
Athens   ●WGTV/8
Atlanta   ●WETV/30
Augusta   ○WCES/20
Chatsworth   ○WCLP/18
Cochran   ○WDCO/15
Columbus   ○WJSP/28
Dawson   ○WACS/25
Pelham   ○WABW/14
Savannah   ○WVAN/9
Waycross   ○WXGA/8

GUAM
Agana   ●KGTF/12

HAWAII
Honolulu   ●KHET/11
Wailuku   ●KMEB/10

IDAHO
Boise   ●KAID/4
Moscow   ●KUID/12
Pocatello   ●KBGL/10

ILLINOIS
Carbondale   ●WSIU/8
Chicago   ●WTTW/11
Olney   ○WUSI/16
Peoria   ●WTVP/47
Urbana   ●WILL/12

INDIANA
Bloomington   ●WTIU/30
Evansville   ●WNIN/9
Indianapolis   ●WFYI/20
Muncie   ●WIPB/49
St. John   ●WCAE/50
South Bend   ●WNIT/34
Vincennes   ●WVUT/22

IOWA
Council Bluffs   ○KBIN/32
Des Moines   ●KDIN/11

Ft. Dodge   ○KTIN/21
Iowa City   ○KIIN/12
Mason City   ○KYIN/24
Red Oak   ○KHIN/36
Sioux City   ○KSIN/27
Waterloo   ○KRIN/32

KANSAS
Topeka   ●KTWU/11
Wichita   ●KPTS/8

KENTUCKY
Ashland   ○WKAS/25
Bowling Green   ○WKGB/53
Covington   ○WCVN/54
Elizabethtown   ○WKZT/23
Hazard   ○WKHA/35
Lexington   ●WKLE/46
Louisville   ●WKPC/15
   ○WKMJ/68
Madisonville   ○WKMA/35
Morehead   ○WKMR/38
Murray   ○WKMU/21
Owenton   ○WKON/52
Pikeville   ○WKPI/22
Somerset   ○WKSO/29

LOUISIANA
Baton Rouge   ●WLPB/27
Monroe   ○KLTM/13
New Orleans   ●WYES/12
Shreveport   ○KLTS/24

MAINE
Augusta   ●WCBB/10
Biddeford   ○WMEG/26
Calais   ○WMED/13
Orono   ●WMEB/12
Presque Isle   ○WMEM/10

MARYLAND
Annapolis   ○WAPB/22
Baltimore   ●WMPB/67
Hagerstown   ○WWPB/31
Salisbury   ○WCPB/28

MASSACHUSETTS
Boston   ●WGBH/2
   ●WGBX/44
Springfield   ●WGBY/57

MICHIGAN
Alpena   ○WCML/6
Detroit   ●WTVS/56
East Lansing   ●WKAR/23

Grand Rapids	●WGVC/35	New	
Marquette	●WNMU/13	Brunswick	○WNJB/58
Mt. Pleasant	●WCMU/14	Trenton	●WNJT/52
University			
Center		**NEW MEXICO**	
(Delta		Albuquerque	●KNME/5
College)	●WUCM/19	Las Cruces	●KRWG/22
		Portales	●KENW/3
MINNESOTA		**NEW YORK**	
Appleton	●KWCM/10	Binghamton	●WSKG/46
Austin	●KAVT/15	Buffalo	●WNED/17
Duluth	●WDSE/8	Garden City	●WLIW/21
Minneapolis	●KTCA/2	New York	●WNYC/31
St. Paul	●KTCI/17	City	●WNET/13
			●WNYE/25
MISSISSIPPI		Norwood	○WNPI/18
Biloxi	○WMAH/19	Plattsburg	●WCFE/57
Booneville	○WMAE/12	Rochester	●WXXI/21
Bude	○WMAU/17	Schenectady	●WMHT/17
Greenwood	○WMAO/23	Syracuse	●WCNY/24
Jackson	●WMAA/29	Watertown	●WNPE/16
Meridian	○WMAW/14		
Oxford	○WMAV/18	**NORTH CAROLINA**	
State College	○WMAB/2	Ashville	○WUNF/33
		Chapel Hill	●WUNC/4
MISSOURI		Charlotte	●WTVI/42
Kansas City	●KCPT/19	Columbia	○WUND/2
St. Louis	●KETC/9	Concord	○WUNG/58
Springfield	●KOZK/21	Greenville	○WUNK/25
		Linville	○WUNE/17
NEBRASKA		Wilmington	○WUNJ/39
Alliance	○KTNE/13	Winston-	
Bassett	○KMNE/7	Salem	○WUNL/26
Hastings	○KHNE/29		
Lexington	○KLNE/3	**NORTH DAKOTA**	
Lincoln	●KUON/12	Fargo	●KFME/13
Merriman	○KRNE/12	Grand Forks	○KGFE/2
Norfolk	○KXNE/19		
North Platte	○KPNE/9	**OHIO**	
Omaha	○KYNE/26	Akron	○WEAO/49
		Alliance	●WNEO/45
NEVADA		Athens	○WOUB/20
Las Vegas	●KLVX/10	Bowling Green	●WBGU/57
		Cambridge	○WOUC/44
NEW HAMPSHIRE		Cincinnati	●WCET/48
Berlin	○WEDB/40	Cleveland	●WVIZ/25
Durham	●WENH/11	Columbus	●WOSU/34
Hanover	○WHED/15	Dayton	●WPTD/16
Keene	○WEKW/52	Oxford	●WPTO/14
Littleton	○WLED/49	Portsmouth	○WPBO/42
		Toledo	●WGTE/30
NEW JERSEY			
Camden	○WNJS/23		
Montclair	○WNJM/50		

OKLAHOMA
Cheyenne ○KWET/12
Eufaula ○KOET/3
Oklahoma
City ●KOKH/25
●KETA/13
Tulsa ○KOED/11

OREGON
Corvallis ●KOAC/7
LaGrande ●KTVR/13
Medford ●KSYS/8
Portland ●KOAP/10
Salem ●KVDO/3

PENNSYLVANIA
Allentown ●WLVT/39
Clearfield/
Unipk ●WPSX/3
Erie ●WQLN/54
Hershey ●WITF/33
Pittsburgh ●WQED/13
●WQEX/16
Scranton ●WVIA/44

PUERTO RICO
Mayaquez ●WIPM/3
San Juan ●WIPR/6

RHODE ISLAND
Providence ●WSBE/36

SOUTH CAROLINA
Allendale ○WEBA/14
Beaufort ●WJWJ/16
Charleston ○WITV/7
Columbia ●WRLK/35
Florence ●WJPM/33
Greenville ○WNTV/29
Rockhill ○WNSC/30
Sumter ●WRJA/27

SOUTH DAKOTA
Aberdeen ○KDSD/16
Brookings ●KESD/8
Eagle Butte ○KPSD/13
Lowry ○KQSD/11
Martin ○KZSD/8
Pierre ○KTSD/10
Rapid City ○KBHE/9
Vermillion ●KUSD/2

TENNESSEE
Chattanooga ●WTCI/45
Cookeville ●WCTE/22

Knoxville ●WSJK/2
Lexington ○WLJT/11
Memphis ●WKNO/10
Nashville ●WDCN/8

TEXAS
Austin ●KLRN/9
College
Station ●KAMU/15
Corpus Christi ●KEDT/16
Dallas ●KERA/13
El Paso ●KCOS/7
Houston ●KUHT/8
Killeen ●KNCT/46
Lubbock ●KTXT/5
Wichita Falls ○KIDZ/24

UTAH
Provo ●KBYU/11
Salt Lake
City ●KUED/7

VERMONT
Burlington ●WETK/33
Rutland ○WVER/28
St.
Johnsbury ○WVTB/20
Windsor ○WVTA/41

VIRGIN ISLANDS
Charlotte
Amalie ●WTJX/12

VIRGINIA
Annandale ●WNVT/53
Harrisonburg ●WVPT/51
Norfolk ●WHRO/15
Norton ○WSVN/47
Richmond ●WCVE/23
●WCVW/57
Roanoke ●WBRA/15

WASHINGTON
Pullman ●KWSU/10
Seattle ●KCTS/9
Spokane ●KSPS/7
Tacoma ●KTPS/62
Tacoma/
Lakewood ●KCPQ/13
Yakima ●KYVE/47

WEST VIRGINIA
Beckley ●WSWP/9
Huntington ●WMUL/33
Morgantown ●WMVU/24

WISCONSIN

Colfax	oWHWC/28	Milwaukee	●WMVS/10
Green Bay	oWPNE/38		●WMVT/36
LaCrosse	oWHLA/31	Park Falls	oWLEF/36
Madison	●WHA/21	Wausau	oWHRM/20

Public Radio Stations[2]

ALABAMA

Birmingham	WBHM (FM)	90.3
Huntsville	WLRH (FM)	89.3
Troy	WTSU-FM	90.1

ALASKA

Anchorage	KSKA-FM	103.1
Bethel	KYUK (AM)	580
Dillingham	KDLG-AM	670
Fairbanks	KUAC (FM)	104.7
Juneau	KTOO-FM	104.3
Kodiak	KMXT-FM	100.1
Kotzebue	KOTZ (AM)	720

ARIZONA

Phoenix	KMCR (FM)	91.5
Tucson	KUAT (AM)	1550
	KUAT-FM	90.5
Yuma	KAWC (AM)	1320

ARKANSAS

Jonesboro	KASU (FM)	91.9

CALIFORNIA

Fresno	KVPR (FM)	89.8
Long Beach	KLON (FM)	88.1
Los Angeles	KUSC (FM)	91.5
Northridge	KCSN (FM)	88.5
Pasadena	KPCS (FM)	89.3
San Bernardino	KVCR (FM)	91.9
San Diego	KPBS-FM	89.5
San Francisco	KALW (FM)	91.7
	KQED-FM	88.5
San Luis Obispo	KCBX (FM)	90.1
San Mateo	KCSM-FM	91.1
Santa Monica	KCRW (FM)	89.9
Santa Rosa	KBBF (FM)	89.1
Stockton	KUOP (FM)	91.3

COLORADO

Boulder	KGNU-FM	88.5
Denver	KCFR (FM)	90.1
Fort Collins	KCSU-FM	90.9
Greeley	KUNC (FM)	91.5

CONNECTICUT

Hartford	WPBH-FM	90.5

DISTRICT OF COLUMBIA

	WAMU-FM	88.5
	WETA-FM	90.9

FLORIDA

Boynton Beach	WHRS (FM)	91.7
Jacksonville	WJCT-FM	89.9
Miami	WLRN (FM)	91.3
Panama City	WKGC (FM)	90.7
Tallahassee	WFSU-FM	91.5
Tampa	WUSF-FM	89.7

GEORGIA

Atlanta	WABE (FM)	90.1

ILLINOIS

Carbondale	WSIU (FM)	91.9
Chicago	WBEZ (FM)	91.5
DeKalb	WNIU (FM)	89.5
Edwardsville	WSIE (FM)	88.7
Peoria	WCBU (FM)	89.9
Springfield	WSSR (FM)	91.9
Urbana	WILL (AM)	580
	WILL-FM	90.9

INDIANA

Bloomington	WFIU (FM)	103.7
Indianapolis	WIAN (FM)	90.1
Vincennes	WVUB (FM)	91.1
West Lafayette	WBAA (AM)	920

IOWA

Ames	WOI (AM)	640
	WOI (FM)	90.1
Cedar Falls	KHKE (FM)	89.5
	KUNI (FM)	90.9
Cedar Rapids	KCCK-FM	88.3
Iowa City	WSUI (AM)	910
	KSUI-FM	91.7
Sioux City	KWIT-FM	90.3

[2]See Figure 7–2 on page 226

KANSAS

Lawrence	KANU (FM)	91.5
Manhattan	KSAC (AM)	580
Wichita	KMUW (FM)	89.1

KENTUCKY

Lexington	WBKY (FM)	91.3
Louisville	WFPL (FM)	89.3
	WFPK (FM)	91.9
	WUOL (FM)	90.5
Morehead	WMKY (FM)	90.3
Murray	WKMS (FM)	91.3
Richmond	WEKU (FM)	88.9

LOUISIANA

New Orleans	WWNO (FM)	89.9

MAINE

Bangor	WMEH (FM)	90.9
Portland	WMEA (FM)	90.1
Presque Isle	○WMEM-FM	106.1

MARYLAND

Baltimore	WBJC (FM)	91.5
	WEAA-FM	88.9

MASSACHUSETTS

Amherst	WFCR (FM)	88.5
Boston	WBUR (FM)	90.9
	WGBH-FM	89.7

MICHIGAN

Alpena	○WCML-FM	91.7
Ann Arbor	WUOM (FM)	91.7
Berrien Springs	WAUS (FM)	90.9
Detroit	WDET-FM	101.9
East Lansing	WKAR (AM)	870
	WKAR-FM	90.5
Flint	WFBE (FM)	95.1
Grand Rapids	○WVGR (FM)	104.1
Houghton	WGGL (FM)	91.1
Interlochen	WIAA (FM)	88.3
Kalamazoo	WMUK (FM)	102.1
Marquette	WNMU-FM	90.1
Mt. Pleasant	WCMU-FM	89.5
Ypsilanti	WEMU-FM	89.1

MINNESOTA

Collegeville	KSJR (FM)	90.1
Duluth	WSCD (FM)	92.9
Grand Rapids	KAXE-FM	91.7
St. Paul	KSJN (FM)	91.1
Minneapolis	KUOM (AM)	770
Moorhead	KCCM (FM)	91.1
Northfield	○WCAL (AM)	770
	WCAL-FM	89.3
Pipestone	KRSW (FM)	91.7
Rushford	○KLSE (FM)	91.7

MISSISSIPPI

Senatobia	WNJC (FM)	90.1

MISSOURI

Buffalo	WBFL (FM)	90.3
Columbia	KBIA (FM)	91.3
Kansas City	KCUR(FM)	89.3
Maryville	KXCV (FM)	90.5
Point Lookout	KSOZ (FM)	91.7
Rolla	KUMR (FM)	88.5
Springfield	KSMU (FM)	91.1
St. Louis	KWMU (FM)	90.7
Warrensburg	KCMW(FM)	90.9

MONTANA

Missoula	KUFM (FM)	89.1

NEBRASKA

Omaha	KIOS (FM)	91.5

NEW JERSEY

Newark	○WBGO (FM)	88.3

NEW MEXICO

Las Cruces	KRWG (FM)	90.7
Ramah	KTDB (FM)	89.7

NEW YORK

Albany	WAMC (FM)	90.3
Binghamton	WSKG-FM	89.3
Buffalo	WBFO (FM)	88.7
	WEBR (AM)	970
	WNED-FM	94.5
Canton	WSLU (FM)	96.7
New York City	WNYC (AM)	830
	WNYC-FM	93.9
Oswego	WRVO (FM)	89.9
Rochester	WXXI-FM	91.5
Schenectady	WMHT-FM	89.1
Syracuse	WCNY-FM	91.3

NORTH CAROLINA

Chapel Hill	WUNC (FM)	91.5
Warrenton	WVSP-FM	90.9
Winston-Salem	WFDD-FM	88.5

NORTH DAKOTA

Belcourt	KEYA-FM	88.5
Fargo	KDSU (FM)	91.9
Grand Forks	KFJM (AM)	1370
	○KFJM-FM	89.3

OHIO

Athens	WOUB (AM)	1340
	WOUB-FM	91.3
Cincinnati	WGUC (FM)	90.9
Cleveland	WBOE-FM	90.3
Columbus	WCBE (FM)	90.5
	WOSU (AM)	820
	WOSU-FM	89.7
Kent	WKSU (FM)	89.7
Oxford	WMUB-FM	88.5
Toledo	WGTE-FM	91.3
Wilberforce	WCSU (FM)	88.9
Yellow Springs	WYSO (FM)	91.5
Youngstown	WYSU (FM)	88.5

OKLAHOMA
  Stillwater   KOSU (FM)   91.7
  Tulsa   KWGS-FM   89.5

OREGON
  Corvallis   KOAC (AM)   550
  Eugene   KLCC (FM)   90.3
                    KWAX (FM)   91.1
  Portland   KBOO (FM)   90.7
                    KBPS (AM)   1450
                    KOAP-FM   91.5

PENNSYLVANIA
  Erie   KQLN-FM   91.3
  Hershey   WITF-FM   89.5
  Philadelphia   WUHY-FM   90.9
  Pittsburgh   WDUQ (FM)   90.5
                    WQED-FM   89.3
  Scranton   WVIA-FM   89.9

PUERTO RICO
  Hato Rey   WIPR (AM)   940
                   ○WIPR-FM   91.3

SOUTH CAROLINA
  Charleston   WSCI (FM)   89.3
  Columbia   WLTF-FM   91.3
  Greenville   WEPR (FM)   90.1
  Sumter   ○WMPR (FM)   88.1

SOUTH DAKOTA
  Brookings   KESD-FM   88.3
  Vermillion   KUSD (AM)   690
                   ○KUSD-FM   89.9

TENNESSEE
  Collegedale   WSMC (FM)   90.7
  Johnson City   WETS (FM)   89.5
  Knoxville   WUOT (FM)   91.9
  Memphis   WKNO-FM   91.1
  Murfreesboro   WMOT (FM)   89.5
  Nashville   WPLN (FM)   90.3

TEXAS
  Austin   KUT (FM)   90.7
  Beaumont   KVLU (FM)   91.3
  College Station   KAMU (FM)   90.3

  Commerce   KETR (FM)   88.9
  Dallas   KERA-FM   90.1
  El Paso   KTEP (FM)   88.5
  Houston   KPFT-FM   90.1
  Killeen   KNCT (FM)   91.3

UTAH
  Logan   KUSU-FM   91.5
  Provo   KBYU-FM   88.9
  Salt Lake City   KUER (FM)   90.1

VERMONT
  Windsor   WVPA-FM   89.5

VIRGINIA
  Harrisonburg   WMRA (FM)   90.7
  Norfolk   WHRO (FM)   89.5
  Richmond   WRFK (FM)   106.5
  Roanoke   WVWR (FM)   89.1

WASHINGTON
  Pullman   KWSU (AM)   1250
  Seattle   KUOW (FM)   94.9
  Tacoma   KTOY (FM)   91.7

WEST VIRGINIA
  Beckley   WVPB (FM)   91.7
  Buckhannon   ○WVPW (FM)   88.9

WISCONSIN
  Auburndale   ○WLBL (AM)   930
  Brule   ○WHSA (FM)   89.9
  Colfax   ○WHWC (FM)   88.3
  Delafield   ○WHAD (FM)   90.7
  Green Bay   ○WPNE (FM)   89.3
  Highland   ○WHHI (FM)   91.3
  Kenosha   WGTD-FM   91.1
  La Crescent   ○WHLA (FM)   90.3
  La Crosse   WLSU (FM)   88.9
  Madison   WERN (FM)   88.7
                    WHA (AM)   970
  Milwaukee   WUWM (FM)   89.7
  Wausau   ○WHRM (FM)   91.9

WYOMING
  Laramie   KUWR-FM   91.9

○ associated stations

Fiscal Year		Funds (millions)	Tra (millions)
1966–67			$0.
1968		2.	0.
1970		2.	0.
1971		4.	0.

Index